Mint Juleps
with
Teddy Roosevelt

THE COMPLETE HISTORY OF
PRESIDENTIAL DRINKING

Mint Juleps
with
Teddy Roosevelt

THE COMPLETE HISTORY OF PRESIDENTIAL DRINKING

Mark Will-Weber

REGNERY
HISTORY

Regnery History™ is a trademark of Salem Communications Holding Corporation; Regnery® is a registered trademark of Salem Communications Holding Corporation.

Library of Congress Cataloging-in-Publication Data

Will-Weber, Mark.
  Mint juleps with Teddy Roosevelt : the complete history of presidential drinking / Mark Will-Weber.
    pages cm
  Includes bibliographical references and index.
  ISBN 978-1-62157-210-7
  1. Presidents--Alcohol use--United States--History. 2. Presidents--United States--Biography. 3. Drinking of alcoholic beverages--United States--History. 4. Drinking behavior--United States--History. I. Title.
  E176.1.W675 2014
  973.09'9--dc23
                              2014006103

Published in the United States by
Regnery History
An imprint of Regnery Publishing
A Salem Communications Company
300 New Jersey Avenue NW
Washington, DC 20001
www.RegneryHistory.com

Manufactured in the United States of America

10 9 8 7 6 5 4 3 2

Books are available in quantity for promotional or premium use. For information on discounts and terms, please visit our website: www.Regnery.com.

Distributed to the trade by
Perseus Distribution
250 West 57th Street
New York, NY 10107

To my late grandfather, Colonel Charles I. Faddis—
U.S. Congressman from Pennsylvania, recipient of the
Purple Heart in both World War I and World War II—
who once said to my mother: "Gertrude, you would be shocked
if you really knew what went on in Washington."

Mark Will-Weber, August 27, 2014

Contents

Prologue

"**N**ot guilty!"

It was Saturday morning, May 16, 1868. The pivotal vote of Kansas senator Edmund Gibson Ross meant that beleaguered President Andrew Johnson—despite an earlier vote for impeachment by the House of Representatives—had escaped charges of "high crimes and misdemeanors."

In the chaotic aftermath (the Senate chamber—both floor and galleries—were packed with spectators), presidential bodyguard William H. Crook raced to the Executive Mansion (the term "White House" was not formally established until Teddy Roosevelt's first year in office, 1901) to inform the president. As Crook stirringly recounted in his memoirs, he covered the distance—slightly more than a mile—with adrenaline-fueled strides:

> I ran all the way from the Capitol to the White House. I was
> young and strong in those days, and I made good time. When

I burst into the library where the President sat with Secretary Welles and two other men whom I cannot remember, they were quietly talking. Mr. Johnson was seated at a little table on which luncheon had been spread in the rounding southern end of the room. There were no signs of excitement.

"Mr. President," I shouted, too crazy with delight to restrain myself, "you are acquitted!"

All rose. I made my way to the President and got hold of his hand. The other men surrounded him, and began to shake his hand. The President responded to their congratulations calmly enough for a moment, and then I saw that tears were rolling down his face. I stared at him; and yet I felt I ought to turn my eyes away.

It was all over in a moment, and Mr. Johnson was ordering some whiskey from the cellar. When it came, he himself poured it into glasses for us, and we all stood up and drank a silent toast. There were some sandwiches on the table; we ate some and then we felt better. In a few minutes came a message of congratulations from Secretary Seward to "my dear friend." By that time the room was full of people, and I slipped away.

I found Crook's remembrance in the early stages of researching this book. Yes, it obviously had the prerequisite connection to alcohol (whiskey in this case, the drink of choice in the Johnson Executive Mansion), but there was also a *human* factor: Johnson, tears of relief streaming down his face; the fetching of whiskey from the Executive Mansion cellar; the president himself performing the honors, tilting the bottle of amber-colored spirits that gurgled into the glasses of his loyalists; and, finally, those glasses raised in a solemn yet celebratory toast. Andrew Johnson—the former small-town tailor from Tennessee—had dodged a political bullet, and they all knew it.

Presidents, as it turns out, drink for many of the same reasons most people drink. They drink in celebration or to be sociable; they drink to confirm solidarity. They drink because they are under pressure or because they might feel lonely, depressed, or trapped. (Harry Truman often referred to the White House as "The Great White Jail.") They drink because their job seems to demand it (knocking back vodka shots with a boisterous Boris Yeltsin or hovering above a snifter of brandy with a cigar-smoking Prime Minister Churchill) or because presenting a lavish state dinner at the White House calls for complementing rounds of wine.

Even presidents who drank lightly or not at all were nevertheless greatly affected by the alcohol consumed by those around them, whether staffers (like Lincoln's inept Ford Theatre bodyguard) or relatives (like Billy Carter, Jimmy Carter's younger brother, often trotted out as the presidential "poster boy" when it comes to alcohol-inspired embarrassments).

This book aims to present an entertaining and accurate portrait of presidents imbibing: from George Washington, who distilled whiskey at Mount Vernon, to President Barack Obama, who requested that his White House kitchen staff conjure up some quite servable homebrew (a key ingredient being honey from Michelle Obama's White House beehives), henceforth known as "White House Honey Ale."

♀   ♀   ♀

Alcohol came with the colonists. In the first Christmas at Plymouth in 1620, the Pilgrims, suffering through a "sore storm of winde and rayne," could not disembark from the *Mayflower* but found some solace in good old English beer, as William Bradford recorded in his diary:

> Munday the 25. being Christmas day, we began to drink water aboord, but at night the Master caused us to have some Beere, and so on boord we had diverse times now and then some Beere....

In Jamestown, Virginia—the first permanent English settlement in North America—beer brewing (although sometimes of dubious quality) was soon established, and the colonists also drank rum and hard cider.

In the eighteenth century, drinking distilled beverages could be safer than drinking water (though the link between contaminated water and, say, cholera, was not yet established), and alcohol was one of the few standard medicinal treatments against colds, flus, fevers, and other ailments.

Alcohol—at least in moderate amounts—continued to have medicinal currency well into the nineteenth and twentieth centuries. Former New York City mayor Phillip Hone—an educated and wealthy man—lamented the death of a friend in 1839, noting:

> He became all of a sudden a total abstinence man, at a time in his life when the experiment was dangerous, and drank nothing but water, when, in my judgment, a moderate use of the good wine he had in his cellar would have been more congenial to his health.

Of course, alcohol consumption also brought social problems, and warnings about the evils of abuse and addiction appeared almost immediately.

In his 1699 travel log "A Trip to New England," English writer Edward "Ned" Ward proclaimed:

> Rum, alias Kill Devil, is much ador'd by the American English, as a dram of Brandy is by an old Billingsgate. 'Tis held as the Comforter of their Souls, the Preserver of their Bodys, the Remover of their Cares, and Promoter of their Mirth; and is a Sovereign Remedy against the Grumbling of Guts, a Kibe-heel or a wounded Conscience, which are three Epidemical Distempers that afflict the Country.

Predictably, alcohol quickly made its way into the lodges of Native Americans, with devastating results. In his autobiography, Ben Franklin recorded this scene of drunken depravity from a 1754 trip to Carlisle, Pennsylvania, for treaty talks with the Six Nations:

We went to Carlisle, and met the Indians accordingly. As those people are extremely apt to get drunk, and, when so, are very quarrelsome and disorderly, we strictly forbad the selling any liquor to them; and when they complained of this restriction, we told them that if they would continue sober during the treaty, we would give them plenty of rum when business was over. They promis'd this, and they kept their promise, because they could get no liquor, and the treaty was conducted very orderly, and concluded to mutual satisfaction. Then they claim'd the rum; this was in the afternoon....

In the evening, hearing a great noise among them, the commissioners walk'd out to see what was the matter. We found they had made a great bonfire in the middle of the square; they were all drunk, men and women, quarreling and fighting. Their dark-colored bodies, half naked, seen only by the gloomy light of the bonfire, running after and beating each other with firebrands, accompanied by their horrid yellings, form'd a scene the most resembling our ideas of hell that would well be imagin'd; there was no appeasing the tumult, and we retired to our lodging. At midnight a number of them came thundering at our door, demanding more rum, of which we took no notice.

Alcohol was and remains a scourge to Native American tribes. Some nineteenth-century American presidents with military experience—such as William Henry Harrison—saw this firsthand and even, like Franklin, knew they could use alcohol to gain an advantage with Native American chiefs.

Ŷ   Ŷ   Ŷ

Although the tax on tea and the subsequent Boston Tea Party gets top billing in junior high school history books, alcohol played a part in igniting the American Revolution. The 1764 tax on sugar—and its predecessor tax on molasses (1733)—rocked the colonials because molasses was needed to make rum, and there were numerous rum distilleries in colonial America, particularly in Rhode Island.

The colonials were also fond of Madeira. This powerful wine (often fortified with rum or brandy) was imported from the Portuguese islands of the same name and was a favorite of such noteworthy devotees as George Washington, Thomas Jefferson, Ben Franklin, John Adams, John Marshall, and John Hancock.

Hancock's interest in Madeira was not solely for his own drinking pleasure. One of the most successful entrepreneurs in colonial America, Hancock imported Madeira to sell. The British seized Hancock's sloop *Liberty* in 1768 because his sailors and dockworkers had hustled off most of the wine and prevented the revenue agents from tallying up the tax bill. The seizure sparked riots in Boston.

And of course on April 19, 1775, the colonial militiamen of Lexington met at John Buckman's Tavern, where they often drank after drilling on the village green, before marching out to trade musket balls with the formidable British regiments.

Ÿ   Ÿ   Ÿ

Alcohol has frequently cropped up in lesser combats—such as political campaigns. The most blatant example of this occurred in 1840, when William Henry Harrison ran as the "Log Cabin and Hard Cider" candidate against New York's dandified Martin Van Buren. The Log Cabin and Hard Cider campaign had its origin in a Baltimore newspaper editorial that was sympathetic to Van Buren and attempted to brand Harrison, "Old Tip," as an uncultured, booze-belting bumpkin from the frontier. But the attempt backfired: Harrison, the Indian-fighting hero of the Battle of Tippecanoe, was embraced as a man of the people, Van Buren was dismissed as an effete snob, and "Tippecanoe and Tyler, Too" (after Harrison's running mate, John Tyler) swept into the Executive Mansion.

Ÿ   Ÿ   Ÿ

Long before candidates raised money with, say, $10,000-per-plate dinner parties in the Hamptons, West Palm Beach, or Beverly Hills, politicians used alcohol to guide voters into making the "right" choice. George Washington did it, Andrew Jackson did it, and Lyndon Baines Johnson was still using booze-for-votes as part of his congressional campaigns in the Texas Hill Country (particularly with German-American and Czech-American constituents) in the 1930s. LBJ outdid most of his political predecessors by allegedly lining up free beer from Anheuser-Busch's St. Louis–based brewery.

Part of Franklin Roosevelt's popularity was due to his stance against Prohibition—specifically, his willingness to repeal the Eighteenth Amendment. In recognition of FDR's election—and the end of Prohibition—a Clydesdale-powered wagon rolled down Pennsylvania Avenue to deliver a free case of Bohemian-style lager to the White House.

♀   ♀   ♀

Prohibition lasted only from 1920 to 1933, but temperance movements had existed for far longer, starting at least from Andrew Jackson's presidency and gaining huge momentum after the Whiskey Ring scandal during the Ulysses S. Grant administration, when government officials profited from illegally diverted liquor taxes.

Teddy Roosevelt lamented that he could not even enjoy a mint julep after a spirited set or two of tennis without fearing a public backlash should word leak out. TR advised his portly successor—William Howard Taft—to avoid contact with the Women's Christian Temperance Union, and Taft, who rarely drank anyway, tried his best.

Even well into the John F. Kennedy years, there were those who wanted to ban booze from official White House functions. Journalist Helen Thomas remembered a party at the White House that drew fire from teetotalers:

> It was held in the State Dining Room where open bars had been set up. In addition, butlers circulated through the rooms with trays of champagne and mixed drinks.

The stories that appeared about the open bar unleashed a furor as certain parts of the country and one group in particular, the Women's Christian Temperance Union (WCTU), weighed in with their outrage. The first couple abandoned the practice, but later on it was quietly resumed, and during such functions, one could walk up to a strategically placed bar for a drink. It's hard to believe in this day and age that something like an open bar would prompt such a backlash—and the practice became White House routine over time.

Eighty years earlier, President Chester A. Arthur had his own run-in with the Women's Christian Temperance Union. When a WCTU representative asked Arthur to commit to an alcohol-free White House, such as former president Rutherford B. Hayes and his wife Lucy had championed, Arthur thundered, "Madam, I may be the President of the United States, but what I do in my private life is nobody's damned business!"

Of course, in today's world of twenty-four-hour news cycles, presidents can rarely sneak a private moment. If a modern president hoists a mug in an Irish pub, the "news" of it zips around the planet almost before he can wipe the foam from his lips and request another round.

Whether that's fair or not is up for debate—but the reality of presidential scrutiny is not. No matter what the era, a drinking president never fails to catch the eye and stir the interest of the American public. It is my hope that this book does much of the same.

CHAPTER 1

George Washington

(1732–1799)

George Washington, America's most famous general, smoothly made the transition to president. His most famous encounter with alcohol occurred when he put down the Whiskey Rebellion in western Pennsylvania. But that had to do with taxes and federal authority. Washington did not have any objection to the potent potable itself; in fact, several years later, Washington had a whiskey distillery set up at his Mount Vernon plantation—a venture that proved quite profitable.

Washington, like other general-presidents, had to draw a hard line on soldiers and officers who drank themselves into states of inebriation. But he also was eager to dispense a moderate rum ration—as was standard practice of the day—when his men needed it or when their efforts deemed them worthy of an extra shot.

Not unlike Thomas Jefferson, Washington enjoyed wines (especially Madeira) and beer (dark, molasses-laced porter) more than whiskey (if, in fact, he drank whiskey at all).

THE WHISKEY REBELLION

When the words "Washington" and "whiskey" appear in the same sentence, they are typically in the context of the Whiskey Rebellion (1791–1794). To pay off the national debt (the Patriots had borrowed heavily to finance their war against England), Alexander Hamilton— Washington's secretary of the treasury—looked to tax whiskey.

Farmers on what was then the frontier of western Pennsylvania railed against the tax, since many saw whiskey as easier to transport across the mountains than regular grain shipments and also because whiskey often served as a currency in remote areas where "hard money" was, in the most literal sense, difficult to come by.

The whiskey rebels harassed government revenue agents and threatened to burn the barns and stills of farmers who complied with the 7.5 percent whiskey tax; some even threatened to torch the town of Pittsburgh. But Washington squashed the uprising in the autumn of 1794, deploying some thirteen thousand militiamen to the most troublesome areas. General Henry "Light Horse Harry" Lee headed the campaign, but Washington also went out to review his troops in the field.

MOUNT VERNON WHISKEY

Coincidently or not, three years after putting down the Whiskey Rebellion, Washington went into the whiskey distilling business.

Washington never drank in the Executive Mansion. (John Adams, the second president, was the first leader to actually live in the Executive Mansion.) He did, however, imbibe almost daily when he occupied the President's House on Market Street in Philadelphia during his presidential years and at Mount Vernon—his splendid plantation in Virginia.

His drinks of choice were Madeira wine, champagne, and porter (laced with molasses for some sweetness). But when it came to making money through his various plantation ventures, Washington had an entrepreneur's taste for distilling whiskey.

James Anderson, a Scottish-born farm manager working for Washington, knew how to make whiskey from rye and corn, and how to build and run a distillery. He pushed Washington early on to expand his two-still operation to five.

In June of 1797, Washington wrote to a friend:

> Mr. Anderson has engaged me in a distillery, on a small scale, and is very desirous of encreasing it: assuring me from his own experience in this country and in Europe, that I shall find my account in it.

"Find my account in it" meant, simply, "make some money." The distillery did in fact prove profitable. Most of Washington's whiskey sales occurred close to Mount Vernon. Swaps were common. For example, one of his neighbors paid in crops of corn and rye—in exchange for thirty-plus gallons of whiskey and some flour ground at Washington's gristmill.

In February 1798, Washington wrote to his relative William A. Washington:

> I make no use of Barley in my Distillery (the operation of which are just commenced). Rye chiefly, and Indian Corn in a certain proportion, compose the materials from which the Whiskey is made.... It has sold in Alexandria (in small quantities from the Waggons)....

The formula seemed to be about 60 percent rye, 35 percent corn, and a very meager amount of malted barley.

Anderson soon convinced his employer on the merits of expansion. When the Polish nobleman Julian Ursyn Niemcewicz visited Washington's Mount Vernon, he found the distillery operating at high throttle, observing:

> Just near by is a *Whiski* distillery. Under the supervision of the son of Mr. Anderson they distill up to 12 thousand gallons a year (they can distill 50 gallons per day if the weather is not too hot); each gallon at 4 Virginia shillings; that alone should bring in about 16,000 doll. I do not know how Mr. Anderson maintains that the distillery produces only 600 pounds.

Niemcewicz was under no illusions that the hard spirits were good for the health of the distillery's steady (or should one say *unsteady*) customers, commenting wryly that it "produces poison for men" but "the most delicate and succulent feed for pigs." Niemcewicz observed that Washington's hundred-plus hog herd was fat and thriving.

At its zenith, Washington's whiskey operation had five copper stills, a boiler, and dozens of "mash pans." While the Andersons oversaw the enterprise, several of Washington's slaves provided the bulk of the muscular labor.

One can visit George Washington's Distillery and Gristmill, precisely reconstructed on a bucolic creek about three miles south of Mount Vernon. Visitors can take the tour (and sample—and purchase—a batch of rye whiskey made authentically to Mount Vernon's original recipe) from April through October.

The modest profits from the distillery benefit various programs at the historical site. There is, however, a cap on how much whiskey the Mount Vernon distillery makes and sells.

As Jim Rees, executive director of Mount Vernon, quipped to a *Wall Street Journal* reporter in 2007: "We have no plans to enter the high stakes liquor business, even though it's tempting, given that the name of George Washington would certainly provide us with a sensational marketing advantage: We could say he was First in War, First in Peace, and First in Smooth Libations."

Sampling the product, the *Journal* reporter said it had the amber color of liquor-store whiskey, but that its taste more closely resembles the wallop of a rougher cousin—the elixir we commonly call "moonshine."

MADEIRA MAN

Washington's character was certainly steered (by his own will) to moderation and control. For example, the general was said to have had a volcanic temper—but he worked diligently to control it. Ronald Chernow, perhaps Washington's greatest biographer, writes that George often drank three glasses of Madeira (a strong wine of close to 20 percent alcohol from the Portuguese islands of the same name) in an evening— not enough to be considered a heavy drinker in his day. He also liked the lighter wines, such as champagne.

Though Washington could be quite reserved with visitors at Mount Vernon, a glass or two helped the master of Mount Vernon arrive at a more congenial disposition. As Robert Hunter Jr., a young Scotsman who visited in 1785, remarked:

> The General with a few glasses of champagne got quite merry, and being with intimate friends laughed and talked a good deal. Before strangers, he is generally very reserved and seldom says a word.

Washington did not tolerate alcohol abuse—particularly among soldiers under his command. Washington did not hesitate to discipline those who got drunk on duty; a "fuddled" soldier might be sentenced to a serious flogging.

Like most wealthy landowners, Washington (Jefferson and John Adams would have felt the general's pain on this issue) sometimes had to endure less than sober employees. In Washington's case, that happened to be the German-born gardener Johann Ehlers—a man who had worked for European royalty. But as Washington bemoaned to his farm manager in 1793:

> The Gardener has too great a propensity to drink and behaves improperly when in liquor; admonish him against it as much as you can, as he behaves well when sober, understands his business, and I believe is not naturally idle; but only so when occasioned by intoxications.

THE HESSIAN RUM

Among the many "Washington myths" that have gained traction over the centuries was that the general led his courageous army across the frigid, ice-chunked waters of the Delaware River en route to his surprise victory at Trenton, assisted by enemy German soldiers who were celebrating a rum-soaked Christmas Eve.

Truth be told, there is no historical evidence that the Hessians were handicapped by drink; just utterly ambushed by a large force of Americans during a snow and sleet storm. If the Hessians had been drinking, it probably was in modest amounts, as they still had a rather large supply of rum on hand.

The rum, however, *did* become a factor because the American troops captured several dozen hogsheads (large barrels, typically containing sixty-plus gallons) of the Jamaican "spirits" from the Hessians. When Washington learned of this, he issued orders to prevent his men from sampling their highly prized booty, but apparently some of the ragtag patriots had already "warmed up" on the recently liberated libation. Given the abysmal weather conditions and the fact that they'd just been through an eighteenth-century version of a firefight with hired German mercenaries, who could blame—or stop—them?

As the historian David Hackett Fischer recorded in his outstanding book *Washington's Crossing*:

> In a word, some of the American victors celebrated their own success by getting gloriously drunk and even more disorderly than usual. John Greenwood (a fifer) remembered a wild scene. The men in his regiment "were much pleased with the brass caps they had taken from the dead hessians." Others began to take them from prisoners. "With brass caps on it was laughable to see how our soldiers would strut,—fellows with their elbows out, and some without a collar to their half-a-shirt, no shoes, etc."

All things considered, Washington wisely retreated back across the Delaware, booty, cannons, and Hessian prisoners in tow. But the re-crossing of the frigid river proved even more problematic than the original attack, as Hackett noted:

> The rum did not help. More than a few Americans tumbled into the icy Delaware trying to leap aboard the boats.

The general was not against dispensing rum or even whiskey to his troops—far from it. It was common practice for British troops, both land and sea, to have their daily rum rations (In fact, the British navy dispensed rum rations to sailors well into the twentieth century). And the newly formed American army followed suit when it was able. Washington's requests to Congress for supplies often asked for rum. But the wise leader absolutely wanted to control *how much* the troops could have and *when* they could have it.

In fact, in August 1777, Washington wrote to John Hancock, proclaiming the need for an occasional dram or two for the soldier in the field and—given the British superiority on the seas—how difficult it would be to obtain alcohol from the usual sources:

> In the like manner, since our Imports of Spirit have become so precarious—nay impracticable on account of the Enemy's Fleet, which infests our Whole Coast, I would beg leave to suggest the propriety of erecting public Distilleries in different States. The benefits arising from the moderate use of strong Liquor have been experienced in All Armies, and not to be disputed.

THE (SOMETIMES) GALLOPING GOURMET

The campaigns of the Revolution did not prevent General Washington from at least attempting to put together a quality dining (and drinking) experience in the field for himself and his top officers. When possible, dinner was served with tablecloth and silverware (decorated with Washington's own family symbol of the mythical griffin) and wine that he and his guests drank from silver cups. Even his French allies were impressed by the quantity and quality of Washington's wartime dining and imbibing.

Not surprisingly, the winter of 1777–1778 at Valley Forge was a notable exception. Even for his Christmas dinner, Washington made due with a meager fare of mutton, spuds, cabbage, and—perhaps worst of all—only water to wash it down with. The lack of alcoholic spirits—coupled with the knowledge that General Howe and his British troops were living quite warm and snug in Philadelphia just a few miles south—proved most depressing to the sickly, tattered troops and their beleaguered officers.

MR. HARE'S PRIZED PORTER

George Washington loved porter—a dark beer—especially Robert Hare's Philadelphia porter. Hare, born in England and the son of a brewer, brought his special skills and recipes with him to America and was already manufacturing the good dark stuff in Philadelphia when the First Continental Congress gathered there in 1774.

In a letter home to his wife, John Adams raved about Mr. Hare's porter, but Washington was equally enthusiastic. They loved it doubly as hostilities with England increased because it meant they no longer had to drink porter imported from London. But long after the Revolution had ended, it was clear that Hare's brew had a loyal following—with Washington close to the front of the line.

On July 4, 1788, Philadelphia (among other cities) put on a celebration called the Grand Federal Procession to honor the ten states that ratified the U.S Constitution. The three-mile-long parade ended with a feast at Bush Hill (near present-day Spruce and 17th Streets), including a generous supply of alcohol—wine, beer, and Robert Hare's much-vaunted porter. Ten toasts were proposed and, without doubt, honored. Each toast was punctuated with the blast of a cannon.

On July 20, Washington wrote to Clement Biddle of Philadelphia, who had served with the Continental Army as a quartermaster, and inquired: "I beg you will send me a gross of Mr. Hairs [sic] best bottled Porter if the price is not enhanced by the copious droughts you took of it at the late Procession." (Could this, by the way, qualify as a humorous jab from General Washington?)

Apparently the cost had not dramatically increased, as Washington—in a follow-up message in August—penned: "As the price of Porter according to your Account has not been enhanced and is good in quality, I beg if this letter gets to hand in time, that you would add another gross to the one ordered...."

Two years later, Tobias Lear—Washington's secretary—was dashing off requests to Philly middleman Biddle:

> Will you be so good as to desire Mr. Hare to have if he continues to make the best Porter in Philadelphia 3 gross of his best put up for Mount Vernon? as the President means to visit that place in the recess of Congress and it is probable there will be a large demand for Porter at that time.

Although it probably did not match Robert Hare's magic potion, Washington used his own porter recipe at Mount Vernon when the Philadelphia porter was unavailable.

WASHINGTON'S "SMALL" BEER

As we know from Washington's letters and invoices, he absolutely *loved* Robert Hare's outstanding Philadelphia porter, brewed in the old English style. But long before George Washington became a famous military officer (let alone president of the United States), he knew how to make (or at least instruct his servants to make) a batch of "small" beer homebrew. The original notation (dated 1757, so pre–French and Indian War, when Washington was still in his mid-twenties), is housed today in the New York Public Library and reads:

> Take a large Sifter full of Bran Hops to your Taste—Boil these 3 hours. Then strain out 30 Gall. Into a Cooler put 3 Gallons Molasses while the Beer is scalding hot or rather drain the molasses into the Cooler. Strain the Beer on it while boiling hot let this stand til it is little more than Blood warm. Then put in a quart of Yeast if the weather is very cold cover it over with a Blanket. Let it work in the Cooler 24 hours then put it into the Cask. Leave the bung open until it is almost done working—Bottle it that day Week it was Brewed.

There are home-brewing enthusiasts who have the expertise to make Washington's "small" beer (presumably with relatively low alcohol content) by following his recipe virtually to the "t"—in fact, knowingly ignoring some slight changes that probably would be more pleasing to taste buds accustomed to beers brewed in modern times, in order to remain more true to something called ... history.

ELECTION LUBRICATION

Washington famously chose the high road in ethics whenever possible. But he also was not a dolt. He had lost (in fact, got slaughtered in) an early election for a much-coveted post in Virginia's House of Burgesses. That taught him some valuable lessons for the future— including that it doesn't hurt one's cause to pony up with some free drinks for the voters.

In July 1758, Washington—who was afield on the frontier, leading his troops against the French and the Indians—directed his primary backers to roll out the heavy artillery (i.e., the barrels of booze) in a spirited effort to secure political victory. According to Chernow's biography, Colonel Washington garnered 309 of a possible 397 votes— an impressive tally.

Similarly impressive was the bill for more than thirty gallons of wine, thirteen gallons of beer, forty gallons of rum punch, and a few bottles of brandy and hard cider thrown in for good measure. Washington appears to have paid the bill of thirty-nine Virginian pounds (a hefty sum in that day) without complaint, given the favorable landslide results.

LAST CALL

Washington could, on occasion, display a sense of humor about alcohol and—in that spirit—named several of his favorite fox hounds "Drunkard," "Tippler," and "Tipsy."

Today, Yards Brewery in Philadelphia produces a "George Washington Tavern Porter" that "reflects Washington's admiration of Philadelphia-style porters and closely follows the general's own recipe."

CHAPTER 2

John Adams

(1735–1826)

John Adams, the second president of the United States (1797–1801), came from Puritan roots. His father had hoped to steer him toward the ministry; instead, he became a lawyer, then a revolutionary, and, eventually, a politician.

Adams helped Thomas Jefferson formulate the Declaration of Independence and helped bring French military might to the American cause. He also assisted in negotiating the Treaty of Paris, which put an end to the hostilities with King George III and England.

As George Washington's vice president, Adams—in typical blunt fashion—described the job as "the most insignificant office that ever the invention of man contrived or his imagination conceived."

As president, Adams found the significance he craved. He was forced to navigate numerous treacherous currents—tightroping a near war with former ally France over the XYZ Affair and political jousting with rivals such as Alexander Hamilton and Thomas Jefferson.

Historians delight that Adams was one of the most forthcoming and prodigious recorders of his era: he wrote copious letters (many to his beloved wife Abigail) and diary entries. Adams could be both wryly humorous and descriptive in his writings—almost all of which pop off the page with a ring of authenticity. The result being that we know a lot about what John Adams thinks—and what John Adams drinks.

CIDER HOUSE RULES

William Henry Harrison went down in history as the "Hard Cider" candidate, but, years before, John Adams could have laid claim to that title.

Adams's insightful writings are laced with references to alcoholic beverages he enjoyed—including rum, whiskey, Madeira, sherry, and various other wines, beer (especially porter), and, yes, hard cider. The Massachusetts native attended Harvard at just sixteen and fondly mentioned that cider was a staple of the college breakfast table. "I shall never forget, how refreshing and salubrious we found it, hard as it often was," he wrote.

Being from New England, where apple orchards abounded (Adams had an orchard on his own modest farm in Braintree), Adams became well acquainted with cider at an early age. His references concerning hard cider typically have a medicinal ring to them; he clearly was not drinking cider each morning in pursuit of a breakfast "buzz." His cider-drinking boost was a habit he carried well into his latter years, as two typical examples from his diary in the 1790s note:

Tuesday

Cloudy and began to rain; the wind at northeast. The men gone up the hill to rake the barley. In conformity to the fashion, I drink this morning about a gill of cider. It seems to do me good.

Thursday

I continue my practice of drinking a gill of cider in the morning, and find no ill, but some good effects.

We rarely hear of "a gill" these days, but in Adams's era it meant approximately three or four ounces of alcohol. This generous shot of hard cider was meant to serve as an "eye-opener" and to ward off cold, or as a preemptive measure against various other illnesses (many of which we rarely deal with today, such as smallpox and cholera and sometimes even malaria) that plagued seventeenth- and eighteenth-century America.

THE PHILADELPHIA STORY

As a Massachusetts delegate to the First Continental Congress in 1774, Adams offset the bureaucrat boredom and bombast with enthusiastic rounds of drinking. Reading between the lines of his letters home and his diary entries, one gets the impression that Adams was initially awed by the amounts of food and drink available to him in the City of Brotherly Love but eventually felt overwhelmed and sickened by these lavish feasts.

Writing to Abigail a few weeks after his arrival, Adams declared:

I shall be killed with kindness in this place. We go to Congress at nine, and there we stay, most earnestly engaged in debates upon the most abstruse mysteries of state, until three in the afternoon; then we adjourn, and go dine with some of the nobles of Pennsylvania at four, and feast upon ten thousand delicacies, and sit drinking Madeira, Claret, and Burgundy, till six or seven and then go home fatigued to death with business, company, and care. Yet I hold out surprisingly.

These gluttonous smorgasbords, supported with generous amounts of imported wines from France and Portugal and Jamaican "spirits" (rum made with molasses from the West Indies), no doubt served as necessary icebreakers. As Adams noted to his wife, the First Continental Congress consisted of "Fifty gentlemen meeting together, all strangers, are not acquainted with each others language, ideas, views, designs. They are, therefore, jealous of each other—fearful, timid, skittish."

Adams may have embellished somewhat concerning the "ten thousand delicacies" of food offerings, but his consistent accounts concerning the amounts of alcohol brim with honesty. The delegates engaged in much of their feasting and imbibing at private homes. There were also intermittent stints at Philadelphia's new three-storied City Tavern (also known as Smith's), conveniently situated on Second Street, less than two blocks from Carpenter's Hall, where the initial Continental Congress met.

Adams's diary entries from his nearly seven weeks in Philadelphia include several other telling references to his own quaffing of alcoholic libations and the similar pursuits of some of his fellow delegates:

September 4, 1774
Spent the Evening at Mr. Mifflin's with [Richard Henry] Lee and [Benjamin] Harrison from Virginia.... An elegant Supper, and We drank Sentiments [toasts] till 11 O Clock. Lee and Harrison were very high. Lee had dined with Mr. Dickinson, and drank Burgundy the whole Afternoon.

September 22, 1974
Dined with Mister Chew, Chief Justice of the Province, with all the Gentlemen from Virginia.... About Four O Clock We were called down to Dinner.... Wines most excellent and admirable. I drank Madeira at a great Rate and found no Inconvenience in it.

Adams later found the Philadelphia beer similarly excellent and admirable—so much so that he penned home to Abigail:

I drink no Cider, but feast on Philadelphia Beer and Porter. A Gentleman, one Mr. [Robert] Hare, has lately set up in this City a Manufactory of Porter, as good as any that comes from London. I pray we may introduce it into Massachusetts. It agrees with me infinitely better than Punch, Wine, or Cider, or any other Spirituous Liquor.

BOOZING WITH BROADBRIMS

John Adams and a few of the other delegates sometimes referred to the Quakers of Philadelphia as "broadbrims"—a derogatory reference to the wide-brimmed hats the Quaker men wore. The religious Quakers, as a rule, did not approve of drinking toasts, but in his diary Adams relates a funny exception, concerning a toast expressing the hope—albeit a fast-fading one—that war with England might still be averted.

1774, October 20

Dined with the whole Congress at the City Tavern ... a most elegant Entertainment. A Sentiment [toast] was give, "May the Sword of the Parent never be Stain'd with the Blood of her Children." Two or three broadbrims, over against me at Table—one of em said this is not a Toast, but a Prayer, come let us join in it—and they took their Glasses accordingly.

HIGH-PRICED HOISTING

Once the Revolutionary War was in full swing, prices for food and drink soared. Adams wrote pleadingly to Abigail in May of 1777:

I would give Three Guineas for a Barrell of your Cyder—not one drop to be had here for gold. And wine is not to be had under Six or Eight Dollars a Gallon and that very bad. I would give a Guinea for a Barrell of your Beer. The small beer here is wretchedly bad. In short, I can get nothing that

I can drink, and I believe that I shall be sick from this Cause alone. Rum at forty shillings a Gallon and bad Water, will never do, in this hot Climate in summer where Acid Liquors are necessary against Putrefaction.

British general William Howe captured Philadelphia in late fall, and Adams was forced to flee west to York. But he managed to find some decent alcohol to drink in that remote refuge.

RUM AND REVOLUTION

Most high school history books focus on England's tea tax. But it was an earlier tax on molasses (1733) that helped singe the tinder of revolution. Molasses was the main ingredient for distilling rum, the drink of choice in the prewar colonies. By the mid-eighteenth century, Massachusetts and Rhode Island contained dozens and dozens of rum distilleries, many participating in the "triangular trade" that sent rum to Africa, where slaves were, in turn, sent to the West Indies. Molasses was then sent to America (as were some slaves), and the process repeated itself for decades.

John Adams readily acknowledged the role of molasses in a letter to a friend in 1818: "Wits may laugh at our fondness for molasses, and we ought to all join in the laugh…." Adams wrote. "General Washington, however, always asserted and proved that Virginians loved molasses as well as New England men did. I know not why we should blush to confess, that molasses was an essential ingredient in American independence. Many great events have proceeded from much smaller causes."

ROAD TRIPS

In February 1778, Adams (with son and future president John Quincy Adams in tow) headed to France to join the esteemed-but-aging Benjamin Franklin in the diplomatic courting of the French to lend even more support (plus formal recognition as a new nation) to the patriots in their struggle against the British. Adams and his son crossed the

Atlantic in the frigate *Boston*. The ship was well fortified with twenty-four guns to fend off ships of the British navy—and also well "fortified" with a rum keg, a cask of Madeira, and a few dozen bottles of port wine, to fend off thirst and boredom during the three-week voyage.

There was no shortage of fantastic wines once the Americans made their way to Paris. Dr. Franklin had access to the Comte de Chaumont's wine cellar—in excess of one thousand bottles. (Adams and Franklin did not mind an occasional brew, either, as noted in an April 8, 1778, diary entry from Paris: "Came home and supped with Dr. Franklin on Cheese and Beer.")

When Adams returned to Europe (again on diplomatic missions) in late 1779, he dined with the French consul and others in Spain, reporting in his diary: "We had every luxury ... the wines were Bordeaux, Champagne, Burgundy, Sherry, Alicante, Navarre, and Vin de Cap. The most delicious in the world."

STOCKING UP

Since war with the British played havoc with their usual sources of rum, the patriots tried to grab it whenever they could. Interestingly, letters of that era often trumpeted the capture of rum supplies from the British or mourned of its loss when the opposite occurred.

In a letter to a rum supplier on November 21, 1778, Adams shows how he tried to stock up when the opportunity arose and, apparently, could even joke about why the order was two bottles short:

> Sir ... yesterday, the Rum was brought here consisting of forty-Eight Bottles. Two I Suppose had been used to wet the Whistle of the Porters. I beg of you to draw upon me the Cost of the Rum which shall be paid immediately.

PRESIDENTIAL KEG PARTY

By the time he ascended to the presidency at sixty-one years old, John Adams was not imbibing with the same vigor that he had when he was a wide-eyed delegate to the First Continental Congress more than two decades prior. But that's not to say the man didn't ever throw a celebration with a little bit of clout.

The president hosted a Fourth of July bash at his home in Philadelphia (the building that was to become the White House was still under construction in Washington), and by most accounts it got rather festive. The overflow crowd devoured massive amounts of cake and guzzled down casks of wine laced with rum. (The wine may have been Madeira, which was commonly "boosted" with rum in the eighteenth century to make a potent libation, typically hovering around 20 percent alcohol.)

LAST CALL

Some of John Adams's earliest ancestors in Massachusetts (dating back to the mid-1600s) were brewers. John's cousin, Sam Adams, also dabbled in brewing and, of course, has a modern-day craft beer named after him. Despite his own fairly heavy consumption of alcohol and tobacco in his early years, John Adams lived to an impressive age of ninety, dying on the Fourth of July, 1826. His alleged last words were: "Thomas Jefferson survives!" He was wrong. Adams could not have known that his one-time rival (and late-life friend) had died just hours before him in Virginia.

CHAPTER 3

Thomas Jefferson

(1743–1826)

He drafted the Declaration of Independence, oversaw the Louisiana Purchase, which more than doubled the size of the country, and unleashed the fury of the U.S. Navy against the Barbary Coast pirates.

But for connoisseurs of fine vintages, Jefferson will always be regarded as the First Father of Wine in the United States. That is not to suggest that there wasn't wine present in America long before Jefferson—wine, like most other kinds of alcoholic drink, arrived virtually with the first Europeans.

Jefferson, however, knew that truly wonderful wine—like art, literature, or architecture—could be something splendid and exhilarating. The "Sage of Monticello" had not used his time in France (1784–1788) solely in diplomatic toil or contemplating the ongoing intrigues of Parisian society. Always keen to pursue both his intellectual and sensual interests, Jefferson went "walk about" for several weeks in southern France and the Italian Piedmont in 1787. He learned firsthand about

European wine culture—from vine to wine cellar, if you will. By the time he returned to the States, Jefferson's wine expertise was quite likely second to none among his countrymen.

Jefferson's love of the best wines, and his urge to constantly share his bottles with his numerous friends and dinner guests, greatly contributed to his precarious financial situation. There were some years in which he spent thousands of dollars just on wine. By the time of his death on July 4, 1826 (just hours before his former foe John Adams succumbed in Massachusetts), the third president of the United States (1801–1809) was on the brink of bankruptcy.

THE BANE OF WHISKEY

Unlike some American presidents who followed him, Thomas Jefferson was not a whiskey man—and, in fact, his zeal for wine was matched by his disdain for hard spirits. As he once wrote to a French acquaintance:

> It is an error to view a tax on that liquor as merely a tax against the rich. It is a *prohibition* of its use to the middling class of our citizens, and a condemnation of them to the poison of whiskey, which is desolating their houses.
>
> No nation is drunken where wine is cheap; and none sober, where the dearness of wine substitutes ardent spirits as the common beverage. It [wine] is, in truth, the only antidote to the bane of whiskey.

Although many of the prominent men of his day were proud whiskey drinkers, Jefferson must have witnessed how overindulgence in hard liquor was a shortcut to ruination. Jefferson was well aware that alcohol addiction shortened the promising lives of both the writer Thomas Paine and the intrepid explorer Meriwether Lewis.

Closer to home, Jefferson's writings reveal that several of his skilled laborers at Monticello—specifically his blacksmith William Orr and cabinet-maker David Watson—drank whiskey to excess and sometimes missed days of work because of it. In addition to their own actual hangovers, the drinking duo must have been a headache to Jefferson, although he apparently overlooked their flaws to benefit from their talents.

WHAT WOULD TOM DRINK?

Jefferson became acquainted with wine well before he traveled to France. At the College of William and Mary, and then as a young law student in Williamsburg, Jefferson was introduced to the stronger Madeira wines and, in fact, had kegs of it in his cellar at Monticello on the eve of the Revolution. (He also may have occasionally drunk some "arrack"—liquor distilled with sugarcane and something of a cousin of rum, minus the molasses.)

But his "education" in France—initially sampling some of the best vintages that Dr. Ben Franklin had in his well-stocked cellar in Paris or from his growing circle of friends in the French aristocracy—gradually pushed him in another direction. His 1787 trip to vineyards in the South of France and northern Italy lifted Jefferson to a higher plateau in his "wine education," and it certainly qualified as some of the happiest days of his life. During this most pleasant trek, he wrote to his secretary, William Short:

> I am now in the land of corn, wine, oil and sunshine. What more can a man ask of heaven? If I should die at Paris I will beg of you to send my body here and have me exposed to the sun. I am sure it will bring me to life again.

As a halfhearted excuse to go on the trip, Jefferson journeyed to a French hot springs spa to rehab a badly injured wrist. But his daughter Martha Jefferson wasn't completely buying that line. She teased her father, writing: "I am inclined to think that your voyage is rather for your pleasure than your health."

Jefferson's favorite wines—once he distanced himself from the fortified wines of his youth—appear to have been top-quality vintages of Bordeaux, Burgundy, and Sauterne. Jefferson also had a special fondness for white Hermitage, ordered it often, and once lauded it as "the first wine in the world without a single exception."

And Jefferson drank wine the rest of his life. Writing to Dr. Vine Utley in March 1821, the seventy-six-year-old Jefferson (after learning that Dr. Benjamin Rush typically drank a glass and a half of Madeira wine each day) noted:

> I double, however, the Doctor's glass and a half of wine, and treble it with a friend; but halve its effects by drinking the weak wines only. The ardent wines I cannot drink, nor do I use any ardent spirits in any form. Malt liquors and cider are my table drinks....

The glasses of wine always came after dinner, with the intention of stimulating conversation and camaraderie. Always keen on inventive flourishes, Jefferson had dumbwaiters on each side of the fireplace so that fresh wine could arrive straight from the cellar with minimal interruption—and emptied bottles could be dispatched downward.

TABLE TIPPLES

Jefferson had such an affinity for wine that it might be easy to overlook other alcoholic beverages that he enjoyed. But Jefferson served beer and hard apple cider as his "table" drinks at dinner.

Prior to the Revolutionary War, Jefferson's wife, Martha, brewed some big batches of beer at Monticello—sometimes as much as fifteen to twenty gallons of "small" beer (which would have been low in alcohol) every several weeks. Martha added a little zip to its taste by including some hops.

In later years, Jefferson brought in an experienced brewer named John Miller—a British soldier who stayed in America after the war. Miller taught the basics of brewing to Jefferson's kitchen slave, Peter Heming.

Although Jefferson is famous for his quotes on wine, he also gave a favorable nod to beer, noting: "Beer, if drunk in moderation, softens the temper, cheers the spirit, and promotes health."

Jefferson longed to establish European vines at his homestead, but his attempts failed due to blight and bad weather. Virginia did produce bountiful apple crops, and good strong cider, like beer, was always plentiful at Monticello.

Visitors to Monticello sometimes commented that Jefferson looked younger than his years. He offset his appetites with vigorous walks (until bouts of rheumatism slowed him down in his last years) and horseback rides around the estate. Tall and relatively athletic, the redheaded Jefferson held his years well, despite the gallons of alcohol (and an abundance of food) at his disposal.

MIND ON THE WINE

Jefferson wrote often about wine. On April 8, 1817, for example, he began a letter to his friend James Monroe—who had just been inaugurated as the fifth president of the United States:

> I shall not waste your time in idle congratulations. You know my joy on the commitment of the helm of our government to your hands....
>
> I promised you, when I should have received and tried the wines I ordered from France and Italy, to give you a note....

Whereupon the Sage of Monticello charged on for several detailed paragraphs about some of the most celebrated vintages grown in Europe and where to buy them.

President Monroe responded the next month by profusely thanking his mentor for his expertise on wine and even offering to expand his order, just in case Jefferson wanted more wine for himself.

John Quincy Adams wasn't enthused about vintage topics. In 1807, when Jefferson was still president, Adams was invited to dinner. In his diary entry, Adams—whose father had been one of Jefferson's rivals—yawningly penned: "There was, as usual, a dissertation upon wines. Not very edifying."

As for Jefferson, he even found wine a suitable simile for friendship itself. In an 1811 letter to Dr. Benjamin Rush, he wrote: "I find friendship to be like wine, raw when new, ripened with age, the true old man's milk and restorative cordial...."

THE DAMAGES

Jefferson was quite diligent about recording how much wine he bought and how much his guests consumed. He bought in very large quantities, but since he entertained almost constantly, the supply inevitably ran low.

As testament to Jefferson's big orders, in 1801 (his first year as president) he would often purchase his Madeira wine by the "pipe"—each pipe holding more than one hundred gallons—at a cost of approximately $350.00. He once ordered 240 bottles of Hungarian wine with a price tag of over five hundred dollars.

As proof that TJ was apt to err on the side of caution, he once estimated that he needed more than four hundred bottles of champagne per year to entertain at the Executive Mansion but robustly rounded up that calculation to five hundred bottles (Why be caught short?). One can readily see how Jefferson's pursuit of both quality and quantity for his wine cellar could rapidly put a dent in the twenty-five-thousand-dollar salary that he drew as president.

Sometimes the wine ran out fast. When the Marquis de Lafayette visited in November 1824, he stayed at Monticello for eleven days. As one might imagine, Lafayette was quite a draw (Jefferson himself had not seen him in thirty-five years, and they greeted each other in a tearful embrace), and so there were several elaborate dinners—and much wine-drinking—at Jefferson's expense. After the famous French patriot had departed, Jefferson's correspondence contained a plea to a Richmond wine merchant for some bottles ("... must pray you send me a box of Claret of about two dozen by the first wagon....") to tide him over—as his own cellar was nearly empty and an expected European shipment was yet to arrive.

An examination of Jefferson's wine cellar in his last years reflects the financial stress he must have been feeling. It was still well stocked, but with less of the expensive wines; the cellar even held some very mediocre domestic vintages.

But even before that, Jefferson—a few years after leaving the presidency—was well aware of his precarious financial situation. In 1813, he petitioned Congress to sell them his personal library of more than six thousand volumes. The idea was to replace the library burned down by the British when the invaders torched Washington, and Congress was receptive. For Jefferson it meant a much-welcomed financial infusion of nearly $24,000. But the majority of that money went to pay some major debts, and certainly Jefferson could not have afforded to return to the high living standards he maintained during his presidential years.

GUY WALKS INTO A WINE AUCTION . . .

Was it the great historical wine find? Or was it the great historical wine *fraud*?

In 2007, the *New Yorker* magazine ("The Jefferson Bottles" by Patrick Radden Keefe) examined the sale of some very expensive wines said to have once been owned—or at least purchased with intent to ship—by Thomas Jefferson. Random House published a book on the same subject—*The Billionaire's Vinegar: The Mystery of the World's Most Expensive Bottle of Wine* by Benjamin Wallace—in 2008. The story revolves around a cache of dark green wine bottles, at least one lettered with the word "Lafitte," the date of "1787," and the initials "Th.J" (the insinuation being this was Jefferson's mark), and extracted from a bricked-up cellar wall in an old Parisian domicile. To believe the story requires believing the premise that these bottles were originally purchased by Jefferson but essentially remained undiscovered from about the time of the French Revolution until well into the twentieth century.

Were the wealthy, modern-day purchasers of the "Jefferson bottles" duped in a grand con? Or are the "Th.J" initialed bottles the real deal? In the legal sense—at least at this writing—much of the controversy is still unsettled.

In 1985, one bottle of the "Jefferson wine" (a Bordeaux) brought more than $150,000 at auction. The London auction house catalog described it as "inestimable" in value. But skeptics might claim "too good to be true" would have provided more accurate phraseology. A historian connected to Monticello, after examining the bottles, said she was dubious that Jefferson ever owned them.

LAST CALL

If the cost of an auctioned "Jefferson bottle" etched with the "Lafitte" name is beyond your means, do not despair. "Jefferson Tavern Ale"—a hefty but affordable libation from Yards Brewery in Philadelphia—can deliver good bang for the buck for the discerning beer drinker.

CHAPTER 4

James Madison

(1751–1836)

*J*ames Madison is often called "the Father of the Constitution" for drafting America's founding document. Madison also deserves partial credit for writing the *Federalist Papers* (with John Jay and Alexander Hamilton). Serving as Thomas Jefferson's secretary of state, Madison helped negotiate the Louisiana Purchase in 1803.

Madison became president in 1809, serving two terms. He presided over the War of 1812 (deemed "Mr. Madison's War" by his political foes) and endured the defeat of American troops at the Battle of Bladensburg, Maryland, and the humiliating burning of Washington (including the Executive Residence) that followed.

Like his good friend James Monroe, Madison was influenced by, and benefitted from, Jefferson's vast knowledge and appreciation of wine. In fact, Madison—like fellow Virginians Jefferson, Monroe, and John Tyler—championed wine (as opposed to whiskey) as a healthier and more respectable choice of alcohol for the American people.

Entertaining at the Executive Mansion or even at Montpelier (his plantation in Virginia), Madison was rarely naturally at ease. But while Madison may not have been the most gregarious host, his charming wife, Dolley, seems to have more than made up for it.

WINE VS. WHISKEY

James Madison Sr., the future president's father, had whiskey at the tobacco plantation—Montpelier—in the bucolic Virginia piedmont. But when it came to alcoholic preferences, Junior followed Thomas Jefferson—his presidential predecessor and fellow Virginian. That meant Madison saw wine as a positive addition to American culture and society and whiskey-swilling as a negative one—except when it could be used to swell the coffers of the U.S. Treasury, of course.

In 1817, Madison wrote to then president James Monroe, lauding his successor for "an overflowing Treasury" at a time when other countries were accumulating crippling debt. In the next flow of the pen, Madison encouraged Monroe to keep up the tax on whiskey—despite its controversial status dating back to Washington's day.

> May it not, however, deserve consideration whether the still tax, which is a moralizing as well as a very easy, productive tax, would not be advantageously retained.... Why not press on the whisky drinkers rather than the tea and coffee drinkers, or the drinkers of the lighter kinds of wine?

Not only that, but Madison was gleefully receptive to the development of native American wines—an idea about which Monroe and Jefferson also were quite keen, although native vineyards struggled to achieve even modest success in their era.

Nevertheless, when the American viticulturist and winemaker John Adlum wrote to Madison stressing the virtues of grapes grown on native ground, he found an enthusiastic ally. After Adlum sent Madison a bottle of native-grown Tokay wine, the former president replied:

It is so long since I tasted the celebrated wine whose name you
have adopted, that my memory cannot compare its flavour
with that of your specimen from an American grape. I am safe,
I believe, in saying that the latter has an affinity to the general
character of the good Hungarian wines, and that it can scarcely
fail to recommend itself to discriminating palates.

In the same letter, Madison writes: "The introduction of a native
wine is not a little recommended" and notes that an American wine
might serve the dual purpose of replacing expensive vintages imported
from Europe *and* encouraging Americans to back off on more "ardent
liquors" (i.e. whiskey and rum) that Madison believed to be so "destructive" to "the morals, the health, and the social happiness of the American people."

THE HARVEST TIME HOP

It was common practice in Madison's day that large landowners
would dole out cups of whiskey to their workers during the strenuous
harvest time. But given Madison's disdain for that powerful liquor, it is
not surprising that the retired president attempted to substitute beer in
place of the hard stuff. That action led to an amusing anecdote (from
Ralph L. Ketchman's *James Madison: A Biography*), as observed by the
early American writer James K. Paulding, when he and Madison were
riding around the grounds at Montpellier.

Mr. Madison had undertaken to substitute Beer in the room
of whiskey, as a beverage for his slaves in Harvest time, and
on one occasion, I remember stopt on a wheat field ... to
inquire how they liked the new drink—"O! ver fine masser"
said one old grey head—"but I tink a glass of whiskey vere
good to make it wholesome!" He [Madison] was excessively
diverted at this supplement of the old fellow, and often made
merry with it afterwards.

THE GREAT CHAMPAGNE EXPERIMENT

In her book *The First Forty Years of Washington Society*, Margaret Bayard Smith provides some insightful scenes from the post-Revolutionary, pre–Civil War era. One such glimpse includes a letter from her husband, Samuel Harrison Smith, involving James Madison and an experiment to see if more than a few glasses of champagne would result in what we today would term a "hangover." The champagne party took place in 1804 (during Thomas Jefferson's first term) when Madison was secretary of state:

> Have just returned, my dearest Margaret, from a dinning party at Genl. Dearborn's, where I met with Mrs. Madison and Mrs. Duval ... I have rarely spent more agreeable hours at a dinner table. Mr. Granger, who was present and who is a very agreeable man, after a few bottles of champagne were emptied, on the observation of Mr. Madison that it was the most delightful wine when drank in moderation, but that more than a few glasses always produced a headache the next day, remarked with point that this was the very time to try the experiment, as the next day being Sunday would allow time for a recovery from its effects. The point was not lost upon the host and bottle after bottle came in, without however I assure you the least invasion of sobriety. Its only effects were animated good humour and uninterrupted conversation.

THE HOUSE WINE

Not all of Smith's historical memories were quite so lighthearted. In late August of 1814, she fled Washington when British troops routed the Americans in the Battle of Bladensburg and occupied the Executive Residence. (It was not yet called the "White House" in Madison's time.) Dolley Madison barely escaped capture; in fact, her dinner (cooked by her French chef and prepared for forty guests at a long table) was still warm when the British sailors and marines stormed the capital.

One British author noted that the wine—bottles of it lying in coolers near the table—was "very good." As a taunting entertainment, British admiral George Cockburn (who was quite keen to start burning down the Executive Residence, primarily in retaliation for the torching of York, Ontario, by American troops earlier in the war) forced a young American bookseller to join the enemy at the presidential table, just before the king's men put the residence to the torch and "the heavens redden'd with the blaze." As Smith wrote in her memoirs:

> The day before Cockburn paid this house a visit and forced a young gentleman of our acquaintance to go with him,—on entering the dining room they found the table spread for dinner, left precipitally by Mrs. M,—he insisted on young Weightman's sitting down and drinking Jemmy's health, which was the only epithet he used whenever he spoke of the President.

The president and Mrs. Madison enjoyed a well-stocked wine cellar (by some accounts, one thousand bottles) at the Executive Residence, but apparently the bulk (but not all) of it escaped both the insult of satisfying British palates and the subsequent conflagration. It was a small consolation to the humbling defeat at the hands of the British Lion. "Mrs. M. lost all her own property," Smith noted. "The wine, of which there was a great quantity, was consumed by our own soldiers."

The reason most of the wine was consumed by retreating Americans was that the French staff member—one Jean Pierre Sioussa—set out buckets of wine and water, anticipating that thirsty troops would be in need of refreshment. Indeed they were hustling through Washington at great haste, the redcoats in spirited pursuit like hounds on a foxhunt back in England.

POP STAR

Years after the "Great Champagne Experiment," Madison—now president of the United States—remained wary of the imported French bubbly. In fact, Madison was aware that the celebratory wine could be explosive—both figuratively and literally.

Isaac Briggs, a noted surveyor of the post-Revolutionary era, visited President Madison a few days before Christmas 1816. (Briggs had performed years of surveying services for President Jefferson after the United States wrangled the vast Louisiana Purchase from Napoleon in 1803 and was on friendly terms with both Jefferson and Madison.) He found the president in a delightful mood and readily accepted when Madison invited him to return in the late afternoon for a "potluck" dinner. Briggs, who had been born a Quaker, was nonetheless amused by an incident that occurred after he "partook of an excellent family dinner." He included this anecdote in a letter to his wife:

> Dolly [sic] attempted to open a bottle of Champagne wine, the cork flew to a distant corner of the room with an explosion as loud as—the sound of a popgun. She looked scared, and the wine seemed to be in a haste to follow the cork. She however dexterously filled 3 large glasses, one for me, one for her sister Lucy Washington [Todd], and one for herself. She handed the bottle to her husband but he would not take more than half-a-glass; I remarked after tasting it that it was very treacherous wine—yes, said the President addressing himself to Lucy, if you drink too much of it, it will make you hop like a cork. Dolly [sic] and Lucy, however, both took 2 glasses, but they soon afterwards left the table and retired—one glass and a half was as much as my head could bear without feeling uncomfortable.

JOHN TODD'S TRANSGRESSIONS

John Todd, Madison's stepson, was a loose cannon who resisted the president's best efforts to steady him. Perhaps it was more Madison's love for Dolley that fueled his willingness even to try, as Todd lost heaps of money through gambling and killed numerous brain cells (apparently in short supply to begin with) through heavy drinking. Madison secretly paid off some of Todd's debts, sparing Dolley the knowledge and shame of her son's destructive habits.

LAST CALL

While a student at the College of New Jersey (which became Princeton University in 1896), Madison—like many college students of that era—enjoyed "small" beer (light beer) and hard cider at the dinner table.... Madison lost one of his earliest elections for a Virginia delegate office when his opponent outspent him and supplied lavish amounts of whiskey to the voters.

CHAPTER 5

James Monroe

(1758–1831)

*N*obody could ever question the patriotism of James Monroe, the man who became the fifth president of the United States (1817–1825). The Virginian was not even nineteen years old when he took a musket ball in his left shoulder as the American army swarmed over the Hessians in the stormy morning-after-Christmas surprise attack at Trenton.

Held in high esteem by General George Washington (though their relationship later soured), young Monroe also formed a lasting friendship with the Marquis de Lafayette during the struggle for independence.

When the Revolutionary War ended, Monroe was called upon to serve diplomatic stints in Paris, France, where he helped negotiate the Louisiana Purchase on behalf of President Thomas Jefferson in 1803 and, like Jefferson before him, furthered his taste for both French cuisine and wines.

Andrew Jackson's great victory over the British at New Orleans in 1815 certainly got the attention of all the European powers. So when

Monroe followed his friend James Madison to the presidency, he inherited one of the most tranquil periods of American history—the so-called "Era of Good Feeling."

Along with his secretary of state, John Quincy Adams, Monroe put forth a strong foreign policy, including the renowned Monroe Doctrine. When not on the job, Monroe enjoyed the finer aspects of life, and that certainly included wonderful wines with his lavish dinners.

THE TRIALS OF THE TOAST

In Monroe's age, diplomats, politicians, and, indeed, anyone claiming to be a gentleman, was extremely sensitive to protocol and slights—real or perceived. Toasts and seating arrangements often brought these incidents of social tightrope-walking to the forefront. Blatant insults, of course, called for some sort of counteraction, perhaps insisting on an apology. But in the crazy heyday of dueling, it was also not unheard of to issue a challenge to meet on the so-called "field of honor." (Monroe, in fact, came quite close to dueling with Alexander Hamilton in 1792, prior to Hamilton's deadly duel with Aaron Burr in 1804.)

One such incident occurred in Monroe's diplomatic career when he was squeezed in between two minor German diplomats at a table in London. When toasts (sometimes called "sentiments" in that era) began, Monroe—testy about a seating arrangement that seemed, at best, an afterthought, if not a deliberate slight, given that German mercenaries had nearly killed him at Trenton—placed his wine glass upside-down in the finger bowl when "The King!" was toasted.

Keeping in mind that the Revolutionary War had ended about twenty years before and the War of 1812 loomed just a few years in the future, relations between England and its former colony remained as chilly as a Scottish loch.

Noticing Monroe's pique, the Russian ambassador stepped up and proposed a toast to the new president of the United States, and Monroe—his diplomatic feathers (and ego) now somewhat smoothed—rose to the occasion. Monroe then reciprocated with a toast to his new ally: "The health and prosperity of our friend, the Emperor of Russia!"

WHAT A PAINE

Thomas Paine—the fiery, hard-drinking author of *Common Sense*—lived in Paris after the American Revolution. But the English-born pamphleteer ran afoul of the hotheads of the French Revolution (by, for example, openly objecting to capital punishment) and found himself imprisoned for ten months in 1794. His detractors claimed alcohol was at least partly responsible for his pigheadedness. As one noted:

> He was a great drunkard [in Paris], and Mr. M., a merchant of this city, who lived with him when he was arrested by order of Robespierre, tells me he was intoxicated when that event happened.

Gouverneur Morris, one of the signers of the Declaration of Independence, was the American minister in Paris and Monroe's predecessor in that office. Morris—a Federalist senator from New York—disliked the radically inclined Paine, as he openly documented in his diary:

> [Paine] came to my house in company with Colonel Oswald, and, being a little more drunk than usual, behaved extremely ill, and through his insolence, I discovered his vain ambition. At present, I am told, he is besotted from morning till night.

So Morris did nothing to free Paine and, instead, concentrated on shipping his own precious wine collection back to the United States. That included some bottles of imperial Tokay that had once belonged to the guillotined queen, Marie Antoinette, as the sly and thrifty Morris had managed to scarf them up at a ridiculously low price. Successful in this venture, Morris embarked on some European travel, while Paine languished in prison.

When Monroe arrived in Paris, he immediately set to work, subtly at first, to free Paine (and the wife of his former brother-in-arms, the Marquis de Lafayette) and finally managed to succeed with both of these delicate cases.

When Paine was sprung, he was suffering from a terrible fever. Monroe's wife, Elizabeth, patiently nursed Paine back to health. Given the times, it stands to reason that alcohol would have been part of that process, and that certainly was a substance with which Paine's body was not unfamiliar.

Paine—drunk, sober, or feverish—plotted revenge against George Washington because he felt that the president (like Morris) had done nothing to help him in his hour of need. But he moved out of Monroe's house before he began to abuse Washington (at least with any real venom). He no doubt realized his benefactor was in a delicate situation—representing the president but harboring one of Washington's most vocal (and rare) critics. As for Monroe, he sensed what was coming and wrote to his friend James Madison on July 5, 1796, expressing that exact worry:

> [Paine] thinks the President winked at his imprisonment and wished he might die in gaol, and bears him resentment for it; also he is preparing an attack upon him of the most virulent kind.

And Paine soon did. In his *Letter to George Washington*, for example, Paine stormed: "The world will be puzzled to decide whether you are an apostate or an imposter; whether you have abandoned good principles or whether you ever had any."

Paine died in Greenwich Village, New York, in 1809. By some accounts he was drinking several bottles of rum a week just prior to his death—but, given the era, it might have been viewed as standard medical strategy to combat his illnesses.

WHERE'S OUR WINE?

Unlike Paine, Monroe was not a consistent imbiber of rum. Ever the Virginia country squire, Monroe usually chose wine. Like his friend James Madison, Monroe was greatly influenced by Thomas Jefferson in regards to wine. Although the Virginians dabbled in attempts to grow their own vineyards (with very little success), they depended primarily on imports for their best bottles.

And so we find James Monroe contacting Madison (and we can almost sense his frustration) about a wine shipment that both men had apparently been anxiously awaiting.

On July 13, 1799, Monroe (soon to be governor of Virginia) felt compelled to write Madison:

> Dear Sir
>
> Have you ever rec. y. wine from Mr. Yard? I hope we shall receive it, since to me, it will be a most acceptable accommodation having had none of any kind for a long time; and if it really is of the quality we are taught to expect of it, it will also be of importance to you.

And then, as if to emphasize the urgency, Monroe pleads: "If you have not written for it, had you not better yet do it?"

THE "LIQUID FURNITURE" FUND

After becoming president in 1817, Monroe embarked on bringing the Executive Mansion decor up to his exacting standards. Given his Francophile tastes, Monroe imported luxury furniture from France and had other pieces made by skilled craftsmen. Congress had provided twenty thousand dollars for these endeavors, but Monroe soon exceeded that amount and brought in some of his own personal furnishings to bolster the redecorating efforts.

Unfortunately for Monroe, he put Colonel Samuel Lane in charge of the payments of the furniture fund, and Lane seemingly made a mess of it. (But the full extent of that mess was not discovered until after Lane's death in 1822.)

One of Lane's questionable maneuvers was the acquisition of 1,200 bottles of Burgundy wine and champagne from France that—carelessly or purposely—got charged to the furniture account. That, and similar errors, resulted in Monroe's unpleasant surprise of finding he owed various creditors several thousands of dollars.

All but Monroe's most ardent enemies believed him to be personally innocent of these miscalculations concerning the wine. As Thomas Jefferson once reportedly said of him: "Monroe was so honest that if you turned his soul inside out there would not be a spot on it."

THE PLANTATION TOUCH

Monroe, like many of the pre–Civil War presidents, owned slaves and brought some servants to the Executive Mansion. The house slaves served dinners and drinks at parties—often called "levees" in Monroe's time. As a Mrs. Tuley of Virginia described a New Year's reception at the Executive Mansion:

> All the lower rooms were open and though well filled, not uncomfortable. The rooms were warmed by great fires of hickory wood in the large open fire-places, and with the handsome brass and irons and fenders quite remind me of our grand old wood fires in Virginia. Wine was handed about in wine glasses on large silver salvers, by colored waiters dressed in dark livery, gilt buttons, etc. I suppose some of them must have come from Mr. Monroe's old family seat, Oak Hill, Virginia.

THE TROUBLE WITH TOMPKINS

The guzzling Thomas Paine was not the only drinker to cause Monroe headaches during his political life. Vice President Daniel D. Tompkins, a New York City politician, provided geographical balance to the Monroe ticket in 1816—but Tompkins also proved to be a problem drinker.

One of Tompkins's main jobs was to preside over the Senate, but he sometimes was too inebriated even to perform the moderate demands of that duty.

Due to his alcoholism, Tompkins was forced to leave Washington for a while, but he returned late in Monroe's second term and appeared to be making a good attempt at recovery. As then secretary of state John Quincy Adams chronicled in his diary entry of January 25, 1824:

> I visited Vice-President Tompkins, who arrived in the city and took the Chair of the Senate last Tuesday. He told me that he had recovered his health, with the exception of sleepless nights, and that he was relieved from all his embarrassments ... and he wished for nothing hereafter but quiet and retirement.

Worried by financial problems, and perhaps compromised by the accumulative effects of his alcohol abuse, Tompkins died within a year of leaving office.

DOUBLE-FISTED

There are two drink recipes associated with Monroe. One is a potentially lethal punch and the second a rather benign-sounding dessert.

Chatham Artillery Punch

It was allegedly labeled "suave and deceitful" by President Monroe when he supposedly sampled some on his 1819 visit to the port city of Savannah, Georgia. The recipe typically features an array of alcohol. Obviously this recipe is intended for dozens and dozens of experienced imbibers:

Ingredients:

1.5 gallons strong tea
1.5 gallons Catawba or scuppernong wine
½ gallon of rum
1.5 quarts of rye whiskey
1 quart of brandy

> 1 quart of gin
> ½ pint Benedictine
> 2.5 pounds brown sugar
> 1 bottle of maraschino cherries
> juice of 18 oranges
> juice of 18 lemons
> case of champagne

Prep: first pour all the ingredients, except for the champagne, into a non-reactive container. Second: Let it rest for a day and a half to two days. Third: Just before the celebration, dump into an extra-large punch bowl or tub over lots of ice, and then add the champagne. Four: Make sleeping arrangements for any over-indulgers, or bring in a battalion of designated drivers.

Syllabub

On the other end of the alcohol recipe spectrum, consider Monroe's "Syllabub" dessert. It requires far less alcohol, far less prep time, and will dispense with the need for extra sleeping bags.

The origins of this dessert trace back to Old England, but the colonials—and then the new Americans—did not hold that fact against it. Syllabub was a light, refreshing dessert that would have been perfect for hot, sultry summer evenings in Virginia.

Ingredients:

> 1.5 cups of whipping cream
> 2 lemons
> ½ cup sugar
> ½ cup white wine
> ¼ cup dry sherry

Prep: whisk the whipping cream until it gets slightly thick. Add the lemon juice, sugar, and white wine and sherry to the cream—one at a time—whisking after each new addition. Whisk this batch until it gets thick, three to five minutes. Pour promptly into parfait glasses and refrigerate overnight. The concoction will separate when it stands. You can top it off with more whipped cream prior to serving.

LAST CALL

As a young officer in the Revolution, Monroe (as did most soldiers) drank whenever the army had—or captured—stores of liquor.... Monroe's immediate superior during the war was Lord Stirling (William Alexander), and allegedly one of Monroe's camp duties was to keep his commander's glass full.... When the Marquis de Lafayette made his U.S. tour in 1824–1825 (about fifty years after the Revolution began), he stopped to see his old friend Monroe (first at the Executive Mansion and then later at Oak Hill), and many toasts were executed in the celebrated Frenchman's honor.

CHAPTER 6

John Quincy Adams

(1767–1848)

The first son of a president to become president, John Quincy Adams was the stereotypical New Englander—flinty, blunt, and slow-to-warm. But at least he was self-aware. The country's sixth president (1825–1829) confessed that he lacked "the honey" to ever be a "true flycatcher."

Like his father, John Quincy Adams was a dedicated diarist—even though he occasionally threatened to abandon the task. Adams certainly did not have the capacity (or urge) for drinking that his father did. Perhaps he was nudged toward moderation by a rare—but memorable—head-butt delivered by John Barleycorn when he was a twenty-year-old law student in Newburyport, Massachusetts. It proved to be a lopsided confrontation: Adams was left with a lingering, three-day hangover and a wary respect for his liquid adversary.

But Adams more than held his own against powerful political opponents of his era, chief among them the volatile Andrew Jackson. Adams, a Federalist, also sometimes clashed with Henry Clay but was not above alliances with Clay (nor Clay with Adams); when it came to battling "Old Hickory," the theory of "the enemy of my enemy is my friend" prevailed.

Adams was a sore loser. When Jackson—his arch nemesis—swept him from office after just one term, JQA bolted for New England before Inauguration Day dawned in Washington. But he eventually returned to the capital, as a senator in 1831. John Quincy Adams died on February 21, 1848, after collapsing in the House chamber. One of his honorary pallbearers was a wet-behind-the-ears congressman from Illinois by the name of Abraham Lincoln.

HARVARD DAYS

Just prior to entering Harvard in 1786, a teenage John Quincy Adams (in a December 31, 1785, diary entry) proclaimed: "Whatever errors, or foibles, may have mislead me ... at least I have not to reproach myself with Vice, which has always been my principle to dread, and my Endeavor to shun."

JQA probably did not pursue "Vice" (even with a small "v") with any real vigor during his year at Harvard (given junior status upon entry, he graduated in 1786), either. But as a member of Phi Beta Kappa, he did sometimes cut loose at their celebrations, as noted at one such gathering: "Wit and wine, the Bottle and the Joke, kept nearly an equal pace. When the Prayer Bell rung we broke up, and attended Prayers."

But in the same year, Adams voiced his disapproval of a celebration that took place on the site of one of the Revolution's early battles (and one that Adams, as a young boy, had witnessed from afar). In his entry of June 17, he records:

> A Dinner was provided for 600 People on Bunker's hill: the havoc of oxen, sheep, and fowls of all kinds ... and I dare say, there was as much wine drank now, as there was blood spilt then.

As for fellow students that did overindulge, Adams (one can almost sense his disdain) does mention some of the more outrageous incidents.

Of one student who broke his leg, Adams reports that he was "drunk as a beast." And he detailed the untimely tumble of another in his diary (November 24, 1786):

> This evening, just after tea ... we were called out by the falling of a fellow, from the top of the stairs. He was in liquor and fell in such a manner, that his head was on the lower floor, and his feet two or three steps up ... the blood was streaming from his head, his eyes appeared fixed, and he was wholly motionless. We all supposed him dead. He soon recovered, however....

JQA'S FANTASTIC FROLIC

In John Quincy Adams's day, going on a "frolick" usually equated to "a bender" or "a binge" in modern terminology.

Although Adams seems to have been quite temperate during his college days, he definitely (though rarely) overindulged as a law student. In fact, JQA was blindsided by a "liquid learning experience" in late September 1787.

It started innocently enough with Adams stopping by to enjoy dinner with friends. But whatever they washed down their supper with (Madeira? Rum? He's not specific) soon got the upper hand. As his entry of September 29, records:

> In the evening I took something of a long walk with Townsend; and as I return'd stopp'd to sup; upon the birds, which Amory and Stacey, had been hunting for in the course of the day. There were three other gentlemen there, Mr. Coffin, Mr. Winslow, and a Captain Cochran. We got to singing after supper, and the bottle went round with an unusual rapidity, untill, a round dozen had disappeared. I then thought it was high time to retreat, and with some difficulty slip'd away from those of the company, who appeared to be the most inspired....

But Adams's "retreat" apparently did not come soon enough, as the next day's entry (despite an initial reluctance to admit that he had over-indulged) soon makes clear:

> Although I had not last night, been guilty of an excess so far as to be intoxicated, yet I had not sufficiently consulted what my feelings would be this day, to be entirely prudent. I therefore arose this morning, with a very disagreeable head-ache, which continued the whole day. I could neither attend meeting nor read, nor write; and pass'd the day with much tediousness.

There is a tone of incredulousness to JQA's entry of October 1, a Monday. He is somewhat stunned that he is still suffering, and the initial claims of not actually having been intoxicated have disappeared, replaced by some regrets.

> I have not yet got over the consequences of our frolick on Saturday evening. Three whole evenings I have by this means entirely lost, for I cannot yet write with any comfort. How inseparably all cases of intemperance, is the punishment allied to the fault!

ONCE BITTEN, TWICE SHY

Less than a month later, Adams indulged at a friend's engagement celebration—but he was among the cautious few.

> At Twelve we went to Mr. Thaxter's lodgings, and found fifty or sixty people heartily at work, in which we readily joined them. At about 2, there were 18 to 20 left who sat down to a table covered with "big bellied bottles." For 2 hours or more Bacchus and Momus joined hands to increase the festivity of the Company. But the former of these deities then of a sudden took a fancy to divert himself, and fell to tripping up their

heels ... by five o'clock they were all under the table except those who had been peculiarly cautious....

Among the "peculiarly cautious" must have been JQA, because the next day's diary entry proudly recorded: "Rose at about 8 this morning, and felt no inconveniency from the scene of yesterday...."

THE ARTFUL DODGER

William Amory, one of Adams's fellow law students in Newburyport, was something of an eighteenth-century party animal. JQA obviously was wise to this fact (particularly after the "frolick" incident), and his diary sometimes refers to his declining to attend potentially damaging get-togethers with Amory. One of those incidents, successfully dodged by the astute future president, occurred in March 1788:

> The lads who dined at Davenport's warm'd themselves so well with Madeira, that at about seven o'clock this evening, they set out upon an expedition to Cape-Ann, to attend a ball there this night. Twenty seven miles in such weather and such roads after seven o'clock at night, to attend a ball, would look extravagant in a common person, but is quite characteristic of Amory.

CLASHING WITH CLAY

Adams knew full well that Henry Clay—an avid enthusiast of gambling and whiskey to the extent that his governmental duties sometimes seemed like an afterthought—wielded considerable political clout. In fact, on more than one occasion in his career, JQA found himself forced to work with—or at least alongside—the famous Kentuckian. Andrew Jackson and his loyalists, of course, insisted that Adams and Clay had colluded—the infamous "corrupt bargain"—to steal the election of 1824 from the "Hero of New Orleans." (It wasn't all that far-fetched a conclusion; Clay had steered his votes to Adams and—after JQA was elected—Adams named Clay as his secretary of state.)

Adams, however, was quite clear about what he thought of Clay's questionable lifestyle, once snidely quipping that the senator's coat of arms should feature "a pistol, a pack of playing cards, and a bottle."

Long before Adams ran for president, he glimpsed Clay's reveling lifestyle at close quarters when both men were in Ghent, Belgium, (1814–1815) to hash out the complicated peace treaty with England following the War of 1812.

In July of 1814, Adams's diary reflected his disgust toward Clay and some of the other American negotiators:

> I dined again at the table-d'hote at one. The other gentlemen dined together, at four. They sit after dinner and drink bad wine and smoke cigars, which suits neither my habits nor my health, and absorbs time which I cannot spare.

And later in the same year, Adams—stirring just before dawn as was his routine—wrote:

> I heard Mr. Clay's company retiring from his chambers. I left him with Mr. Russell, Mr. Bentzon, and Mr. Todd at cards. They parted as I was about to rise.

THE TAZEWELL TOKAY TWEAK

As a man committed to the Andrew Jackson camp, Littleton Waller Tazewell—a Virginian elected to the U.S. Senate in 1824—was a natural foe in the eyes of John Quincy Adams. That fact considered, JQA simply couldn't resist tweaking Tazewell when the opportunity arose.

And that opportunity arose over not some crucial piece of legislation, but wine.

At a well-attended Executive Mansion dinner, Tazewell proclaimed that Rhenish wine and Tokay wine tasted alike. Adams—who had definitely sipped Tokay wine while in Europe—all but sniffed in contempt: "Sir … I do not believe you ever drank a drop of Tokay in your life."

Had someone dropped a fork on the floor, certainly the rattle and clank would have reverberated through the Executive Mansion.

Adams issued what must have been a halfhearted apology (days later and through an intermediary), and Tazewell "officially" accepted it, but undoubtedly like a child forced to swallow a dose of evil-tasting medicine. Adams didn't believe Tazewell's acceptance was genuine, noting (almost gleefully) in his diary: "… the shaft was sped barbed with truth, and it will rankle in [Tazewell's] side till his dying hour."

MY THREE SONS

All of JQA's sons turned out to be hard drinkers, and only one of them—Charles Francis Adams—proved able to function at a high level.

George Washington Adams was the first-born son, but—despite sparks of early promise—he was plagued by debts and alcohol addiction for much of his life. He plunged into the New York Harbor and died in 1829, the remaining mystery being only if his fall was an accident or a suicide.

John Adams II did not fare any better. Born on the Fourth of July, he worked as a secretary for his father when he was president, but he, too, succumbed to drink and met an early demise at just thirty-one years of age.

Charles Francis Adams (who ran unsuccessfully for vice president in 1848 and served as Lincoln's minister to Great Britain during the Civil War), like his grandfather and father before him, faithfully kept a diary. He was usually able to handle his alcohol. But in an incident very reminiscent of his father's, CFA experienced one memorable night—and an epic and awful aftermath—when he drank too much champagne. The incident occurred while playing cards during his Harvard days:

> The great length of the term also had soured us much…. The fact is we were set in for a debauch and one long expected. After the first rubber had been played, the Champagne Wine

which was the provision, was produced and one bottle placed before each man.

After the Harvard students guzzled down their respective bottles, some became rowdy enough (breaking glassware and some furniture) that the proprietor of the tavern had them forcibly removed.

We then went to walk, and returned on a rolling walk. For myself I was sick … as this agitation affected me....

Predictably, the president's son did not feel much better in the morning, and he missed both morning prayers and his classes.

My mouth very parched and I felt under the influence of fever … In fact I never was so much affected by an affair of this kind in my life. I was not intoxicated for I went to bed perfectly conscious of my actions and with a perfect command over myself. But I had drunk nearly a bottle and a half of this Champagne Wine and felt quite loaded in the consequence.

LAST CALL

Like his father, JQA knew his Madeira well. He often drank two or three glasses of the strong wine in a sitting. Famously, JQA reportedly once "taste-tested" fourteen kinds of Madeira—and successfully identified eleven of them. A drinker of the amateur ranks (as one of his biographers concluded) could not have accomplished such a feat.

CHAPTER 7

Andrew Jackson

(1767–1845)

*W*hen the British attempted to invade New Orleans shortly before Christmas in 1814, Andrew Jackson supposedly bellowed: "I will smash them, so help me God!" Which he did (soundly repulsing the British on January 8, 1815) and his battlefield heroics eventually helped him become the seventh president of the United States (1829–1837).

Jackson's election dismayed his political rivals, including Henry Clay of Kentucky, who snidely said: "I cannot believe that the killing of 2500 Englishmen at New Orleans qualifies a person for the various, difficult, and complicated duties of the Chief Magistracy."

Despite being a slave-owner, President Jackson was a strong Unionist and famously faced down John C. Calhoun and South Carolina on the issue of Nullification (the notion that a state has the right to nullify, or invalidate, any federal law that that state has deemed unconstitutional).

Like more than a few general-presidents, Jackson was more skillful on the battlefield than he was in addressing complex economic or banking issues. Some historians believe that the ineptness of Jackson's policies helped create the Panic of 1837 (which occurred on Van Buren's watch and probably cost him a second term)—a severe downturn that featured numerous bank failures and a depression that lasted for several years.

WHISKEY FOR PISTOLS

Like George Washington, Andrew Jackson enjoyed the profits from a whiskey-making still—both at his historic homestead, the Hermitage, and also, prior to that, at his lesser-known Hunter's Hill Farm.

Jackson's letters and account books include more than a few references to whiskey, and it is obvious that he often used the powerful liquor made of rye and corn in place of hard money to pay for various items and debts. He also sold it at some small stores that he owned in the Nashville area. In September 1799, the man who would become famous for defending New Orleans against the British invasion wrote this letter to Robert Hays.

> Dear Sir—This morning your Pistols was handed to me by Mr. Brawley together with your letter for which I thank you. The whiskey you can have at any time in such quantities as you may think proper, or as you may require....

That the brace of pistols were greatly valued by Jackson should not be a surprise; he fought in several serious duels, brawls, and donnybrooks in his lifetime.

TRASHING THE EXECUTIVE MANSION

Jackson supporters would say their hero was—first and foremost—a "man of the people." But Jackson's detractors were equally insistent when they dubbed Old Hickory's most loyal followers "rabble."

In the wild aftermath of Jackson's first inauguration in 1829, it was difficult to argue with the latter assessment. After the new president was sworn in, thousands (crowd estimates ranged from ten thousand to thirty thousand) swarmed after Jackson's carriage as he made his way to the President's House.

Supreme Court associate justice Joseph Story remarked that the overflow included the "highest and most polished ... down to the most vulgar and gross in the nation." He further exclaimed, "I never saw such a mixture. The reign of King Mob seemed triumphant. I was glad to escape from the scene as soon as possible."

The situation became increasingly precarious once the president was in the Executive Mansion. Rough men, their boots caked with street slop, stood on once-dainty chairs to get a view of the Hero of New Orleans. The unwashed and uneducated pressed forward to offer Jackson their congratulations—had his back not already been against the wall, surely they would have slapped him hard between the shoulder blades. At one point, Jackson's men needed to form a protective scrum around the president to prevent him from being crushed by the surging masses.

Liquor played a role in this chaotic scenario. Thousands of Jackson's followers had been drinking toasts at his inauguration earlier in the day, and then they were offered—at the Executive Mansion nonetheless— buckets of spiked orange punch and wine to continue the celebration.

In the end, the rowdy crowd was coaxed outside only after the buckets of punch and wine were dispersed around the Executive Mansion grounds. Old Hickory's supporters climbed out windows to get to the liquor to sooth their throats, most raspy from the repetitive shouts of "Huzzah!" from the hours of jubilation.

In the words of Margaret Bayard Smith, a Washington socialite of the era:

> But what a scene did we witness! The Majesty of the People had disappeared, and a rabble, a mob, of boys, negros [sic], women, children, scrambling, fighting, romping. What a pity! What a pity! No arrangements had been made no police officers placed on duty and the whole house had been inundated.

The President, after having been literally nearly pressed to death and almost suffocated and torn to pieces by the people in their eagerness to shake hands with Old Hickory, had retreated through the back way or south front and had escaped to his lodgings at Gadsby's [tavern].

Cut glass and china to the amount of several thousand dollars had been broken in the struggle to get to the refreshments, punch and other articles had been carried out in tubs and buckets, but had it been in hogsheads it would have been insufficient … for 20,000 people, for it is said that number was there, tho' I think the number exaggerated.

WILD YOUTH

Andrew Jackson was sixty-one years old by the time he reached the Executive Mansion. His hard drinking days were long behind him. He was, in fact, in serious grief over the recent death of his beloved wife Rachel. Even his infamous temper was less easily triggered. The duels he had fought—including one that left bullets embedded in his body—had also taken a physical toll on his health. He was less than robust—except in the political arena, where he was still a formidable force.

His earliest biographers found ample evidence that the young Andy Jackson—who grew up hardscrabble poor in North Carolina and suffered punishment from the Redcoats during the Revolution—had raised his fair share of hell and hijinks.

Jackson biographer James Parton quoted a Salisbury, North Carolina, resident who remembered the young man of Scotch-Irish stock in this way: "Andrew Jackson was the most roaring, rollicking, game-cocking, horse-racing, card-playing, mischievous fellow that ever lived in Salisbury."

Parton (who talked to Salisbury residents for a book on Jackson that was published just prior to the Civil War) landed this gem from a woman, recalling her incredulous reaction when she'd heard Jackson was a candidate for the highest office in the land:

"What! Jackson up for President? *Jackson? Andrew Jackson?* The Jackson that used to live in Salisbury? Why, when he was here, he was such a rake that my husband would not bring him into the house!" (Then she paused and eased up slightly.) "It is true, he *might* have taken him out to the stable to weigh horses for a race, and might drink a glass of whiskey with him *there*. Well, if Andrew Jackson can be President, anybody can!"

Even after Jackson began to ascend the ladder of success (he was already a lawyer at age twenty-one and a congressman by twenty-nine), he never gave up his love of horseracing, cockfighting, billiards, and cards. With such rakish pursuits as his major entertainments, his biographer Parton—with something of a written "wink" to his readers— noted of Jackson's early adulthood:

> Betting in all its varieties was carried on continually.... The whisky bottle—could that be wanting?
>
> In all these sports—the innocent and the less innocent— Andrew Jackson was an occasional participant. He played billiards and cards, and both for money. He ran horses and bet on the horses of others. He was occasionally hilarious over his whisky or his wine, when he came to Nashville on Saturdays. At the cock-pit no man more eager than he. There are gentlemen of the first respectability now living at Nashville who remember seeing him often at the cock-pit in the public square adjoining the old Nashville inn, cheering on his favorite birds with loudest vociferation.

WINE TO THE WOUNDED

Like many "gentlemen" of his era, Andrew Jackson had a keen "sense of honor"—which is to say, he did not take an insult, real or perceived, lightly. Jackson also had a quick-to-the-boil temper. The combination led to several duels and brawls and dozens of other encounters that almost came to ignition.

In 1806, Jackson found himself mano a mano with a deadly skilled marksman—Charles Dickinson—in a pistol duel at a mere eight paces (about twenty-four feet) apart. Not surprisingly, some debts due Jackson from a horserace helped spark the argument, further fueled by an alleged insult to Jackson's wife, Rachel, that eventually escalated into the duel. Wagers around Nashville had Dickinson as the pre-duel favorite, but Jackson—who dressed in a loose frock coat over his tall-but-wiry frame—failed to fall when his enemy's projectile caught him in the ribs, about a half-inch from his heart. In fact, Dickinson was wide-eyed with the assumption (a wrong one, as it turned out) that he had missed Jackson completely. But Jackson lined up his stunned adversary and coolly aimed his dueling pistol. Then, in the words of James Parton:

> The pistol neither snapped nor went off. He looked at the trigger, and discovered that it had stopped at half cock. He drew it back to its place and took aim a second time. He fired. Dickinson's face blanched; he reeled; his friends rushed toward him, caught him in their arms, and gently seated him on the ground.... The blood was rushing from his side in a torrent....

Jackson walked to a nearby house to get his own wound attended to. But in the aftermath, he sent a bottle of wine to Dickinson's doctor to be used in the treatment of the man who had just tried to kill him on the so-called "field of honor." The gesture may have been gallant, but—wine or no wine—the doomed Dickinson died an agonizing death.

THE BUMPKIN'S BEST

Before Jackson ascended to the presidency, his detractors assumed that he was an ill-tempered and inarticulate woodsman from a state—Tennessee—barely beyond the stages of frontier. The post-inauguration party—and the damage inflicted on the Executive Mansion in its presentation—only enhanced those impressions and prejudices.

But Jackson's entertaining at the Executive Mansion soon proved to be a wonderful surprise for even non-supporters who visited. Some of the credit had to go to Jackson's niece, Emily Donelson, who helped Executive Mansion events run smoothly. The dinners were lavish and the libations complementing the copious amounts of food equally impressive.

Jackson would sometimes bring out whiskey for Executive Mansion visitors, occasionally sipping a glass himself. His wine cellar at the Executive Mansion was superb, and like most of the presidents before him, it included the best French wines, red and white, champagne, port, and Madeira.

JACKSON'S MOST FAMOUS TOAST

When Jackson was president, John C. Calhoun (his vice president at that time) was pushing the "states' rights" agenda. At the Thomas Jefferson Day dinner on April 13, 1830—a major affair for the Democrats—the ever-flinty Jackson showed up and proposed a toast: "Our Union!" he emphatically stated, lifting his glass. "It must be preserved!" Then Jackson, his point made, sat down.

This was not what the Nullification wing, mostly Southerners, wanted to hear. Calhoun—the South Carolinian—attempted to counter-toast with: "The Union—next to our liberty the most dear. May we all remember that it can only be preserved by respecting the rights of the States...."

Some accounts claim that Calhoun's hand shook when he made his toast, spilling some wine.

THE HAIR-TRIGGER TEMPER

Although Jackson was quite familiar with alcohol consumption, he didn't see its use as an excuse to tarnish someone's honor—specifically his own—without expecting some consequences.

Samuel Southard, New Jersey senator and the secretary of the navy under John Quincy Adams (himself an anti-Jackson man), made the mistake of bad-mouthing Old Hickory at an 1826 dinner gathering—one in which some wine also was consumed. Essentially, the senator suggested that Jackson's heroics at New Orleans in January 1815 had been exaggerated, and that James Monroe (then secretary of war) deserved the lion's share of the credit for ordering an army into the field to defeat the British in the first place.

Other than insulting his wife, nothing brought Jackson's Scotch-Irish temper to hard-boil faster than any insinuation that his military record had anything less than a spit-polish shine to it. When word of Southard's remarks got back to him, an infuriated Jackson quickly dashed off a letter to his offender, outlining the facts (as Jackson saw them) concerning his defense of New Orleans.

Jackson—with his demonstrated willingness to participate in duels of honor—always had to be regarded as a loose cannon. The Princeton-educated Southard would have been well aware of this and he soon sent back a letter with an "I-can't-recall-exactly-what-was-said" tone to it. Jackson's return letter continued to admonish Southard (and restate his own accomplishments at New Orleans), and, at one point, the general wrote:

> I have therefore to request when on your electioneering tours, or at your wine drinkings hereafter, you will not fail to recollect these historical facts, which indeed you ought long since have known....

Jackson eventually let the controversy fade away and Southard (who became governor of New Jersey) thereby managed to avoid the full force of the future president's infamous wrath. Southard, in fact, might have dodged a bullet—literally.

LAST CALL

Jackson's adopted son, Andrew Jackson Jr., lost most of his father's fortune due to reckless high stakes gambling, drinking, and bad business decisions. When Jackson's beloved Hermitage caught fire in 1834, Old

Hickory was quick to lament: "I suppose all the wines in the cellar have been destroyed?" In the 1950s, Old Crow launched a series of advertisements promoting its bourbon. The ads depicted famous political figures from the nineteenth century, and Andrew Jackson was featured prominently in some of them.

CHAPTER 8

Martin Van Buren

(1782–1862)

artin Van Buren, the eighth president of the United States (1837–1841), notched more nicknames than any other commander in chief. Some of them were nods to his political aplomb, such as "The Little Magician" (which also noted his short stature), "The American Talleyrand" (after the crafty French diplomat), and "The Red Fox of Kinderhook" (which referenced his hair color and his birthplace in New York State).

For the purposes of this book, however, one must mention "Blue Whiskey Van"—a moniker that he acquired while campaigning in Hudson Valley taverns early in his political career. Something of a backhanded compliment, "Blue Whiskey Van" supposedly spoke to Van Buren's ability to drink significant amounts of alcohol sans all the stumbling and mumbling that sometimes plague the less gifted in this dubious pursuit.

Unfortunately, Van Buren was much less steady in addressing the Panic of 1837, which featured bank failures and massive unemployment—

all of which undermined his presidency and helped sink his bid for a second term.

THE KINDERHOOK KID

Politics is full of ironies, and certainly Van Buren's 1840 loss to the onslaught of William Henry Harrison's "Hard Cider" charge qualifies as a prime example.

The political operatives behind Harrison's Whig platform went to great lengths to convince the public that "Old Tip" was a man of humble nature (a log cabin dweller, nonetheless!), while Van Buren (according to the Whigs) was an arrogant aristocrat who resided in a palace, supping on gourmet dinners chased down with expensive wines. While there was some truth to that depiction, Van Buren, by far, emerged from humbler beginnings than Harrison, who was born into a well-to-do Virginia plantation dynasty (before moving west to Ohio and Indiana). In fact, Van Buren—the Jacksonian Democrat—had been born in a tavern in Kinderhook (a small village south of Albany), New York, in 1782.

Abraham Van Buren—the future president's father—fought at the pivotal Battle of Saratoga in the Revolutionary War. He also owned an establishment that served as a watering hole, a spot to sell off the "liberated" belongings of hapless loyalists and, at times, a place to pick up one's mail. Young Martin (whose first language was Dutch) probably had a front-row seat for observing human nature and the intricacies of spirited debate (in Dutch, English, or an evolving hybrid of both) among the masses. It must have seemed logical to proceed to a career in law, followed by politics.

Harrison, by contrast, chose the army route. He took a page from the Andrew Jackson strategic outline: get famous for winning a few battles, then use that fame as a springboard to a political career.

Harrison supposedly was content to drink hard cider (the amounts were modest), but that snooty, affluent Van Buren needed champagne and Madeira, among other European luxuries (such as fancy clothes and a coach), on a daily basis—at least that was the Whig line.

Call it a flimflam, but the result was that Harrison (and running mate John Tyler) steamrolled the incumbent Van Buren in the 1840 presidential election. In fact, one political cartoon depicted just that—"Little Van" running for his life, with a rolling barrel of hard cider about to flatten him. It was an exaggeration only in the literal sense.

STEPPING UP FOR OLD HICKORY

An ardent Jackson Democrat, Van Buren was on hand on April 13, 1830, when Jackson, nicknamed Old Hickory, made his famous "Jefferson birthday dinner" speech to neutralize the anti-tariff Nullifiers—led by Jackson's own vice president, John C. Calhoun of South Carolina.

Jackson, poker-faced but poised to pounce, waited through a series of official toasts offered at the jam-packed Indian Queen Hotel in Washington, D.C. Then he rose to propose the first "volunteer" toast and sternly proclaimed to his audience: "Our Federal Union. It must be preserved." The "Nullies" in the crowd reluctantly rose and sheepishly pretended to sip their wine in solemn acknowledgement of the president's words—strong and unmistakable in their message.

At a mere five feet six inches, Van Buren was in danger of missing the historical moment, as taller and broader men rose before him in tense excitement. Van Buren later admitted: "When the President was called upon for his toast I was obliged to stand on my chair to get a distinct view of what passed in his vicinity."

Calhoun attempted to mitigate the damages from Jackson's preemptive punch, rising (and some observed with a slightly shaking hand on his wine glass) with his own toast of: "The Union—next to our liberty the most dear; may we all remember that it can only be preserved by respecting the rights of the States and distributing equally the benefit and burden of the Union."

Van Buren—then Jackson's secretary of state but destined to replace Calhoun as Old Hickory's vice president—followed with a toast that called for "Mutual forbearance and reciprocal concessions...."

Concessions—or, for that matter, reconciliations—are not traits for which Van Buren's mentor is typically remembered. With rare exceptions, Jackson held grudges.

VAN THE (TOP-SHELF) MAN

It should be said that the bit about Van Buren liking the finer stuff in life, particularly when it came to libations or food, was not without foundation. He liked top-shelf liquor and lots of it.

Like James Buchanan, who occupied the Executive Mansion two decades after him, Van Buren—by many reports—handled his alcohol with commendable expertise. Buchanan was a rather tall, big man, so "The Little Magician's" trickery when it came to avoiding at least the outward appearance of demon alcohol's worst effects seems all the more remarkable. Van Buren biographer Holmes Alexander wrote in 1935:

> It was during this canvas of 1807 that [Van Buren] seems to have developed another reputation for which he was extraordinarily pleased—and to all reports, justly so. The reference here is to his capacity for imbibing enormous amounts of intoxicants without the usual result, and for which he earned the proud title of Blue Whiskey Van ... this stood him in good stead, for most of the electioneering was done in the taprooms.

What did Van Buren drink? Many types of alcohol, though—despite the Blue Whiskey Van nickname—little of that hard liquor, especially in his later years. Van Buren's favorite libations started with the lighter table wines (including champagne), but he also enjoyed the heavier (and more alcoholic) Madeira, sherry, and after-dinner brandy. Van Buren sometimes splurged on the dark red Montepulciano wine from Italy (as did Thomas Jefferson before him).

Like Richard Nixon decades later, Van Buren was not above serving lesser-quality alcohol to his visitors. In November of 1831, Van Buren wrote William Rives, the former U.S. ambassador to France, requesting his help in snagging some top-notch vintages, but also some cheaper bottles "which will be good enough to give to my friends ... a few degrees above what is usually used with water."

THE SCHIEDAM CONNECTION

One drink that the young Martin Van Buren must have sampled (and later offered to guests) was somewhat unique to the Dutch settlers of New York—Schiedam, a powerful clear alcohol. Schiedam got its name from a Dutch city renowned for manufacturing the stuff as early as the sixteenth century. By the seventeenth century, distilleries in Schiedam were shipping their potent product to London, where it apparently hit the lower classes with a head-spinning smack. (England, in turn, shipped much of its grain to Holland, which the Dutch turned into more alcohol.)

The Dutch called this drink *Jenever*—and its English consumers knew it as "Dutch gin," or "Schiedam," in deference to the city that made so much of it. (As if to further testify to its wallop, one who downed a few ounces of Dutch gin—followed by a glass of lager beer as "a chaser"—is sometimes said to have experienced a *kopstootje,* a head-butt, in Dutch.)

Describing one of Van Buren's earliest campaigns (in 1808), historian Holmes Alexander put Schiedam front and center:

> The system of standing drinks in the Dutch counties (of New York) was to gather at the bar over a large loving cup compounded with Schiedam, and to pass it right to left down the line. Then, also from right to left, each man would replenish the cup until each had both bought and drunk a full one.
>
> Considering that Matt [Martin Van Buren] covered as many as a dozen taverns a day, his capacity seems to have been all that was said of it, and for that alone he unquestionably deserved his brother's vacated office of Surrogate Judge.

SOME TALL ORDERS

For a little man, Van Buren placed some rather big orders for alcohol. In his defense, he entertained fairly often, so he certainly was not consuming all of it himself.

For example, in 1819, Van Buren knocked out a letter to Jesse Holt (a lawyer he knew from Albany), asking his friend to secure a sizeable wine order on his behalf. "I want," wrote the future president, "about fifteen or twenty gallons of table wine—say prime Sicily, Madeira, or some other pleasant, but light and low wine to drink with dinner. I wish that you would get Mr. Duer, who takes this, to select it for me, and buy and send it up. Get me also a box of good raisins and a basket of good figs, and send them with the wine."

When he served as ambassador to England (1831–33), Van Buren felt he needed an adequate supply of Lynch's best champagne but ordered cheaper clarets and other wines to get him through less important social visits or gatherings.

Once he retired to Lindenwald, Van Buren—as an ex-president—still felt the need to entertain with a high level of hospitality. That meant multiple dinner courses, properly accompanied by vintages of reasonable merit. As visitor Richard B. Gooch remarked on one such visit to Van Buren's homestead: "There were a dozen courses with wines and champagne. After dinner, liqueurs and brandy were served in the drawing room."

GOUT GUYS

Van Buren and James Buchanan both loved to drink, and they both paid for it in later life. Both men suffered from gout, a disease that is often associated with overindulgence in alcohol and rich food. Van Buren relished oysters and wine, for example—both on the "no-no" list for those suffering from gout.

Van Buren was a prime candidate for gout, as he exercised little (fishing was one of his few activities) and often either attended or entertained with lavish dinners. By the 1840s, a visitor to Lindenwald wrote home to a relative, stating: "Van Buren has gotten fat." The former president was, of course, retired at that point, with little hope of a political comeback—although he did run halfheartedly as the Free Soil (anti-slavery) candidate in 1848, managing just ten percent of the vote in the election won by General Zachary Taylor, Whig and slave-owner.

Suffering from the disease in the last decade of his life, Van Buren journeyed to some health spas in search of relief—including the famed French resort at Aix-Les-Baines, Savoy, in 1854.

But Van Buren did not cut back on his favorite wines, and other alcohol was readily available at Lindenwald. "The Fox of Kinderhook" hosted New Year's Day festivities at his homestead in 1861 and bottles of wine, Schiedam, and a lemonade punch laced with Burgundy were featured beverages at the bash.

By the time of his death in 1862, Van Buren's health was assaulted by various illnesses (in addition to gout), including a bout of pneumonia, severe asthma attacks, and a weakened heart.

LAST CALL

President Van Buren's most talented son (of four) was John Van Buren, sometimes referred to as "Prince John" by his detractors, because he rubbed shoulders with European royalty. A lawyer with promise, John went on to serve in the U.S. Congress, but his reputation suffered from chasing women, drinking too much alcohol, and an addiction to gambling. When it came to vices, he lacked some of his father's restraint. John died just four years after his father, supposedly of exposure, while returning from Europe.

CHAPTER 9

William Henry Harrison

(1773–1841)

With a term that lasted a mere thirty-two days, William Henry Harrison served the shortest stint of any U.S. president. At sixty-eight years old, "Old Tip" was the oldest chief executive until Ronald Reagan entered the White House just a few days shy of his seventieth birthday.

Harrison's untimely death has been strongly attributed to his exposure to the bone-chilling March elements that greeted his Inauguration Day. Harrison himself deserves much of the blame, since he refused to wear a warm frock coat, gloves, or even a hat. To make matters worse, he delivered a tedious speech that lasted the better part of two hours. (And that was even after Daniel Webster edited the bloated text.) Historians chalk up Harrison's demise to pneumonia or pleurisy, but that insidious disease of accomplished men—ego—also played a role.

His doctors used both brandy and wine (and other stimulants) in a futile attempt to cure the fast-fading general. The use of alcohol to treat illness was standard procedure in Harrison's era and for decades after.

Alcohol may have failed to save Harrison, but it certainly played a huge role in his election. There is no other race in the history of American presidential elections that featured alcohol so prominently (and, at times, defiantly) as the rambunctious "Log Cabin and Hard Cider" campaign staged by the fervid backers of the Whig Party candidate. The very roots of the campaign theme came from an attempted slight that was featured in an opposition newspaper, a fact that no doubt made its success all that much sweeter for Harrison's army of supporters.

SON OF FALSTAFF

When the men who became known as the Founding Fathers gathered in Philadelphia for the First Continental Congress, they were not hesitant to play hard in between meetings. We know this from many letters and diary entries of some of the participants, particularly those that flowed from the pen of John Adams. In one such diary entry (September 4, 1774), Adams wrote:

> Spent the Evening at Mr. Mifflin's with [Richard Henry] Lee and Harrison from Virginia.... An elegant Supper, and We drank Sentiments [toasts] till 11 O Clock. Lee and Harrison were very high. Lee had dined with Mr. Dickinson, and drank Burgundy the whole Afternoon.

The Harrison in reference here was the wealthy Virginia plantation owner Benjamin Harrison V—a signer of the Declaration of Independence, governor of Virginia, father of William Henry Harrison (his seventh child), and great-grandfather of Benjamin Harrison. In addition to his bloodline connection to two U.S. presidents, Harrison V—as Adams's observation (he describes Harrison as "a large, luxurious gentleman") suggests—was a voracious lover of rich food and drink.

In fact, Adams also compared Benjamin Harrison V to Sir John Falstaff, the gluttonously rotund rogue of Shakespearean stage, infamous for his quaffing of alcohol, decimation of banquets, and other vices.

Benjamin Harrison V died in 1791, at the age of sixty-five, after a dinner party held at his Berkeley Estate on the James River, Virginia. His health had been compromised by gout, a disease prone to afflict those who overindulge in rich foods and alcohol.

WHISKEY AND THE FORT WAYNE TREATY

Benjamin Harrison V had hoped that William Henry would study medicine. But upon his father's death, William Henry embarked on a career in the army (serving early on as an aide-de-camp for General Mad Anthony Wayne in what was then called the Northwest Territories) and, eventually, upon the battlefield of politics.

The future ninth president of the United States used whiskey to lubricate the signing of a treaty that reaped three million acres of prime farmland. In September 1809, territorial governor William Henry Harrison (he served in that role from 1801 to 1813) gathered chiefs from various tribes to Fort Wayne. Taking a page from Benjamin Franklin's playbook, Harrison made it clear to the chiefs that no whiskey would be forthcoming until their "marks" of consent were on the treaty. As noted in a journal that recorded the events of September 17:

> The Putawatimies waited on the Governor & requested a little liquor, which was refused. The Governor observed that he was determined to shut up the liquor casks until all business was finished.

In addition to whiskey, Harrison (on behalf of President Madison) was authorized to pay some rather meager amounts of money—one thousand dollars to bigger tribes, such as the Miami, and half that to smaller tribes. (Often these sums were paid in actual goods, instead of coin or paper money.)

The Miami chiefs were more reluctant than others to sign the Treaty of Fort Wayne, but it again appears that alcohol played a pivotal and persuasive role. As the journal recorded on September 26:

> The evening the Governor had the greater part of the Miami at his lodgings and in a conversation of some hours.... A Complimentary answer was returned by the Head Chief Paccon & they returned about ten o'clock a little *melowed* with Wine.

In truth, "mellowed with wine" seems to be both a quaint and misleading use of phraseology. "Plied with whiskey" would have been much closer to the mark. Harrison was familiar with the whiskey strategy; he had used it before with other tribes for other land-grabs.

But the Treaty of Fort Wayne did not end Governor Harrison's problems; in fact, it may have accelerated them. Conspicuous by his absence, the war chief Tecumseh (and his brother Tenskwatawa—a reformed alcoholic known as "The Prophet") had no intention of ceding lands that the powerful Shawnee leader believed belonged to *all* the tribes.

TECUMSEH'S WINE QUIP

Set on a martial collision, in August 1810, Harrison had several tense and unfruitful meetings with the Shawnee chief in an attempt to get him to go along with the Treaty of Fort Wayne. Blunt and outspoken, Tecumseh refused to flinch and pointed out the obvious to Harrison—specifically that it would be the warriors such as themselves, and not President Madison, forced to settle the matter on the field of battle. According to some accounts of that era, when Harrison told Tecumseh that President Madison was highly unlikely to withdraw the Treaty of Fort Wayne, the chief replied something (there are slightly different versions, and most smack of flowery embellishment) like:

> As the great chief is to determine the matter, I hope the Great Spirit will put sense enough into his head to order you to give up those lands. It is true, he is so far off; he may sit in his town and drink his wine, while you and I will have to fight it out.

Ironically, it was Tecumseh's death that helped smooth the way for Harrison's ascension to the White House (though it came years later), as the governor-general repulsed an attack by warriors of Tecumseh's Indian Confederacy at Tippecanoe Creek on November 7, 1811, and then proceeded on to burn "the Prophet's" village. And Harrison was in command during the War of 1812 when the warriors (and their British allies) were routed at Thames River in Canada (1813). At Thames River, the Americans left the once-proud Tecumseh dead on the battlefield, his corpse mutilated.

WHISKEY'S WICKEDNESS

Although Harrison sometimes used whiskey to achieve political or military goals with the region's tribes, he well recognized the mass devastation inflicted by "ardent spirits" and attempted to abolish liquor sales by unscrupulous white traders. Harrison's July 29, 1805, address to the Indiana Territory's General Assembly featured a head-on plea for increased enforcement.

> You are witnesses to the abuses; you have seen our towns crowded with furious and drunken savages, our streets flowing with their blood, their arms and clothing bartered for the liquor that destroys them, and their miserable women and children enduring all the extremities of cold and hunger. So destructive has the progress of intemperance been among them that whole villages have been swept away....
>
> And are the natives of North America to experience the same fate with their brethren of the southern continent? It is with you, gentlemen, to divert from these children of nature the ruin that hangs over them.

Harrison had also seen how the abuse of whiskey had an injurious effect on the U.S. Army—not only on the common soldier, but also riddling the ranks of young officers. Arguments and real or imagined insults to honor, more than a few accelerated during drinking bouts, fueled a rash of duels between officers in Harrison's day.

A MAN OF MODERATION

Despite the horrors that Harrison had seen whiskey inflict on others, he occasionally imbibed—at least according to one of his most thorough biographers, James Green. In *William Henry Harrison: His Life and Times*, Green wrote that the general typically had a decanter of whiskey on his sideboard at his home in North Bend, Ohio, and would join guests in a glass or swallow a few medicinal sips himself when exposed to inclement weather. (Did he neglect this practice on the days just after his inauguration?)

As a man of prominence and reputation, Harrison also was expected to entertain. That may explain the sizeable alcohol order he put in to Philadelphia merchants in 1813, requesting if they would "be so obliging to send on to Pittsburgh as soon as possible a quarter cask of best Madeira wine, one ditto of Sherry and ten gallons of best French Brandy.... I wish to have the above articles at Pittsburgh upon my arrival there that I may take them down the river."

LOG CABINS AND HARD CIDER

Despite their similarities (both were military men of note), Andrew Jackson and William Henry Harrison were bitter political rivals. Harrison was active in the Whig Party of what was then called "the West" and unsuccessfully tried to beat Jackson protégé Martin Van Buren in the 1836 presidential race.

But in 1840, the aging Harrison and the Whigs could not be stopped. In one of political history's most clever counter-moves, the Whigs latched onto a Baltimore paper's snide remarks—and eventually rode them all the way to the Executive Mansion. What the anti-Harrison editorial stated was this:

Give him a barrel of hard cider and a pension of two thousand a year and, our word for it, he will sit the remainder of his days in a log cabin by a "sea coal" fire and study moral philosophy.

The Whigs soon re-drew those images and managed to portray Harrison (despite his wealthy Virginian roots and his stately home in North Bend, Ohio) as the friend of the common man. Harrison supporters soon "stumped" the country—building makeshift cabins, hoisting jugs of hard cider (and whiskey, as well), and bursting forth with boisterous songs. There were dozens and dozens of songs of the "Log Cabin and Hard Cider" campaign, with this a fairly typical stanza:

Let Van from his coolers of silver drink wine
And lounge on his cushioned settee
Our man on a buckeye bench can recline
Content with hard cider is he.

The campaign's ditties were designed to show that Harrison was—despite his fame as an Indian fighter—"a man of the people" living the humble life and enjoying its simple joys. Meanwhile, Van Buren was portrayed as a dainty, wine-drinking aristocrat and, therefore, out of touch with the laboring masses. (It did not help Van Buren's cause that the country was mired in an economic mess after the Panic of 1837; some of his enemies mockingly called him "Martin Van Ruin.")

Harrison addressed some of the bigger rallies, particularly one numbering in the thousands held on the Tippecanoe battlefield site in May 1840. Harrison, who drank moderately, took a few token pulls of cider to sooth his vocal cords. His followers—many under the influence of the hard cider flowing from dozens of refreshment stations situated around the grounds—cheered him wildly for it.

The Democratic opposition, well aware that the "Hard Cider" message packed a solid punch, attempted to push back by portraying

Whig supporters as drunken bumpkins and referring to the general himself as "Old Tip-ler" or "Granny" Harrison. But even though Van Buren was the incumbent, the ticket of Harrison and Vice President John Tyler ("Tippecanoe and Tyler, Too!") easily won the election.

THE DISTILLERY SOLUTION

There is some evidence that Harrison had an investment in a whiskey distillery. If so, that puts him in rather lofty presidential company with the likes of Washington and Harrison's political nemesis, Andrew Jackson.

Despite his roots to Virginia's plantation aristocracy, Harrison was not rich. Harrison and his wife, Anna, had ten children (though only four lived long enough to see the general win the Executive Mansion), and any income, from whiskey distilleries or any other enterprise, was probably welcomed. He once lamented in an 1805 letter to President Thomas Jefferson that "my nursery fills up faster than my strongbox."

LAST CALL

Harrison once ordered a beer-making text from a bookseller, so it seems possible that visitors to his North Bend homestead also had an option of drinking homebrew.... In 2005, a company in Indiana (no, it's not all from Kentucky) put out some high-end bourbon whiskey named for William Henry Harrison. One can only wonder how "Old Tip"— given his mixed emotions concerning whiskey—might have felt about such an honor.

CHAPTER 10

John Tyler

(1790–1862)

*W*hen the Whigs searched for a vice-presidential candidate to join General William Henry Harrison's ticket, they looked for someone who could solidify support in the South. John Tyler fit that bill—even if the genteel and mannered Virginian had little in common with those who flocked to Harrison's "Log Cabin and Hard Cider" campaign.

With Harrison's sudden death—after just one month in office—Tyler became America's tenth president (1841–1845) and the first vice president to ascend to the Executive Mansion in this twist-of-fate fashion. The aristocratic-looking Tyler—about six feet tall, thin, with an angular face and Roman nose—took the presidential oath on April 4, 1841. A self-confessed lover of champagne, if he toasted the moment, it was probably with that bubbly French wine.

Tyler fended off numerous assaults on his presidential powers but was almost immediately expelled from the Whig Party that had helped elect him. Tyler pushed to annex the Republic of Texas into the United

States and, as a life-long slave-owner, was perfectly willing to allow slavery to expand there.

Tyler died in 1862, at age seventy-one. Because of his loyalty to Virginia and the Confederacy, Tyler's death was not honored by the U.S. government, making him the only president shunned in this manner. But Tyler is buried in Richmond's Hollywood Cemetery, the final resting place of numerous heroes of the Confederacy, including generals J. E. B. Stuart and James Longstreet and CSA president Jefferson Davis.

CHAMPAGNE: "OUI"
FRENCH CUISINE: "NON"

Despite all the hoopla and huzzahs surrounding the "Log Cabin and Hard Cider" campaign, Tyler—like Harrison's defeated opponent, Martin Van Buren—enjoyed more dignified libations than that made from fermented apple juice or rye. In fact, like Jefferson, Monroe, and Madison before him, Tyler was quite smitten with French wine from the Champagne region.

While still a congressman in 1817, Tyler was invited to dine with President Madison and his wife, Dolley. In a letter to his wife, Letitia, about the event, he spoke glowingly about the hostess and the wine but less so of the food, which he found to be too French and fancy compared to his normal plantation fare.

> I dined on yesterday at the President's. He has invited me three times. Mrs. Madison is certainly a dignified woman, and entertains her company in superb style. In points of intellect, too, she far surpasses the foreign ministers' ladies. I wish the great people here knew something more about cooking. They have adopted the French style, and I cannot relish anything they have for dinner in the eatable way; they have good drink ... champagne, etc., etc., of which you know I am very fond, but I would much rather dine at home.... What with their sauces, and their flum-flummeries, the victuals are intolerable.

THE WHISKEY LETTERS

If Tyler drank whiskey at all, one must assume that he did so very rarely. But, as a venerable Virginian of the higher social order, Tyler no doubt liked to have some good sipping whiskey on hand when guests stopped by.

In a letter written from his Virginia plantation "Sherwood Forest" on February 9, 1858, Tyler makes a request of one Colonel Ware.

> I am about to ask a favour of you the granting of which will I trust, give you but slight trouble. I obtained in 1844 through your friendly agency, two barrels of Whiskey of Lt. Richardson. It is due to truth that all my visitors from time to time have drank and sung its praises, and it has been so great a favorite, that it has shared the fate of most other favorites and has been almost consumed by kindness. The last carton is now all that remains of it. Now my Dr. Sir I wish not only to replenish my stock but to procure a supply for an esteemed friend and neighbor, and should therefore like to get 4 barrels of it. Can you do this for me. It was and is called Richardson's Old whiskey and I should like it to be the same veritable stuff.... Perhaps the stock is nearly run out, if so I should be glad to receive two barrels or even one. I am like yourself a de facto temperance man never drinking spirituous liquors myself, but my numerous visitors would scarcely agree to be placed upon the same list....

But even prior to that, in 1832, then congressman Tyler wrote home to beloved daughter Mary. After starting with some mild admonishment—as Mary apparently had recently kicked up her heels on the party circuit—Tyler closes the letter by noting that he had recently met the famous writer of that era, Washington Irving:

> There is a late work of his, now offered for sale in the bookstores, which I will bring on when I come, if Congress will ever adjourn. We cannot get away sooner than the 1st of July,

and possibly not until the 15th. Harvest will in the meantime
be over; tell John to take good care of the whiskey.

Tyler's reference to "John" is most likely his son. What the future
president exactly means by "take good care" of the harvest whiskey is
somewhat elusive. Did he mean: "Save some for me!"? Or did he mean
that he did not want his son to partake excessively—thereby making sure
his son would save some for guests?

HENRY CLAY'S LATE-NIGHT GAMBIT

John Tyler was playing a game of marbles with his boys in Virginia
when the stunning news arrived that William Henry Harrison had
suddenly died—which meant that Tyler would ascend to the office of the
chief executive.

Almost immediately, the true senatorial powerbrokers of that era—
men like Daniel Webster and Henry Clay—began maneuvering in an
attempt to snip away power from the presidency and add some of it to
their own political arsenals. But Tyler immediately made it clear to
Webster and the other cabinet members whom he had inherited from
Harrison that they could turn in their resignations if they presumed to
dictate policy to the new president of the United States.

Tyler and Clay, in particular, went head to head on the issue of a
national bank. Clay twice introduced legislation for it; Tyler twice vetoed
the bill—much to Clay's frustration.

In a desperate attempt to get Tyler to come around, John J. Crittenden
(Clay's fellow Kentuckian, whiskey-drinker, and the former attorney
general) planned a party of Whig Party powerbrokers and invited the
president. But Tyler, sensing an ambush, conjured up some excuse and
did not attend.

The evening at Crittenden's had suddenly lost its primary reason for
the call to arms, but a few glasses of whiskey (most likely "bourbon," a
term coined in the 1850s) soon got the wilder Whigs thinking of an
alternative plan. As John Quincy Adams recorded in this classic scene in
his diary:

Robert C. Winthrop told me in the House that, after I came away from Mr. Crittenden's Saturday evening, a regular deputation was sent over to the President's house to constrain him to join the party, to which he had been invited but had sent an excuse. On this deputation were Dawson and Triplett. They went over, roused him, if not from bed, after the house had been closed for the night, obtained access to him, took him by storm after the Kentucky fashion, led him over to Crittenden's in triumph, where Clay received him at the door with, "Well, Mr. President, what are you for, Kentucky whisky or champagne?" He chose champagne, and entered into the spirit of this frolicsome agony as if it was congenial to his own temper. But all this was as false and hollow as it was blustering and rowdyish.

PEACHY KEEN

In his book *The Recollections of Thirteen Presidents*, John Sergeant Wise relates an amusing story concerning William Peachy's visit to the Executive Mansion during Tyler's term. Peachy, a Virginia lawyer and an old friend of Tyler's, called while the president was awash in paperwork, but the chief executive begged Peachy to return for dinner, which Peachy did. Tyler soon was abashed to learn there was nothing to sup upon except some leftover ham and turnip greens.

Since Virginia hospitality was considered a serious obligation to a man of Tyler's polished background, he squirmed uncomfortably as the server brought in the meager meal. But then Tyler had a bright idea, as Wise records:

During the meal of ham and turnip greens a happy thought occurred to the President. "I'll tell you what I'll do, Peachy, to atone for this wretched entertainment," said he. "We will send for the keys of the White House cellars, and you shall go there yourself and take your choice." It was no sooner said then done. Peachy knew good wine and loved it dearly.

Accompanied by the butler the two were soon rummaging the dust-covered bottles in the Presidential cellars, and, according to Mr. Peachy's account, he never had such a frolic in his life. Smacking his lips, with the memory of that afternoon's entertainment fresh in his mind, he declared that it was the only time in his life when he had more good liquor than he could drink and not as many people as he wanted to divide with him.

THE SNUB: TYLER'S "SILENT TOAST"

In September 1842, the British diplomat Lord Ashburton was about to depart for home after wrapping up the Webster-Ashburton Treaty, which settled some border disputes between England and the United States. Men of prominence in New York City gathered to give Lord Ashburton a dinner (and proper sendoff) at the Astor House.

As was standard procedure of the era, a series of celebratory toasts were proposed. But so rapidly had Tyler's popularity plunged that when a toast was offered to the president, it was greeted by a resounding ... silence. Even former New York City mayor Philip Hone—certainly far from a "Tyler man"—was appalled at the lack of respect for the presidential office.

A subsequent toast to Queen Victoria was met with rousing applause and acknowledgment—all of which only seemed to add to the absence of respect for the man whose enemies referred to as "acting president" or—even less respectfully—as "His Accidency" or "The Accidental President."

THE PRINCETON DISASTER

It may not be an exaggeration to claim that "Wine, Women, and Song" saved President John Tyler's life—at least on one occasion.

On February 28, 1844, the USS *Princeton*—a new, fast-moving warship armed with state-of-the-art cannons (one called "Oregon" and another dubbed "The Peacemaker")—arrived in Alexandria, Virginia.

Dozens of Washington, D.C., dignitaries, including President Tyler, boarded there, and the *Princeton* sailed off on the picturesque Potomac River. A festive atmosphere (bolstered by food and drinks) dominated the day, and the navy men—including the secretary of the Navy, Thomas Gilmer—were eager to punctuate the pleasantries with some celebratory blasts from the ship's great guns.

Two rounds boomed off from Oregon—much to the delight of the onlookers—but then Gilmer decided that the long-barreled Peacemaker should be brought into the act, the intention to fire off a round in the direction of Mount Vernon, as a resounding salute to George Washington.

As many of the partygoers gathered on deck to hear the Peacemaker's thundering volley, President Tyler lingered below with his twenty-year-old fiancée, Julia Gardiner. He had been engaged in a round of champagne toasts (including what proved to be an ironic one to the Peacemaker itself) and was about to climb the ladder to go up on deck when he stopped to hear a man sing. The wine, his fetching young lady, and this enthusiastic soloist luckily delayed the stately fifty-four-year-old Virginian. Seconds later, the "Peacemaker" blew up—killing six men, including two cabinet members (Gilmer and Secretary of State Abel Upshur), plus Julia Gardiner's father.

Julia Gardiner fainted upon the tragic news that her father was among the dead. Several months later, she (though thirty years his junior) became his second wife and bore Tyler seven children. The most prolific president, Tyler had already fathered eight children with his first wife, Letitia, who had died in the Executive Mansion in 1842.

THE GOODBYE BASH

Tyler's foes snidely called him "a man without a party" because the Whigs had essentially disowned him early into his term. Knowing his days in Washington were numbered, Tyler planned a lavish farewell celebration at the Executive Mansion—inviting a troop of his trusted friends. The event featured a great feast washed down with copious amounts of the best wines from the Executive Mansion cellar.

In addition to his aristocratic appearance and tastes, Tyler possessed a good sense of humor, which he sometimes directed on himself (in a self-depreciating way)—or, when necessary, against his enemies.

At his extravagant send-off, Tyler is said to have beamed: "*Now* they cannot say I am a man without a party!"

LAST CALL

Often in poor health, Tyler died rather suddenly (probably of a stroke) in 1862. As was more or less standard in that era, the president's doctors attempted to treat him with an array of "stimulants"—including mustard plasters, morphine, and brandy.

CHAPTER 11

James K. Polk

(1795–1849)

*I*f James K. Polk, the eleventh president of the United States (1845–1849), was ever drunk on anything, it probably was the concept and implementation of "Manifest Destiny"—the brash idea that the United States would one day stretch from "sea to shining sea," and with God's blessing, to boot.

Polk was the original "dark horse" candidate; he won the Democratic nod for president on the ninth ballot by outmaneuvering such political heavyweights as Lewis Cass of Michigan and former president Martin Van Buren. Polk then beat Kentucky's Henry Clay, the Whig Party candidate, in the election of 1844. His victory brought joy to an aging Andrew Jackson, who long considered Polk his protégé (one of JKP's nicknames was "Young Hickory") and Clay his mortal enemy.

Back in the 1950s, a brand of whiskey marketed under the Old Crow brand ran a series of historically conceived advertisements. Some of those depicted a snow-haired Andrew Jackson drinking bourbon with various notables of the pre–Civil War age, including James K. Polk. But if Polk drank any whiskey, it seems unlikely that he took anything more than social sips.

Polk rarely drank, but he lived in an era when many famous pols were drinkers of hard liquor. Men such as Sam Houston, Daniel Webster, and his rival Henry Clay—not to mention his role model, Jackson—all were imbibers. That fact sometimes made Polk's political life more complicated.

PASS THE BRANDY

Confronting the challenges of the Mexican-American War, facing down John Bull in Oregon, and answering the persistent call of Manifest Destiny were certainly not for the faint of heart. But Polk had already— in the literal sense—been under the knife before he was even out of his teens.

Just short of his seventeenth birthday, Polk suffered from urinary stones. His parents sent him to a renowned doctor in Kentucky—Dr. Ephraim McDowell—to alleviate the excruciating condition. By modern terms, the operation was extremely primitive, intrusive, and painful. The only anesthetic support came in bottle form—specifically, a few pulls of brandy.

Although the operation relieved Polk of his pain (he even sent Doc McDowell a post-op thank-you note), historians speculate that the procedure left Polk sterile and perhaps even impotent.

BOOZE FOR THE VOTERS

With his Presbyterian upbringing, James Polk was well versed in the pitfalls of Demon Alcohol and, therefore, avoided it in excess.

But Polk the politician knew the merits and necessity of the stuff. Supplying liquid refreshment to your would-be constituents was by no means a new concept—indeed, it predated the United States; George Washington supplied liquor to his voting block in colonial Virginia.

Running for a seat in the Tennessee state legislature in 1823, Polk's campaign purchased more than twenty gallons of hard cider, whiskey, and brandy to woo voters. Polk won handily, but apparently the liquid infusions (the other side utilized similar tactics) ignited some rough-and-tumble confrontations on election day. When Polk ran for governor of Tennessee in 1838 (which he won), he gave a speech in Murfreesboro, and by the description of the festive aftermath, it was clear election tactics had not changed dramatically. According to some accounts, the pro-Polk crowd devoured forty sheep, forty piglets, six beeves, hundreds of pounds of ham, bread, and vegetables, and then guzzled "the generous juice of the grape, whiskey, and cognac" to put an exclamation point on the outing.

DEFENDING "BIG DRUNK"

As one of President Andrew Jackson's most trusted allies, Polk fought battles on Old Hickory's behalf while serving in the Senate. Some of those battles were more winnable than others.

One big problem (for both Jackson and Polk) was Sam Houston, the future president of Texas. In the early 1830s, Houston was something of a thin-skinned brute (he was large in stature) with a hair-trigger temper and a weakness for alcohol. In fact, Houston had been nicknamed "Big Drunk" by the Cherokee tribe, with which he had once resided.

In April 1832, an Ohio congressman named William Stanbery insinuated—on the floor of the House—that Houston had been involved in a shady deal with other members of Jackson's administration (concerning bids on food rations to Indian tribes forcibly removed to the West). Infuriated, the future hero of Texas wanted to bash Stanbery on the spot. But Polk hastily intervened and steered the belligerent Houston outside to cool off.

Polk only delayed the inevitable, however. Several weeks later, Houston identified Stanbery on a Washington street. Bellowing that the Ohioan was a "damn rascal," Houston began to throttle him with a sizeable cane carved out of hickory. Stanbery attempted to shoot Houston, but his pistol misfired.

With Stanbery convalescing from his beating, Congress arrested Houston (who was represented in court by lawyer Francis Scott Key of

"Star-Spangled Banner" fame). But Polk (as Andrew Jackson's implement) used his influence and persuasive oratory to water down the punishment. Houston was fined a hefty five hundred dollars, but he skipped off to Texas (and his ultimate destiny of defeating Santa Anna at the Battle of San Jacinto) without ever paying up.

Houston later admitted that on the night before his summons before Congress, he and many of his powerful friends (some of whom were supposed to pass judgment on Houston the next day) had downed lots of liquor in Houston's hotel room. As Houston himself related:

> We sat late and you may judge how we drank when I tell you that Stevenson (Andrew, the Speaker of the House] at midnight was sleeping on the lounge. [Colonel] Baylie Peyton was out of commission and gone to his room and (Tennessee Senator] Felix Grundy had ceased to be interesting.

But Houston (who once jested that Polk's problem was that "he drank too much water") confirmed Young Hickory's reputation for moderation, adding: "Polk rarely indulged and left us early."

THE BASKET OF BUBBLY BET

James K. Polk was serious, hardworking (to a fault, perhaps; those closest to Polk worried that he wore himself down), and pragmatic. But Polk *did* enjoy keeping James Buchanan, his secretary of state, a bit off balance. Polk once "called" Buchanan on his wording in a diplomatic document. As Polk recounted in his diary:

> He insisted that he was right. I then jocosely said to him, I will stand you a basket of champaign [sic] that this letter is not in the usual form as you insist.... He promptly said, Done, I take you up, and rising in fine humour went out.

When Buchanan came back, he was still brimming with confidence. He was armed with a book that he felt certain contained an example in which just such a document had previously been worded. But after quite some time searching, Buchanan's mood faded to one of resignation, as Polk noted:

> He seemed to be disappointed & said, Well, if I don't find such a precedent today I will send you the basket of champaign [sic]. I smiled and told him I would not accept it, and that I had been jesting when I proposed [it], and had done so only to express in an earnest manner my conviction that I was right. But, he said, if I had won it I would have made you pay it, & I will pay it to you.

Polk again refused to accept the champagne. His "victory" (in addition to successfully "tweaking" Buchanan's ego) seemed also to be a refresher course in leadership skills. Polk finished the anecdote in his diary with: "I record this incident for the purpose of showing how necessary it is for me to give my vigilant attention even to the form & details of my [subordinates'] duties."

POLK'S EXECUTIVE MANSION PARTIES

First Lady Sarah Polk banned hard liquor (such as whiskey) and dancing at official Executive Mansion receptions. Wine, champagne, and brandy were served, however.

One wonders whether her husband, always a nose-to-the-grindstone kind of public servant, would have noticed one way or the other. Consider his diary entry of Friday, November 13, 1846:

> This was reception evening, but being much engaged in my office, I did not go into the parlour. I learn from the family that quite a number of persons, ladies & gentlemen called.

Sometimes, in fact, if the president happened to be busy working, Sarah Polk would host receptions without her husband.

BELLIGERENT BENTON

Not all of President Polk's visitors qualified as gentlemen. In Polk's time, it was relatively easy for someone to walk in the door of the Executive Mansion and wait in line to make some request for a political or military appointment. These men were typically called "office seekers," and Polk's diaries are laced with derogatory comments about bothersome callers of this ilk.

To make matters worse, not all of these office seekers were sober, or, in some cases, sane. Security around the president—particularly in a pre-Lincoln era—was surprisingly lax.

As Polk recorded in his diary (on October 25, 1847), one Monday an excitable young man burst into his office demanding an appointment in the army, at the rank of lieutenant, nonetheless.

The situation was complicated by the fact that the man was John Randolph Benton, the son of powerful senator Thomas Hart Benton, known for his volatile temper. In younger days, the elder Benton had brawled in a Nashville tavern with Andrew Jackson, leaving a non-lethal bullet in Old Hickory's frame—something of a permanent souvenir. Polk would have been well aware of this scandalous story.

Polk ("in a mild tone") told him there were no openings, and, if there were openings, his inclination would be to consider men already serving in the Mexican-American War and promote through the ranks. In short, Polk said he could not promise his brash visitor anything. He wrote:

> He left my office in quite a passion, & very rudely, swearing profanely as he went [out] the door. In a loud and boisterous tone.... "By God" he would do something, but I lost the remaining words that he uttered.... Mr. Arthur of Baltimore, who was present, said he smelt liquor on his breath & thought he was drunk. All present expressed their amazement at his conduct.

THE DEVIL AND DANIEL WEBSTER

Intoxicated office seekers were not the only men who made President Polk's life miserable. Congress was notorious for allowing drinking to go on, even during important votes. That included even Daniel Webster, arguably the most esteemed orator of his day, though some claimed his flow of eloquence was directly proportional to the amount of liquor he consumed.

One can almost sense the temperate disgust as Polk remarks in his diary on August 9, 1846, about the "disreputable scene":

> Great confusion, I learned, prevailed in both Houses during this night's Session and what is deeply to be regretted several members as I was informed were excited by drink. Among others I was informed that Senators Webster & Barrow [Alexander Barrow of Louisiana] were quite drunk, so much so that the latter gentleman, it was said, was noisy and troublesome.

LAST CALL

"Blacksmith Harry"—a slave on one of Polk's plantations—claimed in a letter to have won "40 gallons of whiskey" betting that Polk would win the presidency. He assured Polk that he had no intention of drinking it all himself.

Perhaps Polk's temperance was reinforced by the tragedy of Franklin E. Polk (his younger brother), who was a hardcore alcoholic and died at the young age of twenty-eight. Another younger brother—Tennessee representative William H. Polk—also engaged in heavy drinking and according to some reports sometimes reduced himself to slurred speech on the floors of Congress. Polk himself died just a few months after he left the Executive Mansion, probably of cholera.

CHAPTER 12

Zachary Taylor

(1784–1850)

Like Julius Caesar refusing the crown in Shakespeare's play, Zachary Taylor responded with what appeared to be reluctance when word reached him that the Whigs were giving him strong consideration to be their candidate for the Executive Mansion.

In the summer of 1846, just two years before he was elected president, Taylor wrote to his son-in-law: "I shall not interfere with the election ... nor shall I be a candidate for the presidency."

And during the Mexican-American War, when a Whig messenger allegedly visited him in Mexico to breach the subject of his running for the presidency, "Old Rough and Ready" supposedly responded with a scolding quip: "Stop your nonsense and drink your whiskey!" (A great line, if true.)

But by February 1847—after winning bitterly fought victories at Monterrey (September 1846) and Buena Vista (against an army about four times the size of his own)—Taylor was starting to reconsider. "I will not say I would not serve, if the good people were imprudent enough to elect me," he wrote in a letter.

Most scholars and military history buffs—and certainly Taylor himself (given a chance)—would agree that Taylor's battlefield skills eclipsed his abilities in the political arena.

Although Taylor was raised in Kentucky, he found whiskey more of a hindrance than an ally in his challenging military career. He seems to have consumed very little of it (perhaps the occasional toast or medicinal dose) during his life but was frequently bothered by others (such as fellow officers) around him who had an unbridled passion for the stuff.

At any rate, it was not alcohol that killed him, but perhaps tainted cherries. Taylor's term as the twelfth president (1849–1850) was an incredibly short one.

THE "FIRE WATER" FIRE

Zachary Taylor was president for only eighteen months, but he served as a military commander for more than forty years. And his postings were anything but glamorous: Green Bay, Wisconsin, when it was a small fur-trapping village buffeted by the lake weather elements, and deep in Florida, probably camped in some mosquito- and alligator-infested swamp. Taylor also had a problem with whiskey.

It wasn't that he *personally* drank too much of it (he rarely had a few sips, if that)—his problem was keeping it away from his own officers, troops, and Native American tribes, hostile or friendly, in his near vicinity.

One of Taylor's worst experiences with whiskey occurred when he was commanding at Fort Harrison—a small stockade on the Wabash River in present-day Indiana—during the War of 1812. Some six hundred Indians attacked the fort after setting fire to one of the blockhouses. The fire in the blockhouse ignited with a store of liquor, and, as Taylor later recounted, the situation looked beyond bleak:

> ... the fire had unfortunately communicated to a quantity of whiskey and in spite of every exertion we could make use of,

in less than a minute it ascended to the roof, and baffled every effort we could make to extinguish it.

But Taylor organized a bucket brigade, and somehow the besieged and vastly out-numbered Americans were able to extinguish the flames—while others held off the attack with poised rifle fire.

The Indians eventually retreated out of firing range, but the small garrison—Taylor had fewer than twenty healthy men and was forced to press the sick and wounded into service—had lost some food in the whiskey-accelerated blaze and had just a meager amount of dry corn to eat. But reinforcements arrived the next day, and Fort Harrison was saved; Zachary Taylor also notched a crucial victory (no thanks to the "fire water") on his military record.

THE WINTER OF OUR DISCONTENT

There are few places on the planet where whiskey might be as appreciated as in frigid Green Bay, Wisconsin, especially in the winter of 1818. But Major Taylor, then in his early thirties and commanding a garrison at Fort Howard, refused to pay inflated prices for whiskey to the local traders. (The price of whiskey, Taylor fumed, "was calculated to benefit the Speculator ... and not benefit the Soldier.")

Taylor's stubbornness on the price of whiskey did not play well with his officers and soldiers, and after two lieutenants bellyached to the extent that it spread ill will among the troops, he attempted to court-martial them. The charges were later dropped, and the lieutenants escaped court-martial by resigning. As for the soldiers trapped in teeth-chattering Green Bay, more reasonably priced whiskey supplies from the government soon arrived, and Taylor acquiesced to the distribution of their daily gill.

NEW ORLEANS COMES CALLING

Although he himself was little more than an occasional ceremonial sipper, Taylor was not against others enjoying a drink or two.

Once, while awaiting orders in the Rio Grande town of Matamoros in the early stages of the Mexican-American War, General Taylor got word that delegations from both the Louisiana legislature and the citizens of New Orleans were arriving to pay their respects and toast his expected success in the upcoming battles. One of Taylor's junior officers, Lieutenant George Gordon Meade (who would later command against General Robert E. Lee on the fields of Gettysburg) had a front-row seat to the resulting festivities. As Meade wrote to his wife, Margaret, on June 12, 1846:

> The old General received them very courteously and having been warned of their approach, he had a cold collation prepared, at which, through the influence of champagne and other *spirited* things, many patriotic and complimentary speeches were made.

But, according to Meade, the officers (perhaps without Taylor in attendance) earnestly returned the favor to the Louisiana visitors the next day:

> To-day a number of the officers of the army desirous of testifying their sense of the compliment paid them by the Legislature of Louisiana and citizens of New Orleans, got them up a dinner in town, to which all the volunteer officers were invited and you can be assured it was a jolly time. A great quantity of wine was imbibed and an infinite amount of patriotism resulted.

Meade felt compelled to add "To show you I kept sober, I have added these lines after seeing the affair out...."

One assumes that the wise and temperate-minded Zachary Taylor also was listed among the sober ranks through the entire visit from his Louisiana well-wishers.

CROGHAN CARE

Colonel George Croghan grew up in the same area (present-day Louisville, Kentucky) as Zachary Taylor, though he was seven years Taylor's junior. For his brave defense of Fort Stephenson on the Ohio frontier during the War of 1812, the dashingly handsome Croghan (a nephew of the Revolutionary War hero George Rogers Clark) became a much-trumpeted war hero and was eventually awarded a medallion from the U.S. Congress.

But holding Fort Stephenson proved to be the pinnacle of his military career (if not his life). Croghan soon fell into excessive drinking and unbridled gambling, and the collision of both of these diabolical pursuits left him chronically in debt, despite that he often held a decent-paying job as an inspector of fortifications or as the postmaster of New Orleans.

When Croghan showed up on the Mexican border to contribute to the American war effort, higher-ups must have decided that the best man to keep this "loose cannon" in place was his fellow Kentuckian—General Zachary Taylor. In an August 23, 1846, letter to his son-in-law (Dr. Robert C. Wood), Old Rough and Ready was understandably apprehensive about the task, as he penned:

> I very much regret that Co. Croghan had come out as I fear he will expect me to take care of him & there are enough people of that description already here; at any rate to embarrass me not a little; I learn he has been in a tremendous frolic but will get sober before he gets here & will, I expect, keep so while he remains with me.

A "frolic" in Taylor's day was the equivalent of being "on a bender" today. But whatever Croghan's missteps, they must have been minor enough to avoid great notice, and he was said to have conducted himself well during the Mexican-American War (despite suffering from dysentery), particularly during the attack on Monterey. Croghan's luck, however, did not dramatically improve after the war: he died in the devastating cholera epidemic of 1849—the same sweep of disease that took the life of former president James K. Polk in that same year.

WHEN THE SAINTS COME MARCHING IN

It would be next to impossible to pinpoint a more heady time in General Zachary Taylor's much-vaunted career then the end of the Mexican-American War and his arrival shortly thereafter in New Orleans. He was riding the tailwinds of his tremendous victory over Santa Anna at Buena Vista, and the momentum for his candidacy as the Whig candidate for president had already begun.

Given that some of the most prestigious people in New Orleans had already honored Taylor *before* the Mexican-American War in Matamoros, one can picture the festive swell that greeted him when he arrived at the Mississippi port in December 1847.

The city leaders invited the victorious general to a lavish dinner held at the banquet hall in the St. Charles Hotel. Dozens of toasts were proposed, and Taylor was certainly moved. As one observer said:

> The General, evidently affected, rose and made a very neat and pretty speech, which he concluded with the following sentiment: "The Citizens of New Orleans—Unsurpassed for their Hospitality, Intelligence, and Enterprise."

NEXT TIME ORDER THE CHERRY WINE

More than a few historians have suggested that heavy drinking in colonial times (and well into the nineteenth century) occurred, at least in part, because water supplies were unreliable and could, in some cases, cause disease. Food supplies—often not properly refrigerated in an era when an icehouse was considered "high tech"—were similarly suspect.

Taylor is believed to have died after consuming large qualities of iced milk and cherries. Were the milk and/or fruit contaminated? It's possible, but the sixty-five-year-old Taylor had—earlier in his term—already displayed symptoms of poor health while on a tour to Buffalo, New York. The official cause of his death is typically listed as "acute gastroenteritis."

LAST CALL

Even though both the aging President Taylor and Vice President Fillmore barely qualified as sippers, neither could resist an inauguration night visit to Carusi's Saloon, located at 11th and C Streets in Washington, D.C. Carusi's was one of the most popular watering holes in the capital in 1849. Neither stayed very long, and the party— predictably—went on without them when they left.

CHAPTER 13

Millard Fillmore

(1800–1874)

The name Millard Fillmore generally comes up only whenever the topic of obscure presidents is discussed. As with John Tyler's ascendancy to office, Fillmore suddenly found himself in the Executive Mansion after the death of a president (Zachary Taylor, in Fillmore's case). When Fillmore became America's thirteenth president (1850–1853), he faced a plethora of problems that were far more taxing than anything he might have dealt with at the vice-presidential level.

Born in a log cabin in the Finger Lakes region of New York State, Fillmore was one of nine children, and before he was fifteen, he was apprenticed to a hard-driving cloth-maker. He later attended the New Hope Academy in New Hope, New York, where he obtained about a half year of formal education and met his first wife, Abigail. By the time he was twenty, Fillmore had clerked for a judge and learned law; perhaps predictably, he eventually found his way into politics.

At a time when most elected officials were drinkers, Fillmore stood out as a man who rarely took a sip. But, known for his ability to compromise, the Whig from New York had no problem forming political alliances with men who were known to quaff down whiskey—most notably Henry Clay of Kentucky, the silver-tongued Daniel Webster of New Hampshire, and another senator of legendary oratory skills, Stephen Douglas of Illinois. These formidable forces, with President Fillmore's help, pushed through the Missouri Compromise, which delayed the Civil War.

NO DICE FOR VICE

Even as a young man, Millard Fillmore was not a rambler or a gambler and certainly not a drinker of whisky. He once attended a New Year's event that featured all sorts of entertainments, but the future president was mostly reluctant to participate in them. As he later wrote:

> There I witnessed for the first time the rude sports in which people engage in a new country; such as wrestling, jumping, hopping, firing at turkeys and raffling for them, and drinking whisky. I was a spectator of the scene; taking no part, except that I raffled once for the turkey ... and won it. No persuasion could induce me to raffle again; and that was the beginning and the end of my gambling....

THE TEMPERANCE PLEDGE

As a young man in his twenties, Fillmore took the temperance pledge in East Aurora, New York (near Buffalo). Fillmore was already serving as a New York state representative in Albany—a city well known for its revelry—when he embraced the oath. But "taking the pledge" meant no wine, beer, whiskey, rum, or even hard cider—the last almost considered a mythical elixir to tried-and-true Whigs, since hard cider had absolutely helped (at least in strength of slogan) William Henry Harrison capture the presidency in 1840.

Fillmore held (mostly) steadfast to the temperance line. In his later years, Fillmore was asked to speak to college students in Buffalo, and he emphatically stated to the young men: "I have seldom tasted wine and seldom offered it to a guest."

COMMODORE PERRY'S BROADSIDE OF BOOZE

But President Fillmore had no qualms about offering a frightening array of alcohol to foreigners. It was, of course, already a proven strategy that Americans pushing back the frontiers had used with devastating consequences against Native American tribes.

When the United States ventured out to make contact with Japan in 1853, Commodore Matthew Perry (brother of 1812 naval hero Oliver Hazard Perry) was deployed for the mission. (The actual Treaty of Kanagawa did not occur until the following year, on Perry's follow-up mission, when Franklin Pierce was president.)

Perry was armed with all sorts of gifts (pistols, muskets, clocks, John James Audubon's *Birds of America* books, among other items) and a grandly worded letter from Fillmore to the emperor of Japan. But Demon Alcohol absolutely dominated the list—with more than one hundred gallons of whiskey leading the charge.

The United States was looking to establish ties with the reclusive Japanese empire and to guarantee that its ships could count on being refueled, and, in the event of shipwrecks, its sailors would be taken in and cared for. And whiskey, apparently, seemed like a logical bargaining chip in these particular pursuits.

KEG ME

Commodore Perry gifted a small keg of fine Madeira wine to Fillmore, who accepted the gift but insisted on paying duty on it—even though he certainly could have avoided doing so. All evidence shows that President Fillmore then never partook of the contents or even dispensed this fine, potent wine to guests. It was reportedly auctioned off when Fillmore left the Executive Mansion.

THE COMPANY YOU KEEP

Despite the old adage—birds of a feather flock together—Fillmore certainly was the "odd duck" (nod to Mallard Fillmore), that is to say, the non-drinker, if you consider some of his most prominent cabinet members. The Fillmore cabinet featured some of the top imbibers of the era, with Secretary of State Daniel Webster leading the attack.

The cabinet also included John J. Crittenden of Kentucky (a man known to hoist a glass or two of that state's much-vaunted bourbon), Secretary of the Treasury Thomas Corwin, and Secretary of the Navy William Graham. Graham, for example, was notorious for all-male drinking parties at his home on H Street in the capital, of which Ohio senator Benjamin Wade once observed: "the quantity of wine furnished [was] an important topic as anything."

An interesting aspect of the Fillmore presidency days was that the president did not let his coolness toward alcohol stand in the way of his guests. Often the Fillmores entertained twice a week, and some multiple course dinners were supported with eight to ten kinds of wine.

FILLMORE GETS (SLIGHTLY) "FUDDLED"

If this reads like a headline in the *New York Post*, well, it *was*—most definitely—a weird occasion.

"Fuddled" in Fillmore's day (and dating back to the previous century at least) was slang for "drunk" or "intoxicated"—as in: "I went down to the tavern, and my friends kept buying me rum until I was completely fuddled."

A temperate man if there ever was one in the Exectuive Mansion, Fillmore did, nevertheless, once admit to being "slightly fuddled" after touring more than a few wine shops in London. He claimed to be doing little more than moistening his lips with the fine and well-aged vintages, but apparently he did this frequently enough to induce what we might term today as a slight buzz.

But—to paraphrase Shakespeare, with great poetic license—that was in another country, and, besides, it took place *after* Fillmore left office.

MAKING FUN OF FILLMORE

Millard Fillmore, partly because of his name, but primarily because of his obscurity, has been—from time to time—an easy target for pranksters with a political bent.

For example, in 1985 the Associated Press reported that an organization claiming to be "The Society to Promote Respect and Recognition of Millard Fillmore" met at a Baltimore waterfront pub under the pretense of toasting the thirteenth president on the 185th anniversary of his birth.

But it soon became apparent that the event was more roast than toast (although the thirty or so members of the group did a lot of that, too), as they boisterously chanted: "Fill more years! Fill more years!"

Glasses were filled—and certainly emptied—in this toast/roast. All of which led to more barbs. As one attendee cheerfully pointed out: "What [Fillmore] lacked in charisma he made up for in mediocrity."

Fillmore is saluted in a more serious manner in New York State, usually in towns close to his birthplace (near Moravia, New York), but especially in Buffalo, (a city he did much for) by the Millard Fillmore Historical Society and the University of Buffalo.

LAST CALL

After his stint in the Executive Mansion, Fillmore toured the country, including several cities in the South. When he arrived in Savannah, Georgia, the mayor and the top citizens wanted to wine and dine the former president. Fillmore ate well, but—as he often did—he politely declined to participate when his gracious hosts broke out bottles of fine champagne to toast him.

CHAPTER 14

Franklin Pierce

(1804–1869)

*T*he hard-drinking British prime minister Sir Winston Churchill once boasted (not without foundation): "I have taken more out of alcohol than it has taken out of me."

But Franklin Pierce—the fourteenth president of the United States (1853–1857)—could never have made such an outrageous claim. Drinking destroyed Pierce's health and damaged both his public and political image.

One could argue that Pierce had reason to drink, certainly more than most men. Franklin and his wife, Jane Appleton Pierce, had three children, and all of them died young: Franklin (three days after his birth in 1836), Frank Robert (dead at age four), and Benjamin, killed in a horrific winter train wreck, witnessed by his parents, at just eleven years of age.

Pierce was also trapped in the middle of the nation's major controversy: slavery. Despite his New Hampshire roots, Pierce was that rare Northerner sympathetic to the South and that region's insistence on continuing—or even expanding—slavery. As Pierce (a dark-horse Democrat selected on the forty-ninth ballot) prepared to become president, he proclaimed: "I believe that involuntary servitude, as it exists in different States of this Confederacy, is recognized by the Constitution."

The Whigs and abolitionists branded Pierce a "doughface"—a term of derision directed toward Northerners siding with the South on this explosive issue. That label haunted him until his final days.

BOWDOIN BOY

Pierce's father, Benjamin, was a Revolutionary War hero who fought at the Battle of Bunker Hill. Benjamin eventually was elected governor of New Hampshire, although his Federalist adversaries labeled him a profane tavern-owner who swilled much of the liquor he sold. Though not wealthy, the family was able to send young Frank (he was just fifteen when he first arrived) to Bowdoin College in Maine.

At Bowdoin, Pierce made some lifelong friends, including Nathaniel Hawthorne, destined to become one of the country's most renowned writers. Hawthorne enjoyed hunkering down at Ward's Tavern, a rustic watering hole near the Bowdoin campus, drinking wine and playing cards. In fact, Hawthorne was sometimes fined for drinking and gambling. Frank Pierce managed to dodge those bullets, but he did pick up some college fines for skipping church services. But in all likelihood, Pierce—an athletic, engaging, and good-looking (he later acquired the sobriquet "Handsome Frank") young student—imbibed with his college friends at a very early age.

BAD COMPANY

Like most of the early U.S. presidents, Pierce pursued law as a career before careening into the political arena. Riding the Jacksonian Democratic wave, Pierce won a congressional seat and arrived in Washington, D.C., in 1832, as Old Hickory began his second term. Not yet thirty, the poised and well-spoken Pierce showed great promise.

The nation's capital was a backwater swamp in those days; unhealthy is some obvious ways (a hotbed for "bilious fever" and other diseases), and also some insidious ones. Still unmarried at the time, Pierce ran around with other unfettered congressmen, many of whom were no strangers to drinking, gambling, and chasing women, though they usually attempted to exercise some discretion on the last.

Pierce, in fact, did not let party lines stop him from socializing, as he even accepted the top-shelf hospitality of Senator Daniel Webster, the older Whig (and notorious drinker) from Massachusetts. When a fellow Democrat tried to caution Pierce about socializing with the enemy, the congressman made it clear that he would make his own decisions.

THE WILLARD

At the hub of it all was the Willard Hotel. There were hundreds of establishments in the capital, of course, but the Willard was the center of Washington's social beehive.

And liquor made that beehive buzz.

As Hawthorne—Pierce's old friend and first biographer—once advised in an *Atlantic Monthly* article:

> Adopt the universal habit of the place, and call for a mint julep, a whiskey skin, a gin cock-tail, a brandy smash or a glass of pure Old Rye, for the conviviality of Washington sets in at an early hour and, so far I had an opportunity of observing, never terminates at any hour.

DRUNKEN THEATRICS

Pierce married Jane Appleton, the daughter of Bowdoin College president Jesse Appleton, in 1834. Jane was quite reserved, a non-drinker, and not very sociable. She despised Washington, D.C. (as described by Hawthorne), so the young congressman Pierce spent most of his time in the capital alone.

The culture of the U.S. Congress at that time was definitely a drinking one—some members drank openly on the floor. Pierce—who appears to have had the twin misfortune of liking alcohol and lacking an ability to handle it well—did not always pick the best companions.

One of Pierce's worst acquaintances was Edward Hannegan, a U.S. representative (and later U.S. senator) from Indiana. Hannegan was a heavy boozer who, when intoxicated, had a penchant for violence. (In fact, Hannegan later killed his brother-in-law in a drunken rage but somehow got off in court.)

In February 1836, Pierce, Hannegan, and future governor of Virginia, Henry A. Wise—all intoxicated—arrived at a Washington theater. Apparently the tipsy trio was placed in the same box as an army officer who had a "history" with Hannegan, and a tumultuous confrontation soon ensued, with the short-tempered and boozed-up Hannegan yanking out his pistol. Others intervened to stop any further violence, and the military man was transferred out of the city before a duel could be arranged.

Shortly after that disturbing incident, Pierce became very ill with pleurisy. It took him weeks to recover. But it was five years before the future president attempted to quit drinking—a sound decision but not a lasting one.

PIERCE AND "THE PLEDGE"

Pierce won the New Hampshire U.S. Senate seat in 1837 and returned to Washington. But he only managed to break from alcohol when he left the capital city. He resigned from the Senate in 1841 and returned to the Granite State. For the first time in years, he seemingly enjoyed long stretches of sobriety. He also tackled strenuous work on the family farm.

In that time period, Pierce felt confident enough to write his brother-in-law, stating:

> I am now in strong and robust health. I take daily a great deal
> of exercise ... have not used a particle of tobacco in any shape

or taken anything more than black tea & that only in the morning since I got settled here.

Amazingly, Pierce actually signed the temperance pledge. He also pushed to abolish the "using and vending of liquor" within Concord (the New Hampshire capital) city limits in 1843. Clearly, when Pierce receded from politics he also took a step back from the abyss of alcoholism.

SOUTH OF THE BORDER

But when the Mexican-American War commenced in 1845, Pierce (although many New Englanders opposed what they termed "Mr. Polk's War") wanted in on the action. His connections trumped his lack of military experience, and he soon rose to the rank of brevet colonel.

Pierce drifted back to his old habits. Boredom, in its own sneaky way, proved nearly as dangerous as the battlefield. Colonel Pierce (his temperance pledge seemingly forgotten) helped form the "Aztec Club"—essentially a place where officers could hobnob, drink liquor, and gamble.

Once again, Pierce was involved in a potentially fatal incident involving drinking. When one officer accused another one of cheating in a card game, Pierce intervened. The accusing officer made threats and claimed that only Pierce's advanced rank prevented him from challenging him to a duel. The next day, however, sober minds prevailed—apologies were made and accepted—and, with the war coming to an end, the soldiers soon left Mexico for home.

FORNEY'S FORECAST

Pierce, nicknamed "Young Hickory of the Granite Hills," won the 1852 presidential election over Whig general Winfield Scott, crushing "Old Fuss and Feathers" in the electoral vote 254 to 42.

As Pierce traveled to Washington to begin his presidency in 1853, John W. Forney sent a rather disturbing letter to his friend (and future president) James Buchanan. As a newspaperman, Forney was no stranger to hard drinkers and could hold his own in those ranks himself. But even Forney was taken aback by Pierce's vulnerability to alcohol and did not couch his words when writing "Old Buck":

> Pierce has had a fine reception but I deeply, deeply deplore his habits. He drinks deep. My heart bleeds for him for he is a gallant and a generous spirit. The place overshadows him. He is crushed by its great duties and seeks refuge in.... His experience convinces me that a great mistake was made in putting him in at all.

Forney was right to be concerned. Although Pierce periodically quit drinking, his natural inclination to be social (and perhaps a need to dull the tragedies of his life, including Benny's recent death) always brought Pierce back to alcohol.

AN INFAMOUS LINE

When his party failed to support him for re-election in 1856, Pierce allegedly was heard to say: "What can an ex-President of the United States do except get drunk?" (There are other versions of the line that are quite similar.)

But did Pierce *really* say that? Perhaps. His major biographers do not reference it, but the line nevertheless has been widely circulated. It may be just another presidential myth—though perhaps Pierce said something *close* to that, if only in jest or cynical capitulation.

LAST CALL

Because of his prewar sympathies toward the South (and friendships with men like Jefferson Davis), Pierce was regarded almost as a traitor by the most fervent Yankees.... With the death of his wife, Jane (in 1863 from tuberculosis), and his best friend, Nathaniel Hawthorne (1864), Pierce became somewhat reclusive, and his drinking continued unabated. He died of cirrhosis of the liver in 1869. He was just sixty-five years old.

CHAPTER 15

James Buchanan

(1791–1868)

$\mathcal{S}$hortly after James Buchanan's death on June 1, 1868, a Lancaster, Pennsylvania, newspaper published some of his final thoughts. "I have no regret for any public act of my life and history will vindicate my memory from every unjust aspersion," was one of the fifteenth president's (1857–1861) more defensive proclamations.

History, however, did not share Buchanan's enthusiasm. Pennsylvania's only president is typically rated as one of America's worst—cited as timid and indecisive in the face of the rebellion and the 1861 siege against Fort Sumter, leaving incoming president Lincoln to clean up the mess.

If Buchanan—a Democrat—was uncertain during a national emergency, he seemingly was on quite a familiar battlefield when it came to jousting with Demon Alcohol. He began drinking in his mid-teens and kept at it late into life, until complications from gout forced him to reluctantly wave the white flag.

Buchanan was renowned among his contemporaries for his ability to handle large quantities of wine or whiskey without showing the usual telltale effects of intoxication. He also had a taste for the top-shelf stuff and had no qualms about providing champagne and other quality wines for lavish dinner parties or celebrations. In a vivid contrast to Buchanan's marks as a leader, "Old Buck" warrants straight A's when it comes to his ability to handle alcohol.

WELL TOASTED

James Buchanan's collegiate record for "spirited" rambunctiousness arguably rivals that of George W. Bush while a student at Yale.

As a student at Dickinson College, Buchanan drank all sixteen toasts proposed at a Fourth of July gathering in 1808, and then, presumably, indulged in some volunteer "salutes" as well. The young "Buck" (he was only sixteen when he began college) was something of a loose cannon at the Carlisle, Pennsylvania, college and apparently defied institutional rules by smoking cigars and incurring various infractions when he went into town.

Admittedly, there were plenty of bad influences. Jeremiah Atwater— the principal of Dickinson College—complained that "Drunkenness, swearing, lewdness & dueling" held considerable sway over the student body. Some of Buchanan's mild misdeeds might have been the result of peer pressure, as he once admitted that "in order to be considered a clever and spirited youth, I engaged in every sort of extravagance and mischief."

In addition, Buchanan—although obviously bright—was regarded as somewhat arrogant by his professors. In fact, the college suspended him for disorderly conduct at one point, and the future president— "mortified"—had to pull strings to be reinstated.

Although he secured a second chance, Buchanan nevertheless felt snubbed when the college recognized another student, instead of him, as its outstanding scholar.

Proof that he never really forgave the college for that slight was evident decades later when Buchanan retired to his beloved Wheatland. When Dickinson representatives wrote to him requesting a hefty donation to endow a professorship, the former president dismissively replied: "The world is greatly mistaken as to the amount of my fortune."

A SPIRITED VARIETY

Buchanan tried—and liked—many kinds of alcohol, especially as a young lawyer (he often held court at the Grape Tavern in Lancaster) and international diplomat. He obviously loved a variety of wines, from champagne to Madeira, one of his dependable favorites.

In fact, Buchanan's letters from his time as a diplomat in Russia and as a European traveler speak to his willingness to sample whatever the drink of the land happened to be.

From Russia (he served as an ambassador there under President Jackson from 1832–1833) he wrote his friend John Reynolds that the royalty drank less than he expected. As for the working classes, Buchanan said: "The peasants are jolly, good-natured fellows who drive furiously and seem happy. They are rogues, nevertheless."

But Buchanan also noted, perhaps not without a tinge of admiration, that the common Russian "rogue" consumed "a species of hot white brandy enough to kill the Devil." One must assume that he was referring Russian vodka.

When his mission in Russia was completed, Buchanan was anxious to return to America and resume his political career. But he also took time to travel down the Rhine River and also to the Buchanan ancestral home in the north of Ireland.

As he journeyed down the Rhine, drifting past its famous castles, Buchanan remarked: "I felt a little romantic in descending the Rhine ... I never took much to the Rhenish until I got into its native country. There I acclimated to it & now feel that the taste will accompany me through life. But I have some talent in that line."

With Buchanan, it might be a coin-flip to guess whether he was referring to the famous white wines of the region (often referred to as "Rhenish") or the Rhine River culture in general.

From Ireland (his ancestors were Scotch-Irish Presbyterians from County Donegal), Buchanan gleefully wrote to Reynolds: "There I sinned very much in the article of hot whiskey toddy which they term punch. The Irish women are delightful."

The latter statement—about the Irish women—seems to fly in the face of the persistent rumor that Buchanan was gay (in the modern sense of that word, and not as one of his early biographers innocently referred to him as "a gay bachelor with a flair for society"), because he never married and also because he seemed to cohabit (for more than fifteen years) in Washington with Georgia senator William Rufus King prior to becoming president. What letters that survive between Buchanan and King reflect an extremely close friendship—though nothing that proves there was a sexual relationship.

Buchanan was briefly engaged early in life, but it ended in tragedy; when the engagement was broken off (for reasons never quite clear), his fiancée seemingly went to pieces and died just days later.

Since Buchanan never married, the role of first lady fell to his niece, a charming and capable woman named Harriet Lane.

While one might be tempted to debate Buchanan's sexual inclinations, there is nothing ambiguous about Old Buck's attraction to whiskey, wine, and other liquors; the record shows that he consistently enjoyed his libations.

THE BUCHANAN BASH

In January 1846, then secretary of state Buchanan hosted what could be called (in modern terms) "a bash" at Carusi's Saloon, the premier watering hole in Washington at the time. Presumably there must have been quite a few guests and most of them thirsty ones, as the tally for what was consumed included three hundred bottles of wine, 150 bottles of champagne, and liquor with more wallop for hard-core drinkers.

The alcohol washed down some rich dinner selections prepared by the French chef Gautier. The menu included some modern-day mainstays such as ham, turkey, beef, and lobster. But there also were some wild entrees abundant in Buchanan's era, such as venison and pheasant.

FORNEY'S REVELATIONS

John Forney was once Buchanan's political manager and a major cog in Old Buck's 1856 ascension to the Executive Mansion. He once gave a rather eye-opening "rundown" of the fifteenth president's drinking prowess. This litany of Buchanan's ability to quaff massive amounts of liquor, with seemingly mild effect, was printed in Forney's own Philadelphia Press as Old Buck's presidential term was coming to a merciful close.

Leaving room for embellishment, Forney—a man definitely not unaccustomed to hoisting a glass himself—colorfully waxed: "The Madeira and sherry that he has consumed would fill more than one old cellar, and the rye whiskey that he has 'punished' would make Jacob Baer's heart glad." (Jacob Baer was a well-known whiskey merchant in Washington, D.C.)

Forney furthermore stated that Buchanan sometimes coupled a Sunday trip to church with a stop at Baer's to pick up a cask of "old J. B." whiskey, which he liked both for its quality and the fact that the initials matched his own.

And woe to the spirited fellow who felt he could keep pace with Buchanan; Forney claimed it was a contest fraught with disaster against a man of such experience.

Why Forney was so forthcoming on his former boss's ability to consume alcohol is a question worth pondering. Although they had once been fast friends (Forney, like Buchanan, had roots in Lancaster), they were drifting toward estrangement by 1860—partly over the issue of slavery and perhaps also because Buchanan had not offered a position in his administration that Forney felt was worth taking. Forney eventually became a major supporter of Abe Lincoln—with enough zeal that the president's foes sneeringly referred to him as "Lincoln's dog."

THE PROHIBITION PROBE

There is a tendency to think of the Prohibition movement as a product of the early twentieth century. But its peculiar sentiments were stirring even back in Buchanan's day. And while Buchanan may have been wishy-washy on the major issues of his era, he felt sure Prohibition was a fool's errand.

"In [Prohibition], I think, they will entirely fail," he wrote in an 1867 letter. "Lager beer, especially among the Germans, and old rye will be too strong for them. Still, intemperance is a great curse to our people, but it will never be put down by laws prohibiting the sale of all intoxicating liquors...."

The subject of intemperance must have been a curious one for Buchanan to ponder, since the "Sage of Wheatland" himself had such a knack for knocking back alcohol.

OLD BUCK AND THE BEE

Buchanan's own strategy when it came to the emerging forces of temperance seemed to be quite simple: ignore them and pour another drink.

As related in Forney's *Anecdotes of Public Men*, a fuming Pennsylvania judge once charged into then senator Buchanan's office about the judge's harsh treatment in a temperance publication called *The Bee*.

> I [Forney] was sitting with Mr. Buchanan when the irate Judge came in with *The Bee* in his hand. He was a warm friend of the Pennsylvania Senator; and when the latter said, "Won't you take a glass of wine with us, sir?" he said, "I thank you sir, but I came to show you this terrible article against my opinion in *The Bee*. "The what?" said Old Buck, then a very handsome bachelor of fifty. "*The Bee*, sir, said the little Judge in high anger. "And where the Devil is *The Bee* printed, Judge?" "Why Mr. Buchanan, it is printed in this very town, and has a very large circulation among the temperance people and it has given me much pain by its censure of my judicial action, and, by God, sir, I intend to take notice of it from the bench tomorrow!"
>
> These words were uttered with much feeling. The honest and sensitive jurist had been stung to the quick by the little *Bee*, but I shall never forget Buchanan's words as he pushed a cold, bright glass of "Old Wanderer" Madeira to his judicial friend:

"Let me have the honor of a glass of wine with you, sir. I declare to you that I have never to this day heard of the paper you call *The Bee;* but you have made a good record as an honest and impartial judge, and you will be remembered for this long after the name of that paper is forgotten. The faithful public man who feels that he is right, must accept criticism, but he will outlive it as sure as the both of us must die."

DOWN AND GOUT

Buchanan expressed some brief reluctance about running for president due to some minor health issues. He was already in his mid-sixties when he took office.

Letters from Buchanan's post–Executive Mansion years are increasingly laced with references to gout—a disease that's painful to the joints and one believed to be inflamed by a diet riddled with rich foods and too much alcohol.

One of Buchanan's last letters, written to his niece, laments that he attended a lavish dinner at a New Jersey shore resort but felt in an "awkward situation" because he was unable "to drink a drop of wine." His frequent flare-ups of gout might well have been the reason.

LAST CALL

Buchanan allegedly once admonished a wine merchant for sending small bottles of champagne to the Executive Mansion; Old Buck made it clear that big bottles would be required in the future.

CHAPTER 16

Abraham Lincoln

(1809–1865)

braham Lincoln—the sixteenth president of the United States—might well be the most enduring leader America has ever produced. Like a runaway train on the wrong track, the Civil War had been coming from a long way off and the inevitable and devastating smashup happened to occur on Lincoln's watch (1861–1865).

Confederate sympathizers would be quick to say that Lincoln's election accelerated what turned out to be a horrific war. And the venom against him led to the firing of the assassin's fatal bullet at Ford's Theatre mere days after General Robert E. Lee's surrender.

From the trials and tragedies of his personal life, through the initial botched battles of the early war, through Shiloh, Antietam, Vicksburg, Gettysburg, and the end game that led to Appomattox, Lincoln—melancholy and ill-fated—endured it all.

A man of weaker resolve than Lincoln might have easily found reasons to drink—if only to momentarily forget the realities of war or the death of his beloved son Willie in 1862.

Rather than drink, Lincoln told humorous stories as a way to soothe and entertain himself and those around him. Not surprisingly, some of those stories' plots and punch lines were lubricated with alcohol—even if Lincoln very rarely—if ever—touched the stuff himself.

Celebrated by poets and writers like Walt Whitman and Carl Sandburg and, more recently, filmmaker Steven Spielberg, the Lincoln story—both the triumph and the tragedy of it—never seems to fade.

When Lincoln, at the age of fifty-six, was declared dead on the morning of April 15, 1865, Secretary of War Edwin Stanton sadly pronounced: "Now he belongs to the ages."

WEANED IN THE WILD

The pre–Civil War frontier world that young Abraham Lincoln grew up in was still quite rough around the edges. Lincoln was a co-partner at several grocery stores (all of which failed) in Illinois. These stores typically sold liquor, with customers bringing in their own jugs to be filled from kegs.

That William Berry, Lincoln's partner in the New Salem store, drank away any chance to turn a profit may have contributed to Lincoln's personal aversion to alcohol.

TRADING SHOTS WITH "THE LITTLE GIANT"

His ventures into business having failed, Lincoln turned increasingly toward law and politics. Lincoln's greatest rival in the political arena was the Illinois judge named Stephen Douglas (nicknamed "The Little Giant"), and, as the two men battled for a U.S. Senate seat in Illinois in 1858, they took part in a series of debates. Although the future of slavery was a cornerstone topic of these debates, the lengthy speeches occasionally drifted into the bombastic banter so typical of jousting politicians. The topic of alcohol, in fact, was occasionally tossed—like a small, but crowd-pleasing hand grenade—into the fray.

Douglas (known to be partial to whiskey) sometimes called out Lincoln for selling liquor during his days as a store owner. Lincoln responded by noting that *he* had quit *his* side of the counter, but that Douglas was still very much active on the customer's side.

Curiously, Douglas also once taunted Lincoln for *not* drinking, offering him some whiskey during a debate, or—the Democrat demanded—was Lincoln a member of a temperance society? Lincoln unflinchingly replied: "No, I am not a member of any temperance society; but I am temperate in *this:* I don't drink anything."

Lincoln generally denied Douglas's attempts to tie him to a life of liquor, but he did once admit to a crowd (which responded with laughter) that he might have worked one winter at "a little still up the hollow."

THE MISSING SATCHEL

En route to Lincoln's first inaugural in 1861, Robert Todd Lincoln (then a spirited seventeen-year-old) was entrusted with a satchel that contained his father's prepared speech. Robert, who perhaps had become overly festive at several of the whistle stops on the way to Washington, had casually dropped the satchel at a hotel, mixed in with a large heap of other people's luggage.

Rarely one to lose his temper, President-elect Lincoln waded into the heap of bags at the hotel and—using a key—located the missing satchel after a few minutes and some failed attempts on various bags. He then gave the satchel to his sheepish son and, with some emphasis, reminded Robert that he was in charge of it.

WAR AND WHISKEY

Although Lincoln did not indulge in any real drinking, he was reluctant to embrace the temperance force's strict agenda and tired of fending off its periodic assaults on his time. Lincoln often resorted to his favorite defensive foil on these occasions—his dry sense of humor.

A typical example comes from Lincoln's secretary, John Hay. Hay penned this well-written little gem in his September 29, 1963, diary entry:

> Today came to the Executive Mansion an assembly of cold-water men & cold-water women to make a temperance speech at the President & receive a response. They filed into the East Room looking blue & thin in the keen autumnal air, Cooper, my coachman, who about half tight, gazing at them with an air of complacent contempt and mild wonder. Three blue-skinned damsels personated Love, Purity & Fidelity, in Red, White & Blue gowns. A few Invalid soldiers stumped along in the dismal procession. They made a long speech at the President in which they called Intemperance the cause of our defeats. He could not see it as the rebels drink more & worse whiskey than we do. They filed off drearily to a collation of cold water & green apples, & then home to mulligrubs.

SEASICK ASHORE

On June 21, 1864, Lincoln arrived by river steamer at Ulysses S. Grant's headquarters on the James River in Virginia. Grant was preparing for what was to be an exhaustive, costly ten-month siege of Petersburg. Lincoln had just been nominated by the Republicans for a second term and would face the dandified general George B. McClellan, the Democratic nominee, in November.

Although Lincoln had a strong stomach for whatever the dire days of war might put in his path, that strength of stomach apparently did not carry over to extended travel by water. As Admiral Horace Porter noted in his 1897 book *Campaigning with Grant*, the president soon acknowledged these unpleasant issues to Grant and some of his staff officers. When Grant and company stepped aboard, Lincoln and the general exchanged vigorous handshakes and the battlefield commander inquired to the president's health.

"Yes, I am in very good health," Mr. Lincoln replied; "but I don't feel very comfortable after my trip last night on the [Chesapeake] bay. It was rough, and I was considerably shaken up. My stomach has not yet recovered from the effects."

An officer of the party now saw that an opportunity had arisen to make this scene the supreme moment of his life, in giving him a chance to soothe the digestive organs of the Chief Magistrate of the nation. He said: "Try a glass of champagne, Mr. President. That is always a certain cure for seasickness."

Mr. Lincoln looked at him for a moment, his face lighting up with a smile, and then remarked: "No, my friend; I have seen too many fellows seasick ashore from drinking that very stuff." This was a knockdown for the officer, and in the laugh at his expense Mr. Lincoln and the general both joined heartily.

LINCOLN'S LIGHT TOUCH

If one had to start with the lightest-drinking presidents, then Lincoln might well lead the list. The times that he drank are so few and so insignificant that they are actually noteworthy.

Robert Todd Lincoln—when pressed by temperance types concerning his father's alcohol habits—(as quoted in Jason Emerson's *Giant in the Shadows: The Life of Robert T. Lincoln*) allowed this: *

I never saw him use spirituous liquors, and I do not think that he ever did so—I have seen him take a taste of wine at his own dinner table in Washington, but only once or twice and I am sure it was no pleasure to him.

The observations of William Osborn Stoddard, an assistant secretary under Lincoln, in his book *Inside the White House in War Times* (1890) seem to more than confirm Lincoln's reluctance to drink.

There is wine here, and a bottle of champagne has been opened!

A glass of it has been put by the President's plate, and he seems to be taking more than a little interest in it. He takes it up and smells of it, and laughs merrily, but he does not drink. There is a story connected with that glass of wine, and after it is told he has more than one of his own to tell in return.

Some men who worked in the war telegraph office also mentioned that President Lincoln once had "small" beer (low alcoholic content brew) brought to them, and that Lincoln joined them in a few sips. But given these examples of the president's "drinking," one would be hard pressed to list Lincoln even as a lightweight.

AN AVALANCHE OF ALCOHOL

Weirdly, the fact that Lincoln did not drink did nothing to deter people from sending him gifts of alcohol. As Stoddard documented, there was a room at the Executive Mansion overflowing with gifts of liquor.

There are loads of champagne ... red wines of several kinds; white wine from the Rhine; wines of Spain and Portugal and the islands; whiskey distilled from rye, and from wheat, and from potatoes; choice brandy; Jamaica rum, and Santa Cruz rum; and she [Mary Todd Lincoln] suspects one case containing gin.

When Mrs. Lincoln voiced concern about what was to be done with this embarrassment of liquid riches, Stoddard advised giving it to the military hospitals for medicinal purposes. The Lincolns apparently followed that advice.

WHAT THE "OTHER GUY" DRANK

Just days after Richmond fell to the Union forces in 1865, President Lincoln arrived with a small entourage in the city. They went to Jefferson

Davis's home—though the president of the Confederacy had fled the city—and there a house servant still on the premises managed to dig up a bottle, much to the delight of Lincoln's thirsty bodyguard, William H. Crook:

> "Yes, indeed, boss, there is some fine old whiskey in the cellar."
>
> In a few minutes, he produced a long, black bottle. The bottle was passed around. When it came back it was empty. Every one had taken a pull except the President, who never touched anything of the sort.

Jefferson Davis certainly did not limit himself to whiskey. As Union naval commander David Dixon Porter found out (and related in his 1885 book *Incidents and Anecdotes of the Civil War*) upon capturing a British blockade runner in early 1865 and examining its cargo:

> It looked queer to me to see boxes labeled "His Excellency, Jefferson Davis, President of the Confederate States of America.'" The packages so labeled contained Bass ale or Cognac brandy, which cost "His Excellency" less than we Yankees had to pay for it. Think of the President drinking imported liquors while his soldiers were living on pop-corn and water!

THE FINAL HOURS

That Lincoln very rarely—if ever—put alcohol to his lips in his latter years is well established. There is some irony, then, in the fact that men drinking alcohol figured very much in the last hours of the doomed president's life.

On the night of Lincoln's assignation at Ford's Theatre, John Parker, Lincoln's substitute bodyguard, (according to some accounts) ducked next door for a tankard of ale at Peter Taltavull's Star Saloon before the start of the third act of that evening's play, *Our American Cousin*. While

Parker enjoyed his ale, John Wilkes Booth entered the bar. As Taltavull testified in the post-assassination trials:

> [Booth] just walked into the bar and asked for some whiskey. I gave him the whiskey; put the bottle on the counter ... he called for some water and I gave him some. He put money on the counter and went right out. I saw him go out of the bar alone, as near as I could judge, from eight to ten minutes before I heard the cry that the President was assassinated.

Lincoln's regular bodyguard, Colonel William H. Crook (off duty on the night of the assassination), believed whiskey played a role in the president's death. That—and what Crook saw as Parker's abandonment of his post—certainly helped fix Lincoln's fate.

> Booth had found it necessary to stimulate himself with whiskey in order to reach the proper pitch of fanaticism. Had he found a man at the door of the President's box with a Colt's revolver, his alcohol courage might have evaporated.

LAST CALL

Born in Kentucky, Lincoln spent his early boyhood in a place called Knob Creek. Given his famous sense of humor, Lincoln might be amused that today one can buy a premium brand of bourbon named Knob Creek.

CHAPTER 17

Andrew Johnson

(1808–1875)

A ndrew Johnson—the seventeenth president of the United States (1865–1869)—is notorious for two incidents—his inebriated state during his inauguration ceremony for vice president in 1865 and his impeachment by the House of Representatives (and narrow escape in the Senate) in 1868. His political career somehow survived both, but his legacy was tarnished.

Of course, nobody ever really expected Johnson to be president—it took Lincoln's assassination at Ford's Theatre and the failure of one of John Wilkes Booth's fellow conspirators to kill the vice president, as was planned, for that to happen.

Johnson grew up impoverished in North Carolina and was laboring as a tailor in Tennessee when he grasped a rising political ring. He is one of history's most complicated studies: he was (like most presidents before him) a slave-owner—though he eventually emancipated those he owned; he was a man with Southern roots—but a staunch Unionist and a bitter critic of the Dixie aristocrats who he felt riled up the average man for secession behind the guise of "states' rights"; and though a Democrat in the Jacksonian mold, Johnson was chosen to be running mate of Lincoln—the great Republican.

Those who enjoy perusing the rankings of presidents will typically find Johnson near the bottom of the list. Most of his biographers believe Johnson was a moderate drinker (the inauguration fiasco being an exception) for his era. Yet, his political enemies occasionally referred to him as "the drunken tailor."

VP ME!

Abraham Lincoln was disappointed with Hannibal Hamlin, his first vice president. With the 1864 reelection campaign looming, Andrew Johnson emerged from the pack of potential replacement running mates with minimal fanfare. He was given high marks for loyalty when as military governor of Tennessee he withstood a virtual firestorm by siding with the Union, even as his state had thrown its lot in with the Confederacy. Lincoln and Johnson actually ran as the National Union Party ticket.

Lincoln won reelection handily over Democratic nominee General George B. McClellan, whom he'd unceremoniously sacked from command earlier in the war. Johnson, of course, rode Abe's long coattails. But as the inauguration approached, Johnson was quite sick (possibly with typhoid fever), and he alerted Lincoln that, given the unfortunate circumstances, he would prefer not to travel to Washington and deal with the inauguration ceremonies.

But Lincoln would not hear of it. The commander in chief felt it was important that Johnson be on hand for the occasion.

So Johnson reluctantly agreed to make the trip to the capital. It might be a historical toss-up whether Lincoln or Johnson regretted the results of this decision more. That's because when Johnson hit town, he got drunk and stayed that way for a day and a half.

THE FORNEY FACTOR

Johnson's first mistake might have been colliding with John Forney. Forney—the secretary of the Senate—was a newspaper editor, writer, and political operative who had helped his friend James Buchanan get elected president in 1856. Forney had had a previous waltz or two with Demon Alcohol. (John Hay, Lincoln's secretary, described Forney as dangerously drunk on whiskey the night before Abe's Gettysburg Address, for example.)

Of course, it was not unusual in that era to prescribe whiskey as a treatment for various illnesses, and Johnson—feeling somewhat weak from his sickness and the rigors of travel—attended a party hosted by Forney on the evening before the big day. Whiskey certainly would have been offered to the Tennessean to salute his election, as standard hospitality, and perhaps even in the guise of medical treatment. Johnson apparently did not demur.

When Inauguration Day (a dreary, rainy one) came, it was obvious that whiskey, illness, or both still held sway over Johnson. With his speech looming, Johnson asked Hamlin for an additional dose or two— or three—of whiskey. In some accounts, brandy is said to have been the liquor provided, though nobody argues much about the result of whatever Johnson consumed. Ousted from the Lincoln ticket, Hamlin— temperate when it came to his own drinking—perhaps was only too happy to comply. And so Johnson—on one of the most important days of his political career—opted for the dubious "hair of the dog" strategy.

But sometimes the dog bites back.

GRAVE REVIEWS

The outcome was cringe-worthy. Johnson mumbled words that made little sense but weirdly seemed accusatory in nature. The speech was outlined for approximately five minutes, yet Johnson rambled on much longer—pillar to post—like a drunk unable to find his own house.

Finally, mercifully—after more than fifteen minutes inside the stuffy Senate building—Johnson got the equivalent of the "Broadway Hook." Secretary of the Navy Gideon Welles recapped Johnson's spectacular smashup in his diary:

> The Vice-President elect made a rambling and strange harangue, which was listened to with pain and mortification by all his friends. My impressions were that he was under the influence of stimulants, yet I know not that he drinks.

And Welles was not alone in his concern, noting:

> [James] Speed, who was on my left, said, "All this is in wretchedly bad taste;" and very soon he said, "The man is certainly deranged." I said to [Secretary of War William] Stanton, who was on my right, "Johnson is either drunk or crazy." Stanton said, "Something is evidently wrong."

Indeed. Something was wrong and that something was too much booze.

Future president Rutherford B. Hayes was in the audience and wrote home to his wife, Lucy, bluntly stating: "It was lucky you did not come to the inauguration. The bad weather and Andy Johnson's disgraceful drunkenness spoiled it."

The newspapers, of course, did not let Johnson's bizarre, whiskey-infused performance go un-remarked upon, either. The Lincoln administration decided the best possible defense was to play possum: Johnson disappeared for a few weeks, holed up at Francis S. Blair's home. Lincoln—by now quite experienced at defending his generals (chiefly, U. S. Grant) against accusations of drunkenness, tried to reassure his own administrators concerning Johnson. Hugh McCullough, secretary of the Treasury, remembered that President Lincoln assured him several days later that Johnson's behavior was an unfortunate occurrence but not one that likely would be revisited. According to McCullough, Lincoln said:

"I have known Andy Johnson for many years; he made a bad slip the other day, but you need not be scared. Andy ain't a drunkard."

THE WHISKEY PAPER TRAIL

Andy Johnson may not have been a drunkard, but neither was he a stranger to whiskey. If one reads through his letters and bills, there is ample evidence that Johnson possessed a discernible taste for quality whiskey—and was willing to pay good money to get it.

For example, a typical letter to Nashville hotelier Samuel J. Carter (a man who seems to have doubled as Johnson's procurer of whiskey) is this one in August of 1863:

> If you have any pure Simple Whiskey that is good send me some of it—I have enough that is not fit for any one to drink, yet it is called [good] by some.

Several days later, Johnson's correspondence included this note from a whiskey supplier:

> Hon. Andrew Johnson
>   Sir we Sent you a Demijohn of Robinson [Robertson?]
> Co. Whiskey [.] Hoping it will meet with your approval

THE SWING (SWIG?) AROUND THE CIRCLE

In 1866, in an effort to build support for his Reconstruction agenda and perhaps boost his own likeability, President Johnson embarked on what was dubbed the "Swing around the Circle" tour. It started reasonably well, but ended badly and—when it was all said and done—probably hurt Johnson's image.

Johnson surrounded himself with Civil War heroes—General U. S. Grant (a somewhat reluctant draftee), Admiral David Farragut, and the dashing (but doomed) young cavalryman General George Armstrong

Custer. The tour involved banquets at which lavish dinners and numerous toasts were made. Some were held at swanky establishments, such as Delmonico's in New York City.

Fearing that the "Swing" might bolster Johnson's popularity, the abolitionists (who hated the president because they felt he was too lenient on the defeated rebels) began to push back; hecklers soon appeared to badger Johnson at speaking engagements, particularly in the Midwest. And Johnson—a pugnacious man with the stubbornness of a beaten boxer who won't allow his corner to toss in the towel—eagerly engaged these verbal snipers. The result was a chief executive who looked combative (which he was) and undignified.

And, not surprisingly, it allowed the opposition to speculate that Johnson must have been drunk to be so belligerent. There certainly was some drinking on the "Swing"—yet Johnson supporters swore he never over-indulged.

Because of his obvious "slip" at the 1865 inauguration, Johnson could never quite dodge the accusations of his enemies when it came to drinking. In fact, his most vehement detractors often used a double-barreled rhetorical shotgun against him, referring to Johnson as "the drunken tailor"—blasts against both his indulgence of alcohol and his working-class roots.

Somewhat thin-skinned, Johnson insisted that the accusations about his alcohol consumption were grossly overstated and once gave this bristling observation: "It is very strange that some men will be abused like the devil for drinking a glass of whiskey and water, while others ... may almost roll in the gutters, and not a word is said about it."

NOT SO PEACHY

Johnson's enemies—and they were significant in both power and number—soon circled in for the kill. Led by the hard-core abolitionists in 1868, they came incredibly close to ousting Johnson from the Executive Mansion. The House of Representatives did, in fact, impeach Johnson, but the Senate fell short—by one vote—of the needed two-thirds majority.

There is some special justice in the fact that Johnson—in an impromptu ceremony—did not toast his dodging of the impeachment bullet with mineral water or champagne, but instead hoisted some special whiskey from the Executive Mansion cellar. (At least one must assume it was special, as there is ample proof that Johnson liked the best stuff available).

THE ACQUITTAL TOAST

There was no better first-person witness to Johnson's reaction to his acquittal than Executive Mansion bodyguard William Crook. When Senator Edmund Ross of Kansas cast the pivotal vote for acquittal on May 16, 1868, Johnson narrowly escaped the charges of "high crimes and misdemeanors." As Crook recounted:

> I ran all the way from the Capitol to the White House. I was young and strong in those days, and I made good time. When I burst into the library where the President sat with Secretary Welles and two other men whom I cannot remember, they were quietly talking....
>
> "Mr. President," I shouted, too crazy with delight to restrain myself, "you are acquitted!"
>
> All rose. I made my way to the President and got hold of his hand. The other men surrounded him, and began to shake his hand. The President responded to their congratulations calmly enough for a moment, and then I saw that tears were rolling down his face. I stared at him; and yet I felt I ought to turn my eyes away.
>
> It was all over in a moment, and Mr. Johnson was ordering some whiskey from the cellar. When it came, he himself poured it into glasses for us, and we all stood up and drank a silent toast. There were some sandwiches on the

table; we ate some and then we felt better. In a few minutes came a message of congratulations from Secretary Seward to "my dear friend." By that time the room was full of people and I slipped away.

Seward had two reasons to be happy. There was Johnson's acquittal, of course, but also Seward—an aficionado of fine wines—had bet someone a basket of champagne that Johnson would be cleared.

WHISKEY VICTIMS

Writing about the dissipation of Andrew Johnson's sons, Robert W. Winston remarked that whiskey was "the curse of the Old South" and held both Charles and Robert Johnson "in its clutch."

All of this unfolded in waves of grand tragedy, prior to Andrew Johnson's own embarrassing and legacy-marring missteps at his inauguration; so certainly he was very well aware of John Barleycorn's destructive powers.

In May 1860, Robert Johnson wrote a desperate letter to his father, lamenting that he was unable to deter his older brother from an incredible bender during a trip to Charleston, South Carolina.

> I got him about straight before reaching home, and I was congratulating myself … but was doomed to be disappointed, for no sooner had he got home, than went to drinking and is still at it, and I will presume will not quit until it compels him to. . . .

Charles never really shook his drinking habit and died in an accident with his horse. He was only thirty-three years old.

Robert did not fair much better. A Union colonel, Robert eventually had to leave the military because of an alcohol addiction. In 1863, General William Rosecrans, his superior officer, dashed off a letter to then Governor Johnson, lamenting the circumstances and hoping for the best. Rosecrans wrote:

Robert has been drinking so as to become a subject of remark everywhere. I sent for him, told him I wanted him to stop and he promised me he would. If he keeps his word I will do all I can for him....

But Robert was unable to resist the pull of the whiskey bottle. Finally, then Governor Johnson was forced to bring him to Nashville and set him up as his aide. When Johnson became president, he brought Robert along to serve in that position in Washington. But Robert eventually became mired in a serious scandal (prostitutes were spotted coming and going from his Executive Mansion office), and he committed suicide in 1869.

LAST CALL

Gone from the Executive Mansion, Johnson eventually moved back to Tennessee and made something of a political comeback when he was elected to the U.S. Senate in 1874. That he still had lapses with liquor is likely. According to an account by John S. Wise, Johnson spoke to a crowd from a balcony of Nashville's esteemed Maxwell House Hotel just months before his death. Wise wrote:

> It was a pitiful sight to see him standing there, holding on to the iron railing in front of him and swaying back and forth, almost inarticulate with drink.... It was a sight I shall never forget—the bloated, stupid, helpless look of Mr. Johnson, as he was hurried away from the balcony to his rooms by his friends and led staggering through the corridors of the Maxwell House.

Not long after Wise's disturbing observation, the former president suffered a series of strokes and died on July 31, 1875—mere months after his triumphant return to Washington as a senator.

CHAPTER 18

Ulysses S. Grant

(1822–1885)

*I*f you want to start a skirmish among Civil War aficionados—be they scholars or buffs—simply announce: "General Grant was often drunk when he commanded..." or, conversely, claim: "Grant rarely had more than a few sips and anything to the contrary was drummed up to tarnish the poor man's reputation."

Then step back and watch a clash of two opposing interpretations of history collide with great force.

The truth lies, in all likelihood, somewhere in between. Grant could go days or weeks—perhaps even months—without an alcoholic episode. But when Grant did drink, he did not do it well. By some accounts, Grant exhibited low tolerance; he certainly was no match for the rough (and readily available) whiskey of his day. Another general said of Grant: "A single glass would show on him. His face would flush at once."

Born Hiram Ulysses Grant in 1822, the future eighteenth president of the United States (1869–1877) might be better classified as a "bad drinker" than a "big drinker." But there should be little debate that he was, upon occasion, drawn to alcohol.

THE CHARACTER ASSASSINS

U. S. Grant had many enemies in the newspaper industry. One was Murat Halstead, an editor with the *Cincinnati Commercial*, who dashed off a letter to Salmon P. Chase, the former Ohio governor and Lincoln's Treasury secretary. In his letter, Halstead fumed:

> You do once in a while, don't you, say a word to the President, or [Secretary of War Edwin] Stanton, or [Gen. Henry] Halleck, about the conduct of the war? Well, now, for God's sake say that Genl Grant, entrusted with our greatest army is a jackass in the original package.... He is a poor stick sober, and he is most of the time more than half drunk, and much of the time idiotically drunk....

That Chase (a non-drinker) and others expressed their trepidations concerning Grant's issues with liquor is certain. But once Grant took Vicksburg (on July 4, 1863), Lincoln was increasingly deaf to the general's detractors (whether or not one puts any stock in the supposed Lincoln quip: "Find out Grant's brand of whiskey and send some to my other generals..."). And it wasn't long before Lincoln brought Grant to the East and promoted him, with an aim to end the war.

THE MEDICINAL DEFENSE

When Halstead's poisonous letter came to light in 1885, Grant was dead. But General William Tecumseh Sherman, always quick-tempered in Grant's defense, launched a spirited counterattack against the charges, which had been reprinted in the *New York Times*.

New York Times reporter: "The [Halstead] letter states that Grant was drunk at [the Battle of Fort] Donelson and surprised and whipped at Shiloh."

Sherman said:

That is a pure lie. Gen. Grant never was drunk. At Donelson he won a great victory and at Shiloh we had two hard days' fighting; that doesn't much look like drunkenness, does it? Of course, Gen. Grant took a glass of wine or whisky occasionally. It was necessary. I took a glass of whisky myself once in a while. We could never have resisted the climate otherwise. Sometimes we worked knee-deep in water; at others we were exposed to unusual fatigues. But to assert that there was anything like drunkenness is a shameful untruth.

MY FRIEND SHERMAN

One must always view Sherman's comments about Grant through the filter of a friendship forged in the furnace of war. When Sherman suffered something of a nervous breakdown during the Kentucky campaign early in the war, the newspapers hostile to him (some of the same also venomous to Grant) claimed he was insane. But Grant took Sherman under his wing, and, eventually, one of the most successful Union generals was resurrected.

Late in the war, after Sherman captured Savannah, a journalist tried to get him to compare his attributes to Grant's. Sherman snapped: "General Grant is a great general. I know him well. He stood by me when I was crazy, and I stood by him when he was drunk; and now, sir, we stand by each other always."

LONELY DAZE

But the facts show that Grant was a man long familiar with John Barleycorn. And John Barleycorn, unlike most of the Confederate commanders whom faced Grant on the battlefield, knew the man's weaknesses.

Hamlin Garland wrote a sympathetic Grant biography. But, to his credit, Garland did not put on the blinders in regards to the man's drinking habits, which he traces back, most likely, to Grant's stint in the Mexican-American War in his early twenties.

> A very inconsiderable but valuable man was the Lieutenant busily bringing the wagon-train forward, and growing a red beard meanwhile to appear less youthful. He also was acquiring the use of whisky and tobacco.

The majority of American soldiers fighting in Mexico drank whenever they could, so Grant probably never got so much as a second glance.

But a lonely assignment to the Pacific Northwest afterwards was another matter. Most of Grant's biographers trace his problem drinking to that time period. Alone and far from his beloved wife, Julia, and his growing family, Grant—definitely bored, if not actually depressed—appears to have sought solace in the bottle. He allegedly was inebriated on the day he was to hand out pay to the enlisted soldiers. Brought before his commander, Grant wrestled with a difficult decision: either face charges of drunkenness in a court-martial or resign from the army. He opted for the latter. So bleak was Grant's situation that he had to borrow money from another officer just to get back home.

But the all-hands-on-deck crisis of the Civil War rejuvenated Grant's military career. Grant was toiling with his brothers in a leather-tanning shop in Galena, Illinois, when hostilities broke out. His first appointment was as a colonel in the state militia—hardly a lofty perch—but within two years he was rising rapidly in the Union officer ranks.

How did he do it? Grant had, if not flash and brilliance, a gritty, stick-to-it-iveness. And that attribute overrode all his flaws in the long run, including whatever sporadic urges he seems to have had for alcohol.

THE VICKSBURG FIX

The Vicksburg campaign was arguably the most precarious tightrope walk of Grant's military career and, therefore, his life.

Had he failed, Grant could have plunged into the abyss of relative obscurity—yet another hapless commander dismissed by Lincoln—but he did not. That Grant captured the strategic city on the Mississippi River bluff (he accepted the surrender, symbolically, on July 4, 1863) may have happened despite some strongly rumored missteps with alcohol—though, in Grant's defense, (if they did indeed happen) these likely occurred during ho-hum periods of the multi-month siege.

Prior to his capture of Vicksburg, Lincoln was not completely sold on Grant's true value. The persistent rumors of unbridled boozing did not help. Lincoln sent down one of his aides—the journalist Charles Dana—under the pretense of reporting on troop strengths. But Grant deduced that Dana was really there to measure his effectiveness—and, perhaps, to see if his drinking was a hindrance. Grant welcomed Dana into his inner circle, and perhaps Dana downplayed the extent of Grant's drinking when writing his superiors back in Washington.

Sylvanus Cadwallader, a newspaperman from the *Chicago Times*, claimed to have witnessed the general on a classic two-day bender (including a drunken riverboat frolic, followed by a strange, intoxicated gallop along the Yazoo River on a horse called "Kangaroo") during the Vicksburg campaign. Cadwallader's book (*Three Years with Grant*) did not appear until the late 1890s, and, when it did, Grant's most ardent admirers blasted the reports as blatant fabrication.

Whatever the truth, Grant stayed on, captured Vicksburg, and won Abe Lincoln's confidence.

An interesting figure in this brew-ha-ha was Lieutenant Colonel John Rawlins, Grant's chief of staff. Rawlins's principal function seemingly was to prevent Grant from obtaining alcohol. The major was only marginally successful at this thankless—but arguably crucial—job and became dramatically indignant if the general escaped for a "frolic."

Nevertheless, Rawlins took on this task with upmost zeal. Even a gift of Kentucky wine from Grant's mother could send Rawlins into a puritanical rant.

But Rawlins's true angst in this trying role as Grant's Guardian Angel against Demon Alcohol cannot be felt in full unless you read his letters. In late 1863, he wrote to his fiancée, Mary Emma Hurlbut:

> Matters have changed and the necessity of my presence here made almost absolute, but the free use of intoxicating liquors at Headquarters which last nights developments showed me had reached to the General commanding. I am the only one here (his wife not being with him) who can stay it in that direction and prevent evil consequences resulting from it. I had hoped but it appeared vainly that his New Orleans experience would prevent him ever again indulging with his worst enemy.

THE NEW ORLEANS SLIP-UP

Rawlins's reference to Grant's "New Orleans experience" seems to confirm an incident involving the general's spill on a horse during a military review held in his honor there in September 1863—several months after his career-changing victory at Vicksburg.

When Grant and steed crashed to the ground, the general's leg was trapped underneath. Badly injured, it took him weeks to recover. His enemies (and even some of Grant's faithful, such as Rawlins) believed the accident might have occurred because Grant—after attending a post-parade bash—had been intoxicated and riding an unfamiliar and skittish horse.

The predictable gossip about Grant, once again, rose like puffs of cannon smoke above a battlefield. The rumors essentially followed him until the end of the war. As late as December 29, 1864, Secretary of the Navy Gideon Welles wrote in his diary:

> Fox [Gustavaus, assistant secretary of the Navy] says Grant occasionally gets drunk. I have never mentioned the fact to anyone, not to my wife, who can be trusted with a secret. There were such rumors of him when he was in the West....

THE SWING AROUND THE CIRCLE

When Andrew Johnson became president following Lincoln's murder, it was not long before he fell out of favor with factions bent on harsh punishments for the South. In an effort to boost his popularity, Johnson toured the country in what was known as the "Swing around the Circle" in the summer of 1866. To add luster and prestige to the tour, President Johnson was able to persuade certain Union military heroes—a reluctant Grant, Admiral David Farragut, and the brash young cavalry officer George Armstrong Custer—to accompany him.

There is evidence that Grant fell off the wagon during this tour. Repetitive days of train travel and over-feasting (accompanied by fine wines and brandy, no doubt) probably led to tedium—always a trial for Grant. In addition, Grant's chances of an alcoholic episode typically increased when he was required to be apart from Julia for days at a time.

Sylvanus Cadwallader maintained (years later) that Grant gave into the temptations of liquor during the trip. A delegation from Cleveland met the train in New York State and brought food and lots of alcohol onboard, with the general partaking freely of drink.

According to Cadwallader, the result was Grant sprawled out in the back of a railroad car, lying atop "empty mail bags and rubbish." Furthermore, Cadwallader claimed that he and Rawlins (now a general) took turns standing guard to keep the overly inquisitive from discovering the country's most esteemed hero in an inebriated heap.

Claiming illness, Grant skipped the festivities in Cleveland and proceeded by boat to Detroit and wrote to Julia, allowing that he needed rest. (There was no mention of drinking.) President Johnson—though he must have known differently—also told the crowd in Cleveland that the general's absence was due to illness.

THE DONALDSON DIARIES

Once he became President Grant, the general was fairly careful not to overindulge, particularly at official Executive Mansion events. His wine cellar was first-class, and certainly he sipped a glass or two at state dinners, but he was careful before watchful eyes. Nevertheless, as his old army colleague Rawlins could attest, Grant proved elusive when necessary.

Thomas Corwin Donaldson (1843–1898) was a close friend of President Rutherford B. Hayes and something of a mover and a shaker from Columbus, Ohio. Donaldson knew many of the Executive Mansion staffers, too, and put down some insightful comments in a haphazardly kept diary—accounts that have not been widely published in the mainstream media.

Concerning President Grant, Donaldson wrote:

> He had many cronies, and I recall a club room where he used to ... play a social game of cards....
>
> Sen. [T. W.] Osborn of Fla., once told me that John M. Francis of Troy, N.Y., went up to the White House during Grant's first term, played poker with a party, got fuddled—was Grant's partner in this perhaps—did it well, and the next day, to his surprise, was appointed Minister to Greece. Is a good hand at poker a qualification for a foreign Minster?

Donaldson also knew one Samuel Taylor Suit (he was called "Colonel" Suit, but in the honorary Kentucky use of that title), a man familiar to President Grant and other prominent Washingtonians. Although Suit was best known for his whiskey production (delivered in his famous little brown jugs), vast fruit orchards around his Maryland homestead also produced magnificent peach, apple, and cherry brandies.

> President Grant seldom spent an evening at home. He went out dining with his friends. Col. S. T. Suit, who knew him well, once told me he used to meet him at a private club room ... and that he had a partial side for some fine French brandy in his (Suit's) house. Sometimes he was very partial to it.

In 1871, delegations from both Great Britain and the United States met to work out the damages surrounding the case of the infamous rebel raider, the *Alabama* (built by the Brits). President Grant had the meetings held at Suitland—and, one strongly suspects, Suit's much-vaunted libations must have been dutifully sampled by the delegates.

EXECUTIVE MANSION WINE

The hardships of war behind him, Grant transitioned quite smoothly into the high life of living in the Executive Mansion. Grant accumulated a splendid array of wines and took a direct interest in them. As Secret Service man William H. Crook remarked:

> General Grant particularly loved to have a few friends for dinner.... He chose the wines himself, and gave directions that they should be served at the proper temperature ... General Grant was an open-handed lavish host. I remember one wine bill which impressed me very much at the time—$1,800 for champagne alone.

Crook also related a wine-related mishap, involving a particularly esteemed vintage.

> It was brought out for one of the big dinners, and the President went himself, with Henry and Edgar, two of the servants, to have it drawn off into eight large decanters. On the way down, Henry stumbled and fell, breaking the four decanters he was carrying. The President turned and looked at him, but didn't express his feelings further. When they got down-stairs General Grant said to Beckley, the steward:
> "Get four other decanters and go to the garret and fill them, but don't let Henry go again!"

Although Grant was known for treating his staff well, the unlucky servant admitted that the president's disapproving stare had made him wish he could "go through the floor."

THE INDIA INCIDENT

With both war and politics behind him, the Grants and an entourage left for a trip around the world in the summer of 1877. The journey, which took two years, included various stops in Europe (including Germany, where Grant participated in some extensive Rhine wine-tasting), plus China and Japan.

But it in India, visiting the viceroy Lord Lytton, an embarrassing incident seems to have occurred. Lord Lytton wrote about it in a letter, and although the tone suggests embellishment in an effort to humor the reader, it also seems likely that there was at least some truth in the matter. Alcohol, of course, was the catalyst.

> On this occasion "our distinguished guest" the double Ex-President of the "Great Western Republic", who got drunk as a fiddle, showed that he could also profligate as a lord. He fumbled Mrs A, kissed the shrieking Miss B—pinched the plump Mrs C black and blue—and ran at Miss D with intent to ravish her. Finally, after throwing the female guests into hysterics by generally misbehaving like a must elephant, the noble beast was captured by main force and carried (quatre pattes dans l'air) by six sailors ... which relieved India of his distinguished presence. The marine officer ... reports that, when deposited in the public saloon cabin, where Mrs G, was awaiting him ... this remarkable man satiated there and then his baffled lust on the unresisting body of his legitimate spouse, and copiously vomited during the operation. If you have seen Mrs Grant you will not think this incredible.

Since Lord Lytton sent this in a private letter and probably assumed it would not be made public, one must consider he had no serious intent to harm Grant's image. Perhaps an intoxicated Grant *did* indulge in some of these off-color behaviors (although by all accounts, Grant, when sober, was a reserved man who showed the upmost respect for women), if not to the full extent that Lytton portrayed in his letter.

THE GENERAL'S DEMISE

Grant—perhaps when resisting the urge to drink—would often opt for a cigar. He could easily smoke a dozen or more in a day.

In fact, it may have been tobacco—not whiskey—that hastened Grant's death, though medical experts tab both as oral cancer risks. The former president was diagnosed with throat cancer in 1885. To make matters worse, Grant also was essentially bankrupt, having lost his life savings in an investment scam. His financial desperation led the general to sell off most of his personal Civil War collection to erase some of his major debts.

Championed by Mark Twain (Twain helped secure him a fantastic publishing contract), Grant set about writing his memoirs. The memoirs eventually sold more than three hundred thousand copies and brought in more than four hundred thousand dollars in royalties for his widow. He finished the manuscript just days before his death. In an effort to ease his pain, Grant's doctors injected him with brandy and dosed him with cocaine over his final hours. Today we know that that kind of treatment probably hastened Grant's death, but given his painful state—and with his final project completed—that may not have been the worst choice.

LAST CALL

The biggest scandal during Grant's presidency was called the Whiskey Ring—a conspiracy in the mid-1870s that allowed the perpetrators to skim millions of uncollected tax dollars that should have come from liquor production. Although most historians agree Grant seems to have had no direct knowledge of the massive fraud, some of his closest associates were prosecuted for their involvement.

CHAPTER 19

Rutherford B. Hayes

(1822–1893)

Rutherford B. Hayes—a Civil War hero (wounded four times) who went on to become a U.S. congressman, governor of Ohio, and then the nineteenth president of the United States (1877–1881)—did not exactly "sweep" into the Executive Mansion. In fact, his Democratic opponent—the squeaky-voiced Samuel J. Tilden of New York—tabulated more votes. The controversial Compromise of 1877 (basically a deal in which Southern factions consented to support the Republican Hayes if Hayes would agree to remove Union troops from the former Confederate States) allowed Hayes to prevail by a single electoral vote. But Hayes's administration suffered much from congressional backlash, both from defeat-bitter Democrats and Republican radicals who were not yet prepared to pardon the vanquished South.

After such a hotly contested campaign and tumultuous beginning, one might have thought a round of good stiff drinks would have been in order, but the Hayes Executive Mansion left behind a rather different social legacy. Never a big drinker, Hayes had been known to have an occasional beer in his younger days, specifically in Cincinnati's "Over-the-Rhine" German section. However, most likely driven by his wife's wishes (Lucy was a committed teetotaler), the president appeared to embrace a ban on alcohol at Executive Mansion functions, though perhaps with not quite the same conviction as his spouse.

As John Sergeant Wise (a U.S. congressman from Virginia) remarked: "With all her lovable and excellent traits, Mrs. Hayes was more or less a crank on this subject ... President Hayes admired and respected Mrs. Hayes greatly and deferred to her demands about liquor, but I do not think he was himself in the least fanatical on the subject."

THE DAYS OF WINE AND RUSSIANS

Just weeks after President Hayes and his wife moved into the Executive Mansion, the residence was abuzz. The Russians were coming—specifically Alexis and Constantine, the young adult sons of Czar Alexander II. This event was incredibly exciting; but it also created a dilemma.

That dilemma—which arose because it was well known that the first lady had pledged not to serve intoxicating beverages in the Executive Mansion—was what to offer their esteemed and somewhat exotic guests in way of a thirst-quencher?

After much hand-wringing and temple-massaging, it was decided that wine should—and would—be offered. Secretary of State William Evarts took the heat on this incident, insisting that America would look uncultured if its leaders did not offer the Eastern Europeans what they were accustomed to drinking at an extravagant dinner. The young grand dukes from Russia, perhaps oblivious to all the fuss, arrived and drank their wine along with all the trimmings of a state feast. Predictably, President Hayes and the first lady did not imbibe. In the aftermath, temperance forces (which had lent support to Hayes in the recent election) protested that any wine, for any reason, had been served.

Whatever Alexis and Constantine might have done while under the influence would eventually be infamously eclipsed by a fellow Russian. When Prime Minister Boris Yeltsin visited the White House in 1995, Secret Service agents found him as drunk as a Cossack warrior out on Pennsylvania Avenue. Clad only in his underwear, boisterous Boris was attempting to flag down cabs to whisk him off for the culinary delight of a pre-dawn pizza.

THE SIDEBOARD AND THE SALOON

As presidential artifacts go, the "Lucy Hayes Sideboard" is arguably one of the most noteworthy—at least to aficionados of White House decorative history. The sideboard is a valuable piece of art: rich mahogany, ornately carved by one of the most celebrated woodworkers of nineteenth-century America—Henry Fry of Cincinnati. The piece was ordered while Hayes was president and stood in the Executive Mansion dining room along with an accompanying carving table, also made by Fry and his associates.

Since the Hayes Executive Mansion was renowned for not serving alcoholic beverages, the sideboard and table never held or displayed any potent potables. The only liquids to appear on the table were tea, coffee, water, punch, and lemonade. (Lucy Hayes was aptly nicknamed "Lemonade Lucy" by historians, but her defining moniker came after the Hayeses' stint in the Executive Mansion.) The visiting journalists and dignitaries, among others, found this condition especially bleak— and most likely the artistic beauty of Fry's mahogany masterpiece was lost upon those members of the fourth estate.

The sideboard still loomed majestically in the dining room when the Hayes family left the Executive Mansion after one term. James Garfield moved in, but due to an assassin's bullet, his service proved quite brief. When Chester A. Arthur—a polished New Yorker with extravagant tastes—took over the leadership reins, he opted for renovations at the Executive Mansion. In the midst of this zealous makeover, numerous wagonloads of furniture and other items were unceremoniously dumped into the hands of a secondhand junk dealer. The Lucy Hayes Sideboard ended up as part of this hapless haul.

Coincidentally, the secondhand junk dealer promptly sold (for a mere eighty-five dollars) the Lucy Hayes Sideboard to John M. Frank, owner of a Washington brewery and beer garden.

Stirring up even more of a brew-hah-hah, a rumor persisted that the sideboard had been a gift from the Women's Christian Temperance Union, in recognition of Lucy's pledge to keep Executive Mansion events sans alcohol. But the facts suggest that a Executive Mansion official ordered the sideboard at the Hayeses' request. Nevertheless, this notion of the Lucy Hayes Sideboard being a gift from the WCTU is still printed (and presented as fact) today.

In a *New York Times* article (February 28, 1903), John Wesley Gaines, a Democrat from Tennessee, voiced his outrage to his fellow House representatives:

"It is a fact," said Mr. Gaines, "that the mahogany sideboard given to Mrs. Hayes while she was in the White House is down here in a Washington brewery. I saw it there yesterday."

Although it appears Gaines was wrong about the sideboard being a gift from the WCTU or anyone else, he was correct that it was in the hands of the beer garden proprietor. If the sideboard had supported no alcohol during its Executive Mansion era, Frank was making up for lost time—when Gaines viewed the piece it was decorated with various liquor bottles and on the top shelf "a row of fine old German beer steins."

And Frank was not willing to part with it for any reasonable sum. Webb Hayes (one of the former president's sons) offered to buy it from him for hundreds of dollars. But Mr. Frank, apparently, did not want to part with the sideboard for such a modest sum; he was demanding three thousand dollars.

It was more than six decades later, in 1967, that the Rutherford B. Hayes Presidential Center, Inc., was able to purchase the Lucy Hayes Sideboard from Frank's descendants—for a price of $2,500. Visitors to Spiegel Grove—the Hayeses' homestead and museum in Fremont, Ohio— can view the handcrafted mahogany sideboard that caused so much controversy as part of their tour.

PUNCH AND COUNTER-PUNCH

James G. Blaine, the speaker of the House (and a man some Republicans of that day thought should have been president instead of Hayes) from Maine, felt the pain of thirsty visitors to the Executive Mansion. He once arrived rather late in the evening at the Danish Embassy, placed his hands on the shoulders of the ambassador, and—paraphrasing Shakespeare's titular Richard the III—proclaimed: "My kingdom for a glass of whiskey; I have just dined at the White House." (Similarly, Secretary of State William Evarts wisecracked that at Executive Mansion events "the water flows like wine....")

Newspapermen of that day—most of whom were known to hoist a glass or two of wine, beer, or spirits on a regular basis—would certainly have concurred with Blaine and Evarts. Visits to the Executive Mansion in the Hayes term were considered tough duty. There was a rumor that that some of the Executive Mansion staff—taking pity upon the dignitaries, scribblers, and other visiting imbibers at official dinners—soaked the oranges in the supposed non-alcoholic punch with some highly potent rum. The journalists and a few other visitors in on this liquid stealth referred to the spiked punch bowl as "the Life-Saving Station." (Evidence also indicated that some of the frozen orange slices served to guests also might have been rum-fortified.)

But perhaps it wasn't President Hayes and Lemonade Lucy who were fooled. In his diary, former President Hayes staunchly insisted:

> The joke of the Roman punch oranges was not on us but on the drinking people. My orders were to flavor them rather strongly with the same flavor that is found in Jamaica rum.... This took! This certainly was the case after the facts alluded to reached our ears. It was refreshing to hear "the drinkers" say with a smack of the lips, "would they were hot!"

THE HIDDEN BOTTLE

Thomas Donaldson—a fellow Ohioan, Civil War veteran, personal friend, and ally of President and Lucy Hayes—kept some insightful notes during Hayes's (and later Garfield's) Executive Mansion years. Donaldson often stopped by to visit and also was on friendly terms with most of the Executive Mansion staff and was privy to their observations and jokes. Some of those pranks (as with the allegedly doctored punch bowl) inevitably revolved around the no alcohol policy. On June 26, 1880, Donaldson noted:

> Now for a bit of future fun about the north doorway cut from the window into the conservatory at the White House. Before the window jamb was put up, Mr. [Edison S.] Dinsmore, one of the White House [police] officials, got an empty champagne bottle and marked upon the label that it was of the administration of President Hayes, with the date, and put it in the face of the wall. It was closed up by the contractor, and when opened in time to come, there should be fun.

Is it possible that Dinsmore's champagne bottle still resides in the White House wall to this day?

LAST CALL

Hayes's parents once established a whiskey distillery on their farm just north of Columbus, Ohio, in an effort to generate extra income.... As a young lawyer, Hayes belonged to the Cincinnati Literary Club, which served oysters chased with "liberal amounts of Catawba wine," but he also belonged to the Sons of Temperance.... During his presidency, Hayes wished to remove some twenty U.S. diplomats serving abroad whom he strongly suspected of chronic drunkenness.

CHAPTER 20

James Garfield

(1831–1881)

*J*ames Garfield was a Civil War officer who fought at the bloodbaths of Shiloh and Chickamauga. But he had already "seen the elephant" (as Civil War soldiers liked to say) at the lesser-known battle of Middle Creek (Kentucky) early in 1862, when he led his Union troops to a victory against superior odds. Prior to the war, Garfield had been an academic on the fast track, but—catapulted by his success on the battlefield, despite no real prior experience—he won a congressional seat for Ohio in 1863.

Though Garfield was a skilled orator, it was a surprise when he was selected as the Republican candidate for president in 1880. This happened after the "Stalwart" faction (backing Ulysses S. Grant for a third term) and the "Half-Breeds" (initially backing James G. Blaine of Maine) became mired in a stalemate. Garfield often claimed he never had the "fever" to be president. He went on to defeat General Winfield Scott Hancock, the Democratic candidate—by a mere ten thousand votes—to become the twentieth president of the United States. He was president for just two hundred days, and for eighty of those he was incapacitated. Only William Henry Harrison was president for a shorter time period.

Garfield is one of a select group of presidents (Lincoln, McKinley, and John F. Kennedy are the others) who were assassinated while in office. In Garfield's case, the assassin was a deranged and deluded man named Charles Guiteau who believed that the Garfield administration had thwarted his ambitions to be named U.S. ambassador to France.

The bitter man gunned down Garfield (exclaiming: "I am a Stalwart! And now Arthur is president!") at the Baltimore and Potomac Railroad Station on July 2, 1881. Shocked, Garfield uttered, "My God, what is this?" Bullets pierced Garfield's body, damaging his ribs; eighty days later the president died, most likely from septic complications from the very hands of the medical team attempting to save him.

Garfield was a moderate drinker—apparently he liked an occasional beer—but his doctors, as was the thinking of the time, did not hesitate to use brandy and whiskey ("stimulants" as they were typically referred to) in both his initial and continuing treatment after being shot. Dr. Alexander Graham Bell also tried to assist with a metal detector, hoping to help locate the most dangerous bullet—but the projectile, embedded behind his pancreas, was found only after Garfield's autopsy.

ROUGH START

James Garfield was the last American president born in a log cabin. His father, Abram Garfield, was a large-sized character, both in actual size and in legendary deeds. For example, Abram was said to have been a champion wrestler in his region and also a man who (according to one biographer) could drain a sizeable container of whiskey "and no man dared call him coward."

James was educated at Western Reserve (in present-day Cleveland) and Williams College in Massachusetts. There were no reports of feats involving whiskey kegs, but Garfield did once receive criticism for having a keg of ale on campus—though he claimed to have purchased it for medicinal purposes.

BEER BREAK

As if following the example of his fellow Ohioan—the temperance-minded Rutherford B. Hayes—Garfield neither drank nor served wine in the Executive Mansion. Garfield's predecessor, Ulysses S. Grant, had left behind a rather substantial wine cellar, but Garfield's time in the Executive Mansion was so short (barely six months) that there were no receptions there that would have required the serving of quality wines or liquors.

According to the diary of Thomas Donaldson, Garfield did venture out for an occasional beer. Donaldson (a fellow Ohioan who had great access to the Executive Mansion under both Hayes and Garfield) noted this in his writings after some casual chats with Executive Mansion staff.

Washington, D.C., [Wednesday] Jan. 19th, 1881.—[Alphonso T.] Donn, [William D.] Allen and other door-keepers [and ushers] at the White House often speak to me of the habits of the several Presidents they have served under. General Grant was generally out at night, out visiting and with cronies. President Hayes usually walked out in clear and fine weather, and always walked home when out in the evening ... Mr. Lincoln drank nothing. Mr. Johnson drank a good deal and not much wine. General Grant [drank] some, and Mr. Hayes nothing. Mr. Garfield liked to walk out and liked beer and drank but little else.

DODGING THE DRINKING DART

A common political tactic of that era was to accuse your opponent of heavy drinking. Garfield—who, by examining all the evidence, was at most a moderate imbiber—nonetheless had to deal with that political dart during a first defense of his Ohio congressional seat.

In the words of Garfield biographer Allan Peskin:

> There were also some potentially damaging rumors circulating through the district to the effect that Garfield had become a drunkard in the army and was now leading a life of the grossest profligacy in Washington. Garfield was perplexed as to how these charges could be answered. He admitted privately that his life was not spotless: "I have played cards as an amusement with a friend and I have sometimes tasted wine...."

Garfield managed to get reelected, despite the alcohol-related aspersions—and his criticism of President Lincoln, whom he saw as too moderate and plodding on the slavery issue.

BOOZE VERSUS BULLET WOUNDS

As was fairly common practice at the time, the doctors trying to save Garfield's life used alcohol (brandy, rum, claret, and whiskey all were called upon) as part of his medical treatment.

None of this, of course, served to save the president's life. With the huge advantage of hindsight—and the advancement of medical know-how—biographers, historians, and modern medical experts suggest that Garfield might have survived his initial wounds had his doctors not infected him by poking their unsanitary hands and medical utensils inside the patient in an attempt to find the bullet.

PRAYER, BLISS, AND DONALDSON'S WHISKEY

One of Garfield's doctors—D. W. Bliss (whose given first name was actually "Doctor")—allegedly fielded a suggestion from a newspaper reporter that some people believed the wounded president's health had slowly rebounded (Garfield did, for brief stints, seem to gain strength during his ordeal, only to fail again) due to the power of prayer.

Bliss supposedly replied. "They may think so. In my opinion it was whiskey." And the whiskey used in Garfield's treatment most likely came from Thomas Donaldson's very best stock.

In his diary entries, entered in late August, Donaldson optimistically penned:

> I told them at the White House that there were two reasons why Garfield would not die: *first,* He is an Ohio man, and none die in office; [and] *second,* I supplied the whiskey used, 25 years old, and no person was ever known to die while using this whiskey.

Unfortunately, neither prayer nor well-aged whiskey (or being from the Buckeye State) could save Garfield. He died several weeks later—on September 19—at the New Jersey seashore.

PLEA FOR PORT

One of the last letters of correspondence between Garfield and his wife, Crete, (dated June 30, 1881) contained a first paragraph plea from Crete that the president should bring some port to their vacation spot on the New Jersey shore.

> My Darling:
> For two nights I have taken a glass of port wine and conclude that it is one reason that I have slept better, but I have only a little more wine and if you can bring me a little more that you can trust as pure port, I think it may be of advantage to me....

Two days later, while waiting to board a train to New Jersey, the president was shot by his deluded assassin at the Washington, D.C., train station.

PRE-REVEREND BURCHARD

Although Reverend Samuel Burchard's infamous political faux pas of "Rum, Romanism, and Rebellion" inadvertently helped elect Grover Cleveland (in 1884), then U.S. congressman James Garfield had expressed similar sentiments—in fact, four years prior. Fearing that the Republicans (supporting Hayes) had lost the 1876 election to Tilden, he wrote in a private letter to his friend Corydon Fuller on November 9, 1876:

> It is very hard to go on with the work of the great campaign with so much grief in my heart … I spoke almost every day till the election; but it now appears that we are defeated by the combined power of rebellion, Catholicism and whiskey, a trinity very hard to conquer.

The Hayes forces, of course, later prevailed in the electoral vote—with a controversial swing of twenty unresolved votes in Florida, Louisiana, South Carolina, and Oregon coming in for the GOP. But, judging from Garfield's letter, even he thought that the Republicans had lost until those much-contested votes helped Hayes take the Executive Mansion.

LAST CALL

Temperance forces hoped to persuade Garfield to follow the lead of the Hayes Executive Mansion—that is, to ban alcohol from presidential dinners and celebrations. Garfield managed to sidestep their advances and—with the urging of his secretary of state, James Blaine—he intended to bring up some of the fine wines (left over from President Grant's day) from the Executive Mansion cellar. But Garfield died before he had much chance to sample or share those vintages.

CHAPTER 21

Chester A. Arthur

(1830–1886)

A product of the Gilded Age, Chester Alan Arthur spent lavishly on fine clothing (silk top hats included), rich food, and top-quality liquor. His sister—Mrs. Mary McElroy—served as his first lady (and essentially his partner in crime in extravagance), as Arthur's wife, Ellen Herndon, had died suddenly in 1880, prior to his election.

Since Arthur's rise to chief executive came about only after Garfield's assassination, it is perhaps little wonder that few harbored any great expectations for his term (1881–1885). Some contemporaries apparently could not help but register their disbelief: "Chet Arthur president of the United States ... Good God!" was a phrase bandied about. His critics maintained that Arthur's passion for entertaining far outstripped any of his political achievements.

As Teddy Roosevelt would do in the days immediately after the McKinley assassination, Arthur kept a low profile while Garfield hovered near death at the New Jersey seaside. Congressman John Wise found

Arthur holed up in his Manhattan townhouse on Lexington Avenue and described the lodging as "a bachelor establishment, free and easy, with lots of tobacco smoke and decanters...."

Nicknamed "The Gentleman Boss," the former New York pol never disavowed his connection to the Tammany machine. But once he landed in the Executive Mansion, he made it clear that he'd be his own man. He was not chosen by his party to run for a second term, and, despite the rejection he felt, it may have been just as well: Arthur's health was already in rapid decline due to Bright's disease (which included kidney failure), and he would not have lived through a second term.

THE WISE PORTRAIT

In *Recollections of Thirteen Presidents* (published in 1909), Congressman Wise wrote of Arthur, the mutton-chopped twenty-first president:

> Arthur was a high liver. He was not by any means a drunkard, but he was a typical New York man-about-town, and showed it in his fat and ruddiness. He ate and drank too much, and died young from the effects of over-indulgence. He loved good company, and his high-ball, and his glass of champagne, and his late supper with a large cold bottle and a small hot bird.

THE INSIDE "SOAP"

Garfield and Arthur formed something of an uneasy alliance—a classic "marriage" of political convenience that helped the Republicans win the 1880 election. They hardly knew each other prior to the Republican convention, and each man was somewhat wary of the other even after they won. Arthur, after all, was the Tammany Hall man, and everyone in the political sphere assumed that he would represent the interests of Roscoe Conkling, his Gotham-based boss.

As the Republicans prepared to take control of the Executive Mansion, they held some celebratory dinners. One such dinner—

specifically to honor Stephen Dorsey, the national committee secretary who had helped deliver Indiana—took place at Delmonico's in New York City in early 1881. This upscale restaurant-watering hole was familiar terrain for Vice President-elect Arthur, so he must have felt quite comfortable as he arose to address the completely partisan crowd, peppered with a few journalists.

Still flushed with victory (months after the election) and, by most accounts, flushed with a bit too much alcohol, Chet Arthur began to dance dangerously close to the truth about what it takes to win elections. Specifically, Arthur could not help but "crow" about how the Republicans had managed to flip the state of Indiana into the righteous column of Garfield-Arthur.

Some in the crowd (equally inspired by liquid refreshment) began to playfully bellow out "Soap! Soap!" as the key ingredient in the Indiana win. In Arthur's day, "soap" was essentially a code word for spreading around money and other enticements—all in exchange for votes.

But as a veteran product of the Tammany Hall machine, Arthur stopped just short of providing any truly incriminating details; he had not been so tipsy that he did not notice some reporters at the gathering, scribbling down notes.

THE TEMPERANCE ATTACK

James Garfield was hardly buried when temperance forces began pressing their attack on Arthur.

What *exactly* did they want? Surely Arthur—perhaps bewildered by the mere existence of abstainers—must have asked himself that question.

For starters, they wanted Arthur to continue the Rutherford B. Hayes/Lucy Hayes policy of banning wine and other alcoholic beverages in the Executive Mansion. They also wanted Arthur to hang a large portrait of Lucy Hayes, their heroine, in the Executive Residence.

Arthur wanted neither a ban nor a painting. But the temperance forces wouldn't take "no" for an answer.

Finally (one can picture Arthur's already ruddy complexion coloring to a deeper scarlet), the new president had had more than enough. His measured words, his large stature (just over six feet) made his position quite clear:

"Madam," he thundered during a meeting with members of the temperance lobby, "I may be the President of the United States, but what I do with my private life is my own damned business!"

Grant had left some outstanding vintages in the Executive Mansion cellar. Those exquisite bottles had, if anything, improved while slumbering through the Hayes administration. And President Arthur did not intend for them to remain corked and unloved forever.

IN WITH THE NEW—OUT WITH THE OLD

Garfield was not in the Executive Mansion long enough to make dramatic changes, but Arthur immediately declared war on the decor. He spent thousands of dollars on redecorating, even before he moved in. He also chucked out a lot of old furniture and various knickknacks.

Among the items scooped up by junk dealers at bargain basement prices was a splendidly carved sideboard that once belonged to Lucy Hayes (a.k.a. "Lemonade Lucy," in honor of her no-booze stance). The item eventually ended up in a Washington, D.C., beer hall. When it was discovered that the beer-hall owner had decorated the sideboard with various bottles and beer steins, a predictable brew-ha-ha arose. One doubts that Arthur lost any shuteye over the incident. It took decades but—eventually—the sideboard was purchased and brought back to the Rutherford B. Hayes homestead in Ohio.

THE JOCKEY CLUB MADEIRA

A frequenter of Delmonico's, Sam Ward (a.k.a. the "King of the Lobby") knew Arthur before he became president. As a successful lobbyist, Ward also knew how to entice politicians with luxurious gifts.

Apparently, one of the gifts he made to President Arthur included some bottles of old Madeira wine. These particular bottles were said to have been from South Carolina's Charleston Jockey Club. As the story goes, the Jockey Club had hundreds of bottles of aged, precious wine. But when General William Tecumseh Sherman approached the city in 1864 on his "March to the Sea," the aristocratic denizens of Charleston hid the best vintages. (Some supposedly were hidden in the basement of an insane asylum.)

Decades later, much of the Jockey Club wine was sold off to cover debts. Sam Ward ended up with dozens of bottles. He saw fit to send some to Arthur as a gift, and, according to some accounts, these bottles of Madeira were stored in the Executive Mansion cellar, along with a note relating their storied history.

A CONTRARY VIEW

After he left the Executive Mansion in March 1885 (as Benjamin Harrison took office), Arthur returned to New York City with the intention of resuming his law career. But the onslaught of Bright's disease came on rapidly, and the former man-about-town spent the rest of his days cooped up in his Manhattan residence.

The side effects of Bright's disease include lethargy and depression and a gradual wasting away of weight. Arthur's once large and robust frame was a memory during his final weeks of life, but by all accounts he faced his fate courageously.

In an interesting and contrary view, after Arthur's death in November 1886, Dr. George A. Peters (the former president's personal physician) felt compelled to state that Arthur's excesses with rich food and drink were exaggerated.

"The common impression that he was a high liver is a mistaken one," Peters told the *New York Times*. "He was never that in the sense in which it is applied to men who really live high."

Of course, one's definition of "high living"—especially in the Gilded Age—is relative.

LAST CALL

A friend of Arthur's once mentioned that a mutual acquaintance of theirs had been embarrassingly intoxicated. Rather than pry for details, Arthur emphatically stated: "No gentleman ever sees another gentleman drunk...."

CHAPTER 22

Grover Cleveland

(1837–1908)

*D*ecades before a sex scandal nearly destroyed Bill Clinton's chances of winning the presidency, Grover Cleveland demonstrated that a presidential candidate could sidestep a serious sex scandal and still reach the Executive Mansion without much manure sticking to his shoes. In Cleveland's case, the scandal involved his admission that he might have fathered a child out of wedlock with Maria Halpin in 1874. To which the forces of James G. Blaine, the Republican nominee, gleefully trumpeted:

"Ma, ma, where's my Pa?"

After Cleveland won the 1884 election, his Democratic supporters famously blasted back:

"Gone to the White House! Ha, ha, ha!"

If not for William Howard Taft, the most "portly president" designation would be held by Cleveland. Born Stephen Grover Cleveland, "Big Steve" was an early nickname. He later acquired "Uncle Jumbo" as well. An eager eater of meat chops, beefsteaks, sausages, and cheese, and a renowned pounder of beer (plus other forms of alcohol), Cleveland's daily habits led to his corpulence and poor health in general. He rarely exercised, unless you count fishing and some leisurely hunting—both activities suitable to at least a flask for alcoholic refreshment. A newspaper once speculated that he did not attend the theater because there was a real question whether he could fit in a seat. Even by his first term as president (1885–1889; he served a second in 1893–1897), Cleveland—not yet fifty years old—was already limping around with occasional bouts of gout.

RUM, ROMANISM, AND REBELLION

A fateful remark containing the word "rum" may well have helped Cleveland get elected president in the first place.

As the election of 1884 headed into its final days, the Blaine campaign committed two errors—one major and one minor—that may have tipped the election to underdog Cleveland.

The minor error was an extravagant "fat cat" feast at the famed Delmonico's restaurant in Manhattan. Cartoonists had a field day with the so-called "millionaires' dinner," and it allowed the Cleveland camp to tarnish Blaine as the tycoon's candidate.

But the major error unfolded when Blaine attended a meeting of clergymen. During this holy gathering, the Protestant minister Reverend Dr. Samuel Burchard smugly proclaimed:

"We don't propose to leave our party and identify with the party whose antecedents are rum, Romanism, and rebellion!"

Blaine did nothing, at least initially, to distance himself from the minister's inflammatory rhetoric—a thinly veiled slap at Irish Catholics—and soon the statement was spread all over New York City and, eventually, beyond.

Cleveland sensed that Burchard's blunder might prove to be a political godsend, relegating what he called "the Buffalo rumpus" (i.e., the Halpin affair) to the backburner of the red-hot stove of political scandal. In a letter to Wilson S. Bissell (his former law firm partner) a month before the election, Cleveland wrote:

The Catholic question is being treated and so well treated in so many different ways that I shall not be at all surprised if what has been done by the enemy should turn out to my advantage.

And according to most political historians, it did. Irish Catholic voters—some of them having presumably been on the fence prior to Burchard's ill-timed disparagement—flocked to Cleveland's side. Cleveland won New York State (worth thirty-six electoral votes at that time) by fewer than 1,200 votes—and, thereby, the election (218 to 182) over Blaine.

BEER ME IN BUFFALO

As a young lawyer in Buffalo, New York, Cleveland was a frequent visitor to the various German beer halls and gardens in that city. As author Matthew Algeo noted in his book *The President is a Sick Man*, Big Steve could often be found puffing on a fat cigar and hoisting a sweating mug of cold beer.

His favorite haunts were Diebold's, Schwabl's, Gillick's, and Louis Goetz's. On hot summer nights, he was likely to be spotted at Schenkelberger's or one of the city's other German beer gardens, where sawdust covered the floor and not much covered the pretty young frauleins who kept his stein filled.

Perhaps the best beer story from Cleveland's Buffalo days arose from a challenge he had with his friend Lyman Bass when they faced off for the office of district attorney. Familiar drinking partners, Cleveland and Bass agreed to cut down to a mere four beers a day during the campaign. But after some days slowly passed, both men began to regret this stringent vow to which they had committed themselves.

Thirst, however, provides great motivation for problem-solving. Both men agreed they would *still* abide by their four-beer rule—but with one minor adjustment: Cleveland and his friendly rival simply upgraded to a full tankard, essentially doubling the amount of guilt-free brew they could consume.

UNCLE JUMBO'S SECRET OP

Cleveland is the only U.S. president to serve two non-consecutive terms, but rather early in his second stint (1893–1897), he faced a very personal challenge—specifically, an operation to remove what doctors suspected might be a cancerous growth inside his mouth. In addition to his affinity for alcohol, Cleveland—like U. S. Grant—loved cigars. It was fearfully easy, then, to assume that Cleveland—like Grant (who died early in Cleveland's first term in 1885)—had a cancerous tumor.

Piled on top of his own trepidations concerning the operation, Cleveland worried what effect the news might have on the nation in general and the economy in particular. The economy—already suffering from the collapse of some railroads, including the prominent Reading Railroad (which had gone bankrupt)—was in a weakened state and any fear about the president's health, Cleveland speculated, could only add to the negative environment.

What transpired was one of presidential history's most audacious cover-ups—described in detail and spellbinding fashion in Matthew Algeo's *The President is a Sick Man*. Under the guise of a fishing trip on a friend's yacht, Cleveland arranged for half a dozen doctors to remove the vile growth while floating around in the Long Island Sound for several days and thereby out of the sight of nosy newspaper reporters and a prying public.

One can only imagine Cleveland's consternation in the days and hours just prior to the secret operation. But Algeo records that even these dire circumstances did not keep Cleveland from his usual habits. En route by railcar to his clandestine destination, the president lit up a cigar and ordered a glass of whiskey (then had a second) from the porter. One can assume that these actions were more an effort to calm his nerves than they were acts of defiance or bravado.

As for the operation itself (which took place on a table in the yacht's saloon), one must consider it a success; the tumor was removed, and

Cleveland—never the picture of health to begin with—lived another fifteen years. Only one newspaperman managed to dig up the truth, but the Cleveland forces scurried to discredit him. The president had merely been suffering from a bad tooth, said Cleveland's spokesmen, and the public largely bought that explanation.

In something of an ironic display, Big Steve's all-star medical team apparently lit up cigars and brought forth a bottle of whiskey to celebrate the success of their undercover operation on the president of the United States.

THE "FRANKIE" FACTOR

Cleveland modified his bachelor ways after his marriage to the young and attractive Frances Folsom on June 2, 1886. (It was a little weird—some might even say creepy—since Cleveland had known her as a little girl and had been her legal guardian, but that's another story.)

Frances was a fairly devote supporter of the temperance movement; she rarely drank herself. At her wedding ceremony (she was the first to marry an incumbent president in the Executive Mansion) Frances barely touched her lips to the glass during the champagne toast, while Big Steve knocked his wine straight down. Unlike other first ladies of that era, Frances looked the other way when it came to serving wine at the Executive Mansion.

Frankie (as Cleveland called her) also looked the other way when the president imbibed during his "Goodwill Tour" around the country (by railroad) in 1887. Consider that one stop was in Milwaukee—arguably the beer capital of North America—and in Schlitz Park, nonetheless. Uncle Jumbo certainly would have had some foam on his mustache during the stop in Milwaukee.

THE TWAIN ASSESSMENT

Mark Twain and Grover Cleveland both lived in Buffalo around 1870, but the future president was a mere sheriff at that time and, therefore, did not rub social shoulders with the famous writer. Twain, in fact, only lived in Buffalo for about eighteen months. But years later, when Governor Cleveland was the president elect, Twain and Cleveland met, and both men ribbed the other about why they had not associated during their Buffalo days.

If we are to put any belief in Twain's correspondence, however, we must conclude that the great American author held Big Steve in high esteem. Just days before Cleveland's death at Princeton, New Jersey (June 24, 1908, after suffering a heart attack), Twain wrote to his daughter Jean Clemens:

> Of all our public men of today he stands first in my reverence & admiration, & the next one stands two-hundred-&-twenty-fifth. He is the only statesman we have now ... Cleveland drunk is a more valuable asset to this country than the whole batch of the rest of our public men sober. He is high-minded; all his impulses are great & pure & fine. I wish we had another of this sort.

LAST CALL

Cleveland preferred hearty German-American fare to fancy French food. Nevertheless, he inherited Chester Arthur's French chef when he first moved into the Executive Mansion. And so the president once lamented in a letter:

"I must go to dinner, but I wish it was a pickled herring, Swiss cheese, and a chop at Louis' [the Goetz Tavern in Buffalo] instead of the French stuff I shall find."

And, of course, Big Steve—given his druthers—would have chased all that tasty grub at Goetz's with something thirst-quenching—preferably several steins of freshly brewed beer.

CHAPTER 23

Benjamin Harrison

(1833–1901)

*B*enjamin Harrison was the great-grandson of one of the signers of the Declaration of Independence and the grandson of "Old Tip"—President William Henry Harrison. But he probably owed much more of his presidential success to the scheming of Pennsylvania politician Matthew Stanley Quay, who guided his campaign (and somehow helped Harrison steal New York State) than he did his distinguished and historical pedigree. In fact, Harrison bristled if people around him made too big a fuss about his famous ancestors; he wanted to be considered his own man, ascending to the Executive Mansion on his own merit, with a little assistance from God, perhaps.

Like many politicians of his era, emerging from the Civil War as an officer of high rank helped Harrison's credibility with voters in his home state of Indiana.

The growing power of the temperance movement, however, was always a force (and potential source of votes) to be considered. Therefore, like most savvy politicos of his era, Republican presidential candidate

Harrison—en route to becoming the twenty-third president (1889–1893)—did not go out of his way to showcase the moderate amounts of alcohol he consumed. Considering that Harrison was both preceded and followed by known beer-lover Grover Cleveland, perhaps alcohol consumption was not such a determent to political fortune as one might have imagined.

KING ALCOHOL VS. THE TITANS OF TEMPERANCE

A decade before the Civil War, Harrison—a lawyer by trade—was already branching out into the political arena. He was once asked to share his views on temperance to a Hoosier crowd. The speaker before him apparently had already "handed down the tablets" on the subject and also confessed that he had suffered the evils of drink before he saw the light.

Fearing it might be a tough act to follow, Harrison more or less petitioned the crowd for a bit of understanding in advance because he was "inexperienced not only in making temperance speeches, but in drinking whiskey."

> ... for unlike the reformed drunkard who addressed you so powerfully, I can recount no life spent in the service of King Alcohol; nor can I speak of a home made desolate by its ravages.

All that said, Harrison (knowing his crowd) emphatically added that "drunken demagogues" should be ousted from legislative and judicial positions and their spots filled by "honest temperance men." Obviously he considered himself one of the latter. Harrison was not exactly a teetotaler, however.

WHISKEY WARRIORS

A pious man by practice, Harrison was nonetheless pulled into the mass horror of the Civil War. He served as a general with the 70th Indiana Regiment and held prayer meetings at his tent.

Harrison's letters from the field seem to hint that he drank a bit more than he might have as a civilian back home in Indiana, but those records also stress that his consumption was moderate. And they do not hide his disdain for his fellow officers (or even his superiors) who fell under the firm spell of Demon Alcohol.

When some of his fellow officers got their hands on some quality bourbon and knocked back a few measures, Harrison humorously penned to his wife Carrie:

> Some of the officers got quite mellow and I laughed more than I did for a year before at the antics of some of them, particularly Col. Dustin.

But did the future president of the United States imbibe in a sip or two of the char-barreled nectar too? He allowed to his wife that he might have "touched it very lightly myself."

NO LOVE FOR HOOKERS

Harrison may have confessed to his own "light touch," but he was no fan of heavy-handed whiskey sluggers, either. When it was learned that General Joseph "Fighting Joe" Hooker was coming in to a branch of the Union Army that included Harrison's Indiana unit, the future president was much chagrined. Writing to his wife in April 1864, Harrison feared that "whiskey … would be the ascendant now, if the stories about Hooker are well founded."

Some of those stories came from men very high up in President Lincoln's administration. As Secretary of the Navy Gideon Welles noted in his diary in 1863 (a year before Harrison "inherited" Hooker):

> [Francis] Blair, who was present, said [Hooker] was too great a friend of John Barleycorn.

And furthermore, Welles wrote:

> From what I have since heard, I fear [Hooker's] habits are not such to commend him, that at least he indulges in the free use of whiskey, gets excited, and is fond of play. This is the result of my inquiries....

Hooker's arrival also meant the reassignment of General Howard, a man who, like Harrison, was quite religious (and not a drinker). It was no wonder that Harrison viewed the switch as a lose-lose situation. To make matters worse, Hooker had a sidekick—General Ward—who also liked his liquor. Harrison refers to Ward in his writings as getting "beastly drunk" and also as a "lazy sot."

Like General George Washington, Harrison did not turn a blind eye when men below him mucked up the army's efficiency by lifting the whiskey jug with drunken intent. He once fired a regiment postmaster for chronic intoxication.

WHISKEY WARMTH

Nevertheless, Harrison knew that alcohol had both its charms and uses. Slogging through inclement weather on a march against the Confederates, Harrison was sympathetic to the plight of the rank-and-file soldier, as he mentioned to his wife:

> Some of the wagons did not get in until noon the next day and the rear guard was forced to stand all night in a swamp

and without a fire to do any good. I went out four miles the next day and took a ration of whiskey to them.

Last night when we and all our bed clothes were wet it turned cold and froze quite hard this morning. We got up stiff all over.

In contrast to the enlisted man's whiskey ration, Harrison—who enjoyed the occasional benefits of dining under more refined conditions—spoke to the attributes of moderation concerning "a pleasant, cheerful dinner of the kind where only enough wine is taken to give vivacity to the mind."

JOHN S. WISE WEIGHS IN

In his *Recollections of Thirteen Presidents,* John S. Wise had this take on Benjamin Harrison:

He did indeed have two prominent traits of the Harrisons, for he was fond of shooting and a religious enthusiast. . . .

He utterly lacked another family trait, for many of the Virginia branch have dearly loved whisky. My father, who knew them all and loved them, but had a way of saying what he pleased, generalized Harrison traits that he never knew a Harrison who was not a gentleman, but some were inclined to run to extremes—some in the love of God, and others in the love of whisky.

President Benjamin Harrison was quite "inclined" toward God (though he was not entirely unfamiliar with whiskey) and, in fact, gave the Lord great credit for his winning of the Executive Mansion.

"Providence has given us the victory!" Harrison exclaimed to Republican chairman Senator Matthew Quay shortly after securing the 1888 election victory. In a cynical aside to a journalist, Quay blurted out: "Think of the man! He ought to know that Providence hadn't a damned thing to do with it...." Quay also said that Harrison would never know how many underlings had been "compelled to approach the gates of the penitentiary" in order to get him elected.

CARNEGIE'S "CONGRESSIONAL" CARGO

Industrial magnate Andrew Carnegie loved to send casks of fine scotch whisky to people he deemed worthy. Mark Twain, for example, had long been a recipient of Carnegie's liquid kindness, once observing that it was "the smoothest whisky now on the planet."

As president of the United States, Harrison made the Carnegie gift list. Carnegie sent Harrison a keg of scotch from John Dewar & Sons, and (like Twain) the sender spoke most highly of its contents.

The Scottish-born Carnegie must have also sent some sort of amusing message with the keg, because Harrison's thank-you note for the precious cargo mentioned: "It was very nice of you to think of me as to needing a 'brace' this winter in dealing with congress."

If Carnegie was pleased with sending the gift of Scottish spirits, and Harrison seemingly quite content to receive it, perhaps only Thomas R. Dewar (son of the distillery's deceased founder, John Dewar) outstripped them in his enthusiasm concerning the shipment.

"It was the very best kind of advertising I ever had and certainly the cheapest.... Inquiries and orders flowed to us from all parts of the States," said Dewar once word spread concerning the delivery of whisky to the Executive Mansion.

A few months after shipping Carnegie's keg, a traveling Dewar swung by the Executive Mansion, as he documented in his book *A Ramble Round the Globe*. Dewar did not get to meet President Harrison, but a tour guide showed him around:

> He was expatiating proudly on the fact that everything was American-made, when I mentioned that he must not forget that there is something from Scotland in the cellar. At first he looked hurt; but when I gave him my card, and he saw who I was, his *countenance* relaxed, and the meaning smile which

beamed over it proved that he was well aware as I of what had travelled from Perth to Washington, some months previously

HARRISON'S ANCESTORS

Most presidential history buffs are well aware that William Henry Harrison, Benjamin's grandfather, won the Executive Mansion on the infamous "Log Cabin and Hard Cider" campaign.

But Benjamin Harrison—"Little Ben's" great-grandfather—most definitely fit John S. Wise's description of the family branch fond (in the extreme) of whiskey. The portly delegate from Virginia was one of the original signers of the Declaration of Independence, and was sometimes dubbed "The Falstaff of Congress." His gluttony resulted in decades of suffering with gout.

LAST CALL

Special events at the Benjamin Harrison Presidential Home in Indianapolis have included a croquet tournament and a Civil War dinner—the latter accompanied by wine and a "guest" dressed up as General Benjamin Harrison. Confirmation is still pending on whether there might be a keg of Carnegie-sent scotch hidden somewhere on the site.

CHAPTER 24

William McKinley

(1843–1901)

One can argue that William McKinley lived through two Civil Wars—the bloody struggle between North and South (in which McKinley served as an officer under Rutherford B. Hayes) and the emerging conflict between "wet" and "dry" factions that eventually led to enactment of Prohibition during Woodrow Wilson's second term.

Yet another president from Ohio, McKinley (the twenty-fifth president, 1897–1901), knew that being a successful politician in the Midwest meant showing at least some deference to the temperance movement—if not actually completely embracing the teetotaler gospel.

Despite, or because of, his own experiences in the Civil War, McKinley initially resisted the "war hawks" who were drumming up a reason to boot the Spanish out of Cuba. But he eventually gave way to pressure from the likes of Teddy Roosevelt (McKinley's second-term vice president) and Henry Cabot Lodge. The public's reaction to the sinking of the *Maine* in Havana Harbor provided the necessary tinder to touch off what some deemed "a splendid little war."

WHAT'S IN A NAME?

In one of his early elections, an 1876 contest for a U.S. congressional seat, McKinley had to fight off accusations that he had frequently been intoxicated during the Civil War. (McKinley rose to the officer ranks after he heroically risked his life at the Battle of Antietam, resupplying Union soldiers under intense fire at what is now known as the Burnside Bridge.)

Two facts made McKinley's defense against these political snipes somewhat tricky. One, there had been another officer—a John McKinley (no relation to the future president, but also in the 23rd Ohio Regiment)—who did, in fact, get notoriously blasted. Soldiers fighting in the same theater of war might have easily associated the name McKinley with drinking binges.

The second fact was a bit stickier. Though hardly a chronic boozer, William McKinley apparently had, on at least one occasion, drank to excess at a social reception hosted by General George Crook, in Cumberland, Maryland. The incident was recorded in a letter from Colonel James Comly to Colonel (and future president) Rutherford B. Hayes, who had been home on leave at the time. Comly wrote:

> ... a grand party. The belle of the evening was Chf. Quartermaster Farnsworth, who parts his hair in the middle. Gardner was the best dancer ... and from what Kennedy tells me of the latter end of the thing, McKinley must have been the drunkest. I guess they had a little difficulty about it.

As for the other McKinley, Hayes wrote in his diary in 1862, lamenting that he had encouraged the sergeant to visit his homestead in Ohio while on leave:

> Heard from home. Sergeant [John] McKinley, with letter and watch—tight, drunk, the old heathen, and insisting on seeing the madame! I didn't dream of that. He must be a nuisance, a dangerous one too, when drunk. A neat, disciplined, well-drilled

soldier under rule, but what a savage when in liquor! Must be careful whom I send home.

Given that description, it's no great surprise that Major William McKinley (despite whatever indiscretions he may have committed at Crook's ball) did not want to be mistaken for a chronic offender such as Sergeant McKinley.

Hayes, the future president, had nothing but *good* to say about William McKinley, however, describing him in a letter home to his wife (in December 1863) as "an exceedingly bright, intelligent, and gentlemanly young officer. He promises to be one of our best...."

MODERATE MCKINLEY

Although he was raised as a fairly strict Methodist, McKinley did have an occasional glass of wine with dinner and served wine to his guests at the Executive Mansion. He also often sipped and savored a glass of whiskey as a nightcap.

But if McKinley had a true vice (if you can call it one), it was smoking cigars. He allegedly could smoke several dozen in one week and liked to enjoy them on a porch at the Executive Mansion, where he could not be readily observed.

McKinley obviously knew smoking was not the most healthful of habits. In fact, he did not like having his photograph taken while he had a cigar in hand or mouth, fearing that a president who smoked would set a bad example for the young men of America. He tried to be equally stealthy when it came to his moderate drinking habits.

CARNEGIE'S SECRET CARGO

As was his generous habit over several presidential administrations, industrial titan Andrew Carnegie relished supplying the Executive Mansion with a liquid gift—a barrel of scotch whisky, typically from the Dewar distillery in Scotland.

With "dry" sentiment in the country on the upsweep, most of the presidents who had terms that coincided with Carnegie's years tried to keep the steelmaker's generosity a secret, with varying success.

At any rate, McKinley got his barrel of scotch from Carnegie, too, with instructions to pass it on to those who might appreciate it if the president did not want to keep it for his own consumption.

CARRIE "THE HATCHET" NATION VS. BREWERY BILL

Carrie Nation—the volatile, hatchet-wielding nemesis of all things bacchant—suspected that McKinley was something of a closet drinker and referred to him as "the brewer's president." Given McKinley's moderate habits, it seems a bit overstated, but Nation was not a matron given to compromise. For example, she once destroyed a saloon painting depicting the Egyptian queen Cleopatra at the baths because she deemed it filth. She came back and destroyed a good amount of liquor bottles later and was about to chop up the bar itself when local law enforcement intervened.

Nation often toured the country and delivered her fiery spiel to what were typically receptive audiences. She happened to be speaking at Coney Island, New York, just days after McKinley's assassination in September 1901. While McKinley lingered in a state of near-death, the hostile hag dispensed not an ounce of sympathy concerning the president's grave condition.

According to one news report, Nation bellowed:

"Bill McKinley deserves to die. He is a friend of the brewer and the drinking man.... He deserves just what he got."

Hundreds in the crowd almost instantly booed and hissed at her, whereupon the reformer snarled back, referring to them as "hell hounds" and "snakes" and "sots." Nation's manager wisely hustled her off as some of the most hostile began to menacingly approach the speaker's stage. Soon after, the crowd broke out with three hearty cheers for McKinley.

MCKINLEY'S DELIGHT

McKinley—like most politicians of his day who weren't blatant "dry" candidates—did his best to tap-dance around the issue of drinking alcohol. It must have been with (at best) mixed emotions, then, that—as the election of 1896 gathered steam—the Republican's most rabid supporters toasted him with concoctions dubbed "McKinley's Delight."

The powerful cocktail, supposedly first created by a St. Louis barkeep during the 1896 GOP convention held there, is really just a basic Manhattan but with a tweak or two. Sometime after the Spanish-American War, the drink's name morphed into a libation titled "Remember the Maine" But regardless of its name, the recipe is something (this is a stronger, less sweet version) like this:

McKinley's Delight/Remember the Maine

Ingredients:

3 ounces rye whiskey (shoot for at least 100 proof)
1 ounce sweet vermouth
2 dashes of cherry brandy
1 dash absinthe

Shake it up, pour over ice. Serve in a Manhattan bar glass.

Taverns and bars with a Democratic lean countered with something called a "Free Silver Gin Fizz" (McKinley was a strict backer of the gold standard)—a bit bogus since their candidate, William Jennings Bryan, was a strong temperance advocate. (Sometimes called "Our Fearless Leader" by his supporters, Bryan was lampooned as "Our Beerless Leader" by drinking men of all political stripes.)

THE ASSASSIN'S ELIXIR

McKinley's murder brought no cries of restricting guns or background checks in that era. But the most radical prohibitionists were quick to point out that alcohol had certainly played a role in most of the presidential assassinations. All the more reason, the teetotalers insisted, to ban John Barleycorn from American life.

In his book *The Challenge of Pittsburgh* (1917), the Reverend Daniel Lash Marsh asked his readership:

> Are we interested in abolishing crime? All the persons implicated in the assassination of Abraham Lincoln were drunkards, and had been drinking the night before the great President was killed....
>
> President Garfield's assassin, Charles Guiteau, was a drunkard. The man who killed President McKinley was the direct spawn of the saloon. [Leon] Czolgosz was an ex-bartender, was reared in a saloon, and was at a saloon just before the assassination, and confessed before his execution that it was the talk he heard in his father's saloon that determined him to murder President McKinley.

LAST CALL

As a lawyer in Ohio, McKinley worked to stop the sale of liquor to students at Mount Union College.... As president, McKinley once complained that he could not sip a glass of wine or touch a deck of cards without drawing fire in the press.... Whiskey and other stimulants were used in a vain attempt to keep McKinley alive after he was shot by Czolgosz at the Pan-American Exposition in Buffalo on September 14, 1901. He died several days later.

CHAPTER 25

Theodore Roosevelt

(1858–1919)

*I*n his poem "Three Presidents," Robert Bly presents Teddy
Roosevelt as a larger-than-life figure, with a dash of myth and
majesty—and a heap of tongue-in-cheek braggadocio tossed in
for good measure.

> When I was President, I crushed snails with my bare teeth
> I slept in my underwear in the White House
> I ate the Cubans with a straw, and Lenin dreamt of me every
>   night.

Roosevelt proponents, of course, can make a plausible case for their man
being one of history's most noteworthy presidents, and a man who
brought forth "the right stuff" long before he was in the White House.
(The official "White House" name was established during TR's first year
in office.) He was the "Hero of San Juan Hill," leading his Rough Riders
through the snap and buzz of projectiles; the man who challenged the

corruption of New York, both city and state; the prolific author and winner of the Nobel Peace Prize; the man who finished a lengthy political speech while still bleeding from an assassin's bullet ("It takes more than a bullet to kill a Bull Moose!"); and the president who oversaw the building of the Panama Canal (though it was not finished until 1914).

One might expect a man of Teddy Roosevelt's historical stature to have hoisted a few rounds in a gigantic silver goblet or something fittingly grandiose, but that's not how he rolled. Drinking alcohol, it seems, was one of the few pursuits in which TR engaged on a rather modest scale. In fact, President Roosevelt (1901–1909) was not only a moderate imbiber—but proud of it, too.

THE SUNDAY SOLUTION: SEVENTEEN BEERS, ONE PRETZEL

Although Roosevelt did not spend an inordinate amount of time in bars, pubs, or taverns, more than a few of his famous confrontations were set in such establishments.

Serving as New York City police commissioner (1895–1896), Roosevelt tried to stop Gotham's saloons from serving up the shots and suds on Sunday—and also to crack down on rampant corruption within the police department. Teddy even chased down a cop he caught drinking on duty.

For his efforts on sans-booze Sundays, TR drew intense fire—including from someone who claimed he "dined on a champagne dinner at the Union League Club" while prohibiting the working class men from enjoying a brew or two on their day off. The majority of the city's newspapers (especially the German-language ones) were against him on the saloon issue, and Roosevelt proved easy to zing when these publications needed a political target.

Roosevelt himself admitted that his campaign was only marginally successful. In his autobiography, he wrote:

> As regards the Sunday closing law, this was partly because public sentiment was not really with us.... All kinds of ways

of evading the law were tried and some of them were successful. The statute, for instance, permitted any man to take liquor with meals. After two or three months, a magistrate was found who decided judicially that seventeen beers and one pretzel made a meal—after which decision joy again became unconfined at least in some of the saloons and the yellow press gleefully announced that my "tyranny" had been curbed.

Nevertheless, an appointment to the position of assistant secretary of the Navy helped Teddy move on with his pride still in tact, although there were suspicions that his enemies supported this would-be promotion just to get him out of town. No doubt the beer flowed freely that first Sunday after Roosevelt's departure.

THE BRAWL-ROOM BLITZ

Adversaries—be they foreign powers or individuals attempting to intimidate him—underestimated Roosevelt at their own peril. Despite serious asthma issues that plagued him most of his life, TR robustly pursued physical activities—both indoor and out. One of his indoor specialties, honed to at least practical proficiency while an undergraduate at Harvard, was boxing. The lessons learned in the gym apparently came in handy later in life.

In his autobiography, Roosevelt describes a confrontation with a drunken cowboy in a barroom on one of his many trips out West. His gun-wielding aggressor brazenly addressed TR as "four eyes" (a reference to his trademark spectacles) and insisted that Roosevelt would treat the locals to a round of drinks.

Accordingly, in response to his reiterated command that I should set up the drinks, I said, "Well, if I've got to I've got to," and rose looking past him.

As I rose, I struck quick and hard with my right just to one side of the point of his jaw, hitting with my left as I straightened out, and then again with my right. He fired the guns, but I do not know whether this was merely a convulsive action of his hands or whether he was trying to shoot at me. When he went down, he struck the corner of the bar with his head ... and if he had moved I was about to drop on his ribs with my knees; but he was senseless.

There is a similar story of TR decking an antagonist—a rival Democratic politician named John Costello, who reportedly referred to Roosevelt as that "damned little dude"—in an Albany, New York, saloon. Roosevelt was a new representative in the New York State Assembly, but that did not prevent him from displaying his pugilistic skills when such obvious insults were hurled within earshot.

Curiously, Teddy does not mention this incident in his autobiography, but friends who witnessed it claimed that he ordered Costello to clean himself up (all the while lecturing him on how to behave when around gentlemen)—and then insisted on buying the humiliated pol a peacemaking beer.

SELF-DESCRIBED ASS

If TR's offer to buy a round was a good gesture in the aftermath of the Albany affair, he was perhaps a bit overzealous when he wanted to buy a round—a rather big round, in fact—in San Antonio, Texas, in 1898, during training camp. The recipients of TR's generosity were the troopers of the 1st U.S. Volunteer Cavalry Regiment—the men who would become the much-storied Rough Riders of San Juan Hill fame during the Spanish-American War in Cuba.

In Roosevelt's defense, the weather in Texas in mid-May was already scorching and, therefore, quite capable of provoking a thirst for which warm and fetid canteen water simply had no answer. After a mounted drill that the men must have performed to TR's satisfaction, he sought to reward them. Allowing the men to dismount at the Riverside Fairgrounds, their leader festively announced that they could drink "all the beer they want, which I will pay for!"

This declaration obviously made Roosevelt quite popular with his Rough Riders. But his more experienced commander, Colonel Leonard Wood, knew the enthusiastic New Yorker might later regret this blatant generosity. That evening Roosevelt was requested to appear before Wood, who sternly pointed out the potential pitfalls of rubbing shoulders with enlisted men, particularly when that fraternization was lubricated with alcohol. An embarrassed Teddy—in a rare moment of silence—snapped off a salute and then abruptly left headquarters. In a few minutes, however, he sheepishly returned before Wood and readily acknowledged his mistake:

"Sir, I consider myself the damnedest ass within ten miles of this camp," declared the future president. "Good-night, sir."

THE "BIG STICK" STRIKES IRON ORE

Although the young TR was not above buying a round of beers for others (an intoxicated, pistol-toting cowboy withstanding), in his later years he took great offense at the mere suggestion that he himself might be a hard drinker.

In 1913, Roosevelt broke ranks with the Republican Party to head the Progressive Party (also known as the "Bull Moose Party") in an effort to defeat both Democrat Woodrow Wilson and the portly GOP incumbent, William Howard Taft. In the course of the race, an obscure newspaper in Michigan's Upper Peninsula—the Ishpeming *Iron Ore*—ran an editorial that outrageously claimed: "Roosevelt gets drunk, and that not infrequently, and all his intimates know it."

Sick and tired of such attacks from small-minded, rumor-mongering "rags," Colonel Roosevelt (as the *New York Times* typically referred to him) launched a vigorous counter-attack. The man who made the phrase "Speak softly and carry a big stick" famous also slammed Newett with a ten-thousand-dollar libel suit, with full intention of sending a message to other would-be character assassins. TR also traveled to Marquette County Courthouse in Michigan to testify at the trial in person.

A *New York Times* pretrial piece noted that George A. Newett, the editor of the paper and author of the accusations, "will assert that the article was privileged as comment on a public figure running for office, and as a secondary line of resistance attempt to prove that the editorial was true."

Roosevelt's line of defense was not unlike the contents of a letter he once sent to William Hatfield Jr. when explaining his practice of controlled imbibing:

> It happens that I am, as regards liquor, an exceedingly temperate man. I drink about as much as Dr. Lyman Abbott—and I say this with his permission. I never touch whisky at all and I have never drunk a highball or cocktail in my life. I doubt if I drink a dozen teaspoons of brandy a year.

Dr. Abbott was a former pastor and theologian, in addition to being one of TR's most trusted friends and allies. He testified by letter that if Teddy drank too much of anything, that liquid might be milk. Other key witnesses (including some newspaper men who had covered Roosevelt during his political career) took the stand on TR's behalf—as did the former president himself. Teddy charmed the courtroom with his tales of adventure around the world, recounting the very occasional drinks he might have had.

After five days in court, Newett finally capitulated and admitted that he had been wrong to write an editorial claiming that Roosevelt was frequently drunk. TR did not offer to buy his foe a reconciliatory post-trial beer, but he did magnanimously drop his monetary damages down to the lowest allowable amount—a mere six cents. When reporters asked him what he might spend the six cents on, Roosevelt allegedly quipped that it was just enough for "a *good* paper." (The *Iron Ore* sold for half that price.)

TR'S WHISKY LETTER

About a year before Roosevelt charged—legal guns blazing—into the *Iron Ore* libel case, he fired off a letter to one of his Progressive

Party colleagues (George H. Payne) that underscores just how sensitive he was to any accusations linking him to hard alcohol. The letter is short and to the point:

> I never drank whisky at all, and on none of these trips have I even drunk any wine. But I am told that on several trips other members of the party have drunk whisky and that bills have been submitted and paid for showing that whisky was drunk. In view of the absolute scoundrelishness of our political foes, it would be quite possible that they would obtain possession of these bills in order to show that I had drunk the whisky in question. Under the circumstances, therefore, I shall ask you to see that no whisky, in fact no liquor of any kind, and no wine is carried on the trip by the Pullman people. Of course I do not mean that you should search each individual's luggage to see if he carries whisky! I merely mean that no whisky is to be carried or used at the expense of the Committee, or paid for by the Committee, or by any person directly or indirectly responsible for my campaign. I do not drink it myself and I do not intend that any scoundrel of the type of some of our opponents shall be able to assert that I do drink or have drunk it.

THE MINT JULEP CAVEAT

Despite TR's sworn aversion to whiskey and claims that he never touched the stuff, there remains at least one contrary fact: his admission for a very occasional indulgence in mint juleps, made with fresh mint grown on the White House grounds.

In the *Iron Ore* trial, the colonel allowed: "There was a fine bed of mint at the White House. I may have drunk a half dozen mint juleps in a year."

Roosevelt's lawyer, the esteemed James H. Pound of Detroit, drew some hearty laughter from the packed courtroom when he asked TR: "Did you drink them all at once?"

Regardless of how many TR drank and in what time frame, the fact remains that a mint julep's primary fortification comes from whiskey—Kentucky bourbon, or whiskey not technically a bourbon, but TR's variation (mixed by White House steward Henry Pinckney) seems to have used several ounces of rye whiskey and a quarter ounce of brandy instead. So when the old Rough Rider said he "never" drank whiskey, a more accurate statement should have included "except when presented with fresh mint sprigs, a sugar cube, and finely crushed ice."

TENNIS AND POST-MATCH REFRESH-MINT

Had the editor's attorney had access to the letters of Colonel Archie Butt—Teddy Roosevelt's aide (and later, William Howard Taft's)—he might have at least given the judge some pause or an inquisitive rise of the eyebrows.

In various letters to his mother and sister-in-law, Butt mentions that TR often liked to break out the mint juleps after a few sets of tennis—and he liked to play tennis, several days a week, rain or shine. As Butt noted (in a letter) after one particular match:

> It was a pleasant afternoon. He was in his best humour, and during the afternoon Longworth and his wife, Mr. Pinchot, the forester, and some others came in. The President had already ordered four mint juleps, but before they were served they had got up to eight. As each guest would arrive he would say to someone inside:
>
> "One more mint julep, please," and then laugh with glee.
>
> Finally, when they were served on the lawn by the side of the tennis court, he offered a toast to his new aide.
>
> "Wouldn't dear old Fairbanks [his VP, Charles W.] give a great deal to be able to sit down and enjoy one of these without fearing that a photograph fiend was hidden behind the bushes?" he said. "It is almost worth being called a drunkard by Wall Street to feel free to take a julep such as this without shocking the public."

Just then Secretary Garfield [James R., son of the late president] said hurriedly:

"Look out, here comes a sightseeing automobile by the White House."

The President grabbed his glass, and with mock fear put it under the table.

"That is the first evidence of fear I have ever seen in you, Mr. President," laughed the Secretary.

"Not for *my* reputation, Garfield, but for you. After all Wall Street has said about me mine can't be injured, but you, my dear boy-faced Secretary, you may yet need the vote of the teetotaler."

The juleps were certainly good, especially after the seven sets of tennis. The President and I finished ours first....

TR'S MINT JULEPS AND THE TENNIS CABINET

Thanks to Archie Butt's keen observations, we have a good idea how Teddy Roosevelt had his courtside mint juleps made (prepared by White House steward Henry Pinckney, not actually TR himself) that made the president giggle with glee when they were served courtside to his guests—typically cabinet members or staffers whom had been cajoled into playing tennis with him.

The main deviation from a southern-styled mint julep is that Teddy opted for rye whiskey instead of bourbon, and he added a splash of brandy. While no true Kentuckian would ever dream of using anything other than bourbon in this drink so tethered to Churchill Downs tradition, TR never had a problem with going his own way.

TR's Courtside Mint Juleps

Ingredients:

10 to 12 fresh mint leaves "muddled" (until it resembles a paste) with a splash of water and a sugar cube

2 or 3 oz. of rye whiskey
¼ oz. of brandy
sprig or two of fresh mint as a garnish

First fill a bar glass with the muddled mint, then fill the glass generously with finely crushed ice. Top off with the rye whiskey, brandy, and mint garnish.

BUTT'S REBUTTAL

Despite all the excitement over a few courtside mint juleps, Archie Butt (who lost his life when the RMS *Titanic* went down on April 12, 1912) would have been the first to defend Teddy Roosevelt against charges of overindulgence. He wrote:

> I am really amused to hear the reports so often made and more astonished to find that many believe them: namely, that the President is a hard drinker. I have dined with him several times and lunched most informally with him, and he never serves at luncheon, even when he has guests, anything but a Rhine-wine cup, and at dinner he takes hardly anything himself, usually confining himself to white wine.

CHAMPAGNE-BUZZED BEARS STALK TR

Late in 1902, Roosevelt went hunting for bears in Mississippi. In a rare occurrence, he could not claim "a kill," and the press (and some politicians) could not resist teasing TR about coming up empty.

At the Gridiron Club dinner, held in Washington, D.C., on December 1902, two rather unique "guests" arrived. Both were bears. One was the real deal—a trained bruin that had been performing in vaudeville clubs around the capital city. The other was an intrepid journalist—the *Washington Evening Star*'s Rudolph Kauffmann—concealed in an extremely authentic bearskin costume. As Arthur Wallace Dunn recorded in his *Gridiron Nights*: *Humorous and*

Satirical Views of Politics and Statesmen as Presented by the Famous Dining Club:

> Both bears looked the same size and when they came into the dinning-room with the keeper between them it was hard to say if both were real, both imitation, or which was which. Arriving at the center of the room, both bears took seats at the table. Pint bottles of champagne were brought and both bears stood on their hind legs and inserting the neck of the bottle in their mouths began to drink, but the real bear beat the imitation at that game and soon emptied his bottle.

For those who could not figure out fake bear from real bear, Kauffmann finally spoke: "The President seems to be having a hard time finding bears in Mississippi and we thought we would come here and look for him."

The audience—always up for a "roast" and a toast—roared at Kauffmann's quip. Meanwhile, the real bear supposedly was led backstage whereupon he quaffed more champagne ("of which he was very fond")—certainly a better proposition than being shot at by the Hero of San Juan Hill.

THE LION'S ROAR AND A FEW SIPS OF BRANDY

In March 1909 (just after his presidency ended), TR embarked on a hunting expedition to Africa. As if to support his claims of temperance, Roosevelt mentions that a case of champagne and a bottle of good brandy were part of the expedition's supplies. But he emphasized that the alcohol was used almost exclusively for medicinal purposes—treating fever and dysentery and other such ailments.

In Roosevelt's book *African Game Trails*, he addresses his sparing use of brandy:

> There are differences of opinion as to whether any spirituous liquors should be drunk in the tropics.... Not liking whiskey

I took a bottle of brandy for emergencies. Very early in the trip I decided that even when feverish or exhausted by a hard day's tramp, hot tea did me more good than brandy, and I handed the bottle over to Cuninghame [R. J. Cuninghame, Roosevelt's hunting guide]. At Khartoum he produced it and asked what he should do with it, and I told him to put it in the steamer's stores; he did so, after finding out the amount that had been drunk, and informed me that I had taken just six ounces in eleven months.

HAT IN THE RING: TR'S GRAND GARNISH

Upon his return from Africa in 1910, Rooseveelet became increasingly disenchanted with President Taft, TR's former secretary of war. In fact, in February of 1912, Roosevelt announced he would run against Taft (and eventual Democratic winner Woodrow Wilson) thundering: "My hat is in the ring, the fight is on, and I am stripped to the buff!"

As if to honor the "hat in the ring" battle cry, a Chicago hotel/bar entrepreneur fashioned a drink in Teddy's honor. The drink ingredients in the "Teddy Hat" cocktail were nothing unusual:

Teddy Hat Cocktail:

Fill a cocktail glass with crushed ice
Add several dashes of orange bitters
1 pony (1 oz.) of gin
Half pony of raspberry syrup
Half pony of dubonnet
Shake vigorously and strain into glass

But it was the garnish that made this drink famous! As its name suggests, the lemon was cut into the shape of TR's famous Rough Rider hat and—with a bit of ceremony—tossed into the glass (i.e., the "hat in the ring").

Another cocktail in honor of TR had preceded the "Teddy Hat" in 1910 and was billed in the *Baltimore Sun* as "A New Roosevelt Cocktail." What the drink may have lacked in creative garnish, it more than made up for in potential alcohol wallop (perhaps it should have been dubbed "The Big Stick Cocktail"), as its creator claimed it could motivate "a milksop" to "thrash a Rough Rider." The recipe looks like this:

New Roosevelt Cocktail

1 half jigger of San Juan Rum
¼ jigger of vermouth
¼ jigger of dry gin
a dash of absinthe
a dash of Kirschwasser

The recipe advises it be served in a Venetian cocktail glass; one presumes over ice.

LAST CALL

TR aficionados who visit Washington and crave a drink might find Teddy & the Bully Bar near Dupont Circle just the place to go. There is plenty of TR-related art and drinks dubbed "The Trust-Buster" and "The Rough Rider".... If TR was wary about overindulgence, he had good reason: his brother Elliott (father of Eleanor) died at age thirty-four after a lengthy battle with alcohol and a failed-but-injurious suicide attempt. TR's son, Kermit, also suffered from alcoholism and depression, resulting in his suicide in 1943.

CHAPTER 26

William Howard Taft

(1857–1930)

*W*illiam Howard Taft loved being part of the judicial process, he loved riding horses, he really enjoyed playing golf (although he would have been no threat to make the PGA tour), and—alert the media—he absolutely loved eating. (At just under six feet tall, Taft's weight peaked at 340 pounds.) But it would be a stretch to say he liked being president (1909–1913) very much. When his bid to return to the White House failed in 1912, it cleared the way for Taft to get a position he truly relished: chief justice of the United States Supreme Court. Presidential trivia buffs might note that Taft is the only man to serve both as president (the nation's twenty-seventh) and chief justice (the tenth).

In the months after leaving the White House, Taft was able to bring his weight down to a self-reported 270; not a bad effort, but one that he said required abstention from all alcohol, potatoes, and fatty meats, such as pork. No doubt removing the stress of being president helped, too.

Theodore Roosevelt more or less groomed Taft—his secretary of war and fellow Republican—to be his presidential successor in the election of 1908. TR advised Taft on how to deal with the growing power of the temperance movement. TR's strategy was essentially to avoid all contact with the teetotalers, if possible—the message, seemingly, was that there would be political points to be lost, and few to be gained, by any messy confrontations.

BIG BOOZER ... OR BIG SNOOZER?

William Howard Taft *looks* like a guy with whom one would like to hoist a few. His walrus-like appearance, considerable girth, and natural affability all seem to suggest that he would be quite at home grasping a sweating glass with a large paw. Can you picture Taft with an extra-extra-large T-shirt on advertising some surf shop, bellying up to a thatched-roof beach bar for some magically mixed, rum-laced cocktail in a glass made to look like a coconut? Absolutely!

But it would not be true. William Howard Taft—despite his considerable bulk (requiring a specially sized bathtub to accommodate him in the White House)—must, when it comes to alcohol consumption, be considered a mere lightweight.

While all the evidence shows that Taft was not a big boozer, he *was* (apparently without the help of alcohol) a big snoozer. Much to the embarrassment of his staff, Taft would sometimes fall asleep at inopportune moments—such as funerals or public performances or even upon sitting in a chair waiting for an appointment.

ARCHIE BUTT WEIGHS IN

The presidential aide Archibald Butt summed up Taft's attitude toward alcohol in a letter to his sister-in-law, Clara. Butt could not fathom that the boredom of political life could be endured without at least *some* alcohol, noting:

The President never takes anything to drink at all, but is most profligate in making others imbibe. I do not see how he sits through these long dinners and banquets without taking enough to merely exhilarate him, but he takes no alcoholic liquors of any kind and seems to be the better for it.

Along the lines of "making others imbibe," Butt mentioned that one of the less pleasant aspects of working for Taft was that the president would occasionally trap him to share in some boring political meeting—using scotch (which Taft knew Butt loved) as bait. As he lamented to Clara of a 1910 incident:

Saturday night [in Albany] when he and Governor Hughes sat down in the library after coming in from a late banquet, I tried to slip upstairs and get to bed, for I was worn out; but he saw my maneuver, I think, for he said: "Governor, I am sure Captain Butt would like a Scotch and soda with you," and he made a motion for me to remain, so down I sat and never got up again for two hours and did not get to bed until after half-past two.

THE GREAT CHAMPAGNE SWITCH

President Taft instructed Colonel Butt to buy some of the best French champagne for guests at a dinner celebrating the passing of the controversial Payne-Aldrich Tariff Act. But Butt—concluding that many of those attending might not have the fine-tuned palates to fully appreciate the good stuff—served run-of-the-mill bubbly to most of the attendees. A chosen few were to be served the superior wine. (Note: this was decades before the term "Pulling a Nixon" came into the esoteric vocabulary of presidential history buffs.)

But a problem arose when Congressman Nicholas Longworth (who was married to TR's eccentric daughter, Alice) deduced this slight-of-hand. As Archie related to his sister-in-law in a letter:

I was sitting next to Nick Longworth, and to my horror I noticed that the waiter, in serving the wine, passed me by and filled up Longworth's glass and later came back to serve me from the vintage wine, which I had not told him to do. I was drinking Scotch and soda. I loathe the taste of champagne. Nick promptly fired an arrow into the sky in the shape of a remark that I was serving two kinds of wine and possibly palmed off inferior brands on the unsuspecting.

Butt recovered to laugh off the accusation and ordered the waiter to keep Longworth's glass brimming with the good stuff. This seemed to satisfy the suspicious politician, much to Archie's relief, as he declared: "I never would have heard the last of it."

NO-BRAWL BILL

Residing in Cincinnati (one of the country's famous beer-brewing cities, along with Milwaukee and St. Louis), young Bill Taft appears to have visited the "Over-the-Rhine" section of the Queen City. This German section of Cincinnati was, of course, brimming with breweries and beer gardens. But, according to one of Taft's earliest and most prolific biographers (Henry F. Pringle), the future president was quite moderate when it came to alcohol—even after he graduated from Yale and attended the University of Cincinnati College of Law.

[Taft and his friends] went to the beer gardens, which abounded in the section called "Over the Rhine," across the canal. They would have dinner with beer or wine and enjoy the music. One night, during the 1880 campaign, some politicians began to argue vociferously ... Taft reached for the check and suggested to his companions that they leave before beer bottles started to fly.

Similarly, Taft—again according to Pringle—seems to have been low-key at Yale, despite the fact that he was a member of the Skull and Bones fraternity. He is described as "a model young man" who did not smoke and drank "only an occasional glass of beer." And furthermore, he declined to tag along with "rowdy youths who broke loose, from time-to-time, and cavorted through the streets of New Haven."

BRONX COCKTAILS IN ST. LOUIS

A brief shake-up—not even a short-lived scandal—emerged during a 1911 road trip to the western states. In St. Louis, the Taft contingent was treated to a breakfast that included something called "Bronx cocktails"—a brunch with an alcoholic punch, if you will. Though it is doubtful that Taft indulged, teetotaler forces in Missouri labeled the gathering as something of an outrage. Among other things, they surmised that there must have been whiskey in those Bronx cocktails!

The *New York Times* rose to the occasion (and, coincidently, the defense of President Taft) and in a September 24, 1911, article (with the tone of an editorial) launched a counterattack against the Missouri ministers and their anti-alcohol crusaders. Put forth the *Times*:

> An annoying feature of President Taft's journey through the West has been the controversy caused by the presence of Bronx cocktails at a breakfast party he attended. One does not have to be a clergyman or a total abstainer to reprehend the practice of drinking cocktails before breakfast. The Taft breakfast, however, was in St. Louis and was really dejeuner, but that word is not tolerated in Missouri. It is not the time of day that seems so objectionable, but the mere fact of the controversy. When this Republic grows older, and mellows a little, such controversies will not be conducted in public....

One preacher, for example, declared that a Bronx cocktail contains whisky.... So for a large part of Missouri from this time forward, the Bronx cocktail will contain whisky.

So far as that particular cocktail is concerned, or, indeed, any other concoction of that type, we do not care; it is the deplorably deficient culture of our country that depresses us....

Can it be that these Missouri clergymen are not college men? Anyhow, there is no whisky in a Bronx cocktail.

Although the Bronx cocktail seems rarely to get a mention these days, it is worth noting that it was typically composed of gin, with perhaps a little bit of vermouth and orange juice worked into the formula. And, in direct contrast to the fire and brimstone dispensed by the Missouri clergymen, the Bronx cocktail should be served up icy cold.

INTOXICATING TROUT

Before a political rift in 1912 pushed them apart, Taft and Teddy Roosevelt were good friends and political comrades in arms. TR, in fact, put all his might behind Taft's election (the big fellow was something of a reluctant draftee) in 1909.

One of TR's strategies that Taft often employed was to avoid, whenever possible, any meeting with radical factions of the women's temperance movement (such as the hatchet-wielding Carrie Nation.)

But once when Taft was on a swing through Colorado, he was ambushed—somewhat sweetly—by a contingent of Women's Christian Temperance Union (WCTU) sister-soldiers when he stepped off a train in Glenwood Springs. They were waiting for the hulking president with, of all things, a platter of trout that they wished to present to him.

Seeing no chance to follow the strategy set forth by the Hero of San Juan Hill (i.e. run away!), Taft could not resist "tweaking" the WCTU ladies. Were the women absolutely *sure* these trout were completely free of all intoxicants?

The stern-faced women assured the president that the trout were sans intoxicants—after all, *they* were total abstainers!

When Taft had safely returned to the train, he turned to a traveling companion (a Bishop Brewster, nonetheless!) and stated, with a tight-but-knowing smile: "It is my experience ... that the good women of the temperance movement are usually totally devoid of humor."

WHOA, NELLIE!

If Taft was restrained when it came to alcohol, his wife—Helen "Nellie" Taft more than made up for it. Her diaries and letters even from her teen years are laced with references to her drinking—beer (acquired in the storied beer gardens of Cincinnati's German "Over-the-Rhine" section), cocktails, and champagne—leading the list.

On her 1888 honeymoon to Europe, for example, Nellie declared: "It seems impossible to go through Germany without drinking beer ... I am very fond of it. What they call Pilsner is delicious."

Once in the White House, Nellie drew some flak from the WCTU by serving champagne punch to the diplomatic corps. But she had no intention of letting them ruin her fun. She also played cards in the White House, sometimes even on a Sunday.

A stroke in 1909 temporarily slowed down the first lady. But if there was a health risk that made Nellie susceptible to stroke, the culprit arguably had much to do with her *other* vice—smoking cigarettes. She managed to rebound to a great degree and lived until 1943.

ARCHIBALD BUTT'S EGGNOG EXTRAORDINAIRE

Even if the President himself had an aversion to "hard stuff" he certainly had no qualms when Archie Butt indulged. Butt frequently savored a scotch and soda at the White House.

Butt, however, was most proud of his signature dish (it proved too thick to be labeled a drink); New Year's eggnog, concocted strictly to his dear mother's recipe. As he glowingly penned his sister-in-law in 1910:

Major Cheatham came in to help me with the eggnog, and the people went wild about it when they ate it. It was too thick to be drunk. Here was what was in it:

Ten quarters of double cream whipped very stiff, twelve dozen eggs, six quarts Bourbon whisky [sic], one pint rum. I rented a huge punch bowl and kept the rest in tubs in the pantry. That at the bottom was as thick as that at the top. It was made by mother's recipe and for fear you don't know it I will send it to you, for I have never tasted any eggnog equal to it.

This eggnog was, obviously, a high-caloric, high-cholesterol, high-alcoholic-laced bomb of pure pleasure. But there is no record that Big Bill Taft ever sampled even a cup of it.

THE BOURBON HALL OF FAME

On December 17, 2009, some of the heavy-hitters of the art of making Kentucky bourbon flocked to the Old Governor's Mansion in Frankfurt to honor—and toast—William Howard Taft.

Since we know that Taft was *not* a whiskey drinker, one might find Big Bill a curious choice as an inductee to the Kentucky Bourbon Hall of Fame.

But, according to bourbon whiskey expert/historian Michael Veach, Taft deserved the honor because of the "Taft Decision" on whiskey that the president offered on December 27, 1909. Taft's legislation essentially answered the serious question of "What is Whiskey?"

The Taft Decision defined the various whiskey categories—"Straight," "Blended," and "Imitation"—that the distilling industry still utilizes. As Veach noted in his Filson Historical Society blog:

Kentucky is the state that made the decision necessary because before this decision people would move to Kentucky and rectify a product and call it "Kentucky Bourbon" because they made it in Kentucky even if it had no aged whiskey in it at all. Because of this decision, William Howard Taft is the father of modern Bourbon Whiskey.

LAST CALL

Taft was in Montreal in 1921 when he got the word of his appointment to chief justice—a position he had always longed for—and, in a rare fit of jubilation, toasted his accomplishment with a glass of champagne.... The mega-rich steel-mill tycoon Andrew Carnegie once sent Taft a case of scotch whisky, thinking that he might need a restorative swig during the 1912 election.... Nellie Taft recovered from her stroke and, in her golden years, traveled to Mexico, where, armed with the word "*cerveza*" (beer), she reportedly had a fine time.

CHAPTER 27

Woodrow Wilson

(1856–1924)

orn in Virginia, Thomas Woodrow Wilson graduated from Princeton University and later became its president. Wilson was serving as the governor of New Jersey when—as the Democratic Party nominee and champion of "progressive" reforms—he was swept into the White House in 1912. He defeated Republican incumbent William Howard Taft and former President Theodore Roosevelt (representing the "Bull Moose Party"), plus socialist candidate Eugene Debs in that famous election. He became the twenty-eighth president, serving from 1913–1921.

In his second term, Wilson attempted to keep America out of World War I—a stance that became increasingly impossible to hold due to Germany's policy of unrestricted submarine warfare and hawks (such as Wilson's political adversary Henry Cabot Lodge) in the Senate pushing for U.S. involvement. After the war, Wilson championed the League of Nations, although—much to his lament—the United States itself did not initially join the organization designed to promote understanding and peace.

Some people wrongly assume that Wilson must have pushed for Prohibition, since the Eighteenth Amendment (the Volstead Act) was passed during his second term. But, in fact, Wilson vetoed it on October 28, 1919—only to have Congress override him.

Prior to his veto, Wilson had suffered a serious stroke. Most historians and biographers believe that his second wife, Edith, (with assistance from Dr. Cary Grayson,) virtually ran the country in Wilson's last years in the White House. Wilson died in 1924 after a more serious stroke at his home on S Street in Washington, D.C.

WILSON—THAT'S ALL!

Wilson made some enemies when he was the president of Princeton University. One of his Princeton faculty foes—Professor Henry Duffield—once claimed that Wilson was "drunk with egotism."

Wilson's own words sometimes seem to suggest that he was not a man eager to embrace compromise, having once stated to an Ivy League audience:

> I am one of those who are of the seed of the indomitable blood, planted in so many parts of the United States, which makes good fighting stuff,—the Scotch-Irish. The beauty of a Scotch-Irishman is that he not only thinks he is right, but knows he is right. And I have not departed from the faith of my ancestors.

Neither did Wilson depart from the favorite *drink* of his ancestors—scotch whisky.

Although none of Wilson's opponents—academics or politicians—ever claimed he overindulged, the Virginian-born future president was far from a teetotaler. He may have *looked* like a stodgy academic (our only president with a Ph.D.) in his dark suits and top hat, but Wilson was, in fact, a moderate imbiber with a preference for high-quality whisky.

Coincidently, in the early 1900s, there was a popular scotch whisky called "Wilson" (distilled in Baltimore, Maryland, and claiming to date back to 1823), and the product's slogan was: "Wilson—That's all!" The obvious advertising implication being: "If you can have Wilson's whiskey—Why ask for anything else?"

Woodrow Wilson's Democratic campaign essentially co-opted this slogan (it was bandied about even when he ran for governor of New Jersey in 1909), and it appeared on campaign posters. "America First" appeared at the top of the poster—above a rather serious looking portrait of Wilson against a backdrop of the American flag. And below Wilson's picture, in bold letters, appeared: "That's All!"

But the poster was certainly out-done by a jaunty, banjo-strumming campaign song titled—you guessed it—"Wilson, That's All!" that was played and sung at campaign rallies during Wilson's White House run.

The verses brim with references to Democratic fellowship and alcohol consumption:

> Now convention days are over
> And election time is near
> From East and West, from North to South
> There's just one name in ev'ry mouth
>
> When a fellow meets a fellow
> And he says to him: "What's yours?"
> He says, "I think I'll have to drink
> To the Democratic cause!"
>
> It's "Wilson, that's all, Wilson, that's all!"
> Who strikes the public sentiment
> Say who will be our President?
> It's Wilson, that's all
>
> You'll hear them call, "Tammany, Tammany"
> While on the street or on the car

While at your home or at the bar
It's "Wilson, Wilson, Wilson, that's all!"

CHAMPAGNE ON CHAIRS

As the president of Princeton University, Wilson, first wife Ellen, and their children lived in the prestigious Italianate Victorian mansion called "Prospect House." Wilson may not have qualified as a "party animal," but he certainly knew how to welcome in the new year.

As the stroke of midnight approached, Wilson gathered everyone in the dining room and filled up the champagne glasses. Then everyone perched themselves on dining room chairs, put one leg up on the table top, and toasted in the new year—while singing the classic Scottish ballad "Auld Lang Syne."

VOLSTEAD VETO

Because Prohibition unfolded during Wilson's presidency, it might be assumed that he approved, or even pushed for, anti-liquor laws in the United States. But Wilson vetoed the Volstead Act—only to be overruled by Congress.

Wilson attempted a compromise; the war in Europe was ending and with it the need to keep wheat and other grains purely as food sources for soldiers in the field. So when President Wilson addressed the Sixty-sixth Congress in 1919, he raised eyebrows by pointing out the obvious:

> The Demobilization of military forces of the country has progressed to such a point that it seems to me entirely safe now to remove the ban upon the manufacture and sale of wines and beers. But I am advised that without further legislation I have not the legal authority to remove the present restrictions.

A backlash came from several directions. A minister from Ohio soon pronounced Wilson's declaration as: "Very unbecoming for an elder in the Presbyterian Church [which Wilson was], and a man holding so high an office as that of President of the United States."

Others suspected that German-American brewers were manipulating the White House—and, of course, anti-German sentiment was still running high in the country.

For their part, the "wets" felt Wilson's remarks did not go far enough; they wanted *all* liquor—not just beer and wine—to be made available to Americans.

SQUIRREL WHISKEY

Like other U.S. presidents (Lincoln and LBJ come readily to mind), Wilson enjoyed telling stories that featured liquor as a humorous ingredient. One revolved around "squirrel" whiskey.

On December 14, 1910, Wilson gave a speech to the New York Southern Society, staged in the grand ballroom of the Waldorf-Astoria Hotel in Manhattan. William G. McAdoo served as the toastmaster and welcomed Wilson with a lofty prediction: "I invite you, gentlemen, to drink to the health of a future President of the United States."

In return, Wilson—in a matter of seconds—regaled the crowd (their toast to Wilson was already their third of the night, having previously toasted William Howard Taft, the current president, and "the ladies") with his tale about squirrel whiskey—which he used to tell the crowd that he was not exactly sure in *which* direction the future might take him.

> I find myself in one respect (I hope in only one respect), resembling certain individuals I heard of in a story that was repeated to me the other day. A friend of mine in Canada with a fishing party was imprudent enough to sample some whiskey that was called "squirrel" whiskey. It was understood that it was called "squirrel" whiskey because it made those who drank it inclined to climb a tree. This gentleman imbibed too much of this dangerous liquid and the consequence was that when he went to the train to go with the rest of the

company, he took a train bound South instead of a train bound North. Wishing to recover him, his companion telegraphed the conductor of the south-bound train: "Send short man named Johnson back for the north-bound train. He is intoxicated." Presently they a got a reply from the conductor: "Further particulars needed; there are thirteen men on the train who don't know either their name or their destination."

(Wilson continued)

Now, I am sure that I know my name, but I am not as sure as Mr. McAdoo that I know my destination, and I have at the present so much to do that I don't think I am very concerned where I land....

Wilson unleashed his squirrel whiskey story on several other occasions. The president even regaled British prime minister David Lloyd George with the tale during a brief respite at the Paris Peace Conference in 1919.

DRAWING THE LINE

When Wilson launched his run for governor of New Jersey, a Judge Hudspeth gave him a good-natured warning.

"Dr. Wilson," Hudspeth stated, "you need not be surprised that sometime during your trip around the State, some exuberant voter will slap you on the back and say: 'Come, Woody, old man, let's have a drink!'"

Wilson responded with a good-natured laugh, allowing: "The intimate introduction is all right, but I would draw the line on liquoring up!"

PEACE TALKS AND PROHIBITION

The summer of 1919 proved to be a hectic one for Woodrow Wilson. While wrapping up the Paris Peace Conference in Europe (with his trusty friend and personal physician Dr. Cary Grayson, a former admiral, by his side), the American contingent was well aware that when they arrived "home" that the United States would (at least officially) be a "dry" country, as of July 1.

If Wilson and Grayson had *not* remembered that Prohibition was indeed looming in the very near future, European leaders were only too pleased to remind them. The day Wilson, British prime minister Dave Lloyd George, and France's Georges Clemenceau signed the controversial Treaty of Versailles in the Hall of Mirrors on June 28, Dr. Grayson wryly noted in his diary:

> Clemenceau had tea served for the party. He also had wine brought in and proposed a toast to the peace and good health of the party. After the toast had been drunk he turned to me and said: "You had better have another one because you will not be able to get any of this (wine) when you get back home."

Wilson was somewhat willing to poke fun at the situation, judging from a discussion (in the spring of 1919) with Lloyd George—one that started out being about sparrows. As Dr. Grayson recorded in his diary:

> The subject turned to birds, particularly the English sparrow. The President said that the English sparrow in America was a menace because it whipped away the thrush, the robin and other songbirds. Lloyd-George was surprised to hear that, because, he said, "it was such a quiet bird at home in England." The President said: "How do you account for the fact that it is so peaceful at home and such a fighter with us?" Lloyd-George said: "I think it is due to the fact that your climate is more energetic; that you have more champagne in the atmosphere." The President said: "That may have held good in the past but it will not hold good now, because we are dry...."

WILSON'S WINE CELLAR

Wilson stocked an impressive wine cellar at the White House. Rather than leave it to the incoming Warren Harding and his cronies (who surely would have guzzled it down in rapid order), Wilson wisely opted to move it to his new residence prior to leaving the White House.

This reasonable request actually required special approval from Congress since—technically—it was illegal (under the Volstead Act) to transport liquor.

In addition to wine, Wilson liked an occasional sip or two of scotch whisky. In the latter stages of his life—despite the Volstead Act—correspondence signed with Wilson's name appeared to acknowledge his use of scotch whisky to combat the challenges of a serious stroke that left him in a fragile state.

A typical example was a June 14, 1921 letter that Wilson sent to Louis Seibold (a journalist trusted by the Wilson circle—he once conducted an interview intended to show that President Wilson had recovered from his stroke) that read:

> My dear Seibold:
> The goods arrived as per Grayson's schedule and I am very grateful. You certainly know what is wanted and when.
> With warmest regards from us all;
> Faithfully and gratefully,
> Woodrow Wilson

As Seibold acknowledged in a note to Katharine E. Brand, "the goods" were six bottles of rare scotch whisky, which he passed on to Dr. Grayson for delivery to the former president. At another time, Seibold noted: "I personally delivered to Mister Wilson's house some very good Rhine wine—Berncastler Doctor—as a gift from my father."

LAST CALL

Wilson's vice president, Thomas R. Marshall, is most famous for his quote: "What this country needs is a really good five-cent cigar!" But Marshall also was a reformed alcoholic who sometimes made speeches on behalf of the temperance movement, which allowed the Wilson-Marshall ticket to win votes from some of the "bone-dry" contingent.

CHAPTER 28

Warren G. Harding

(1865–1923)

A ban on the "transportation of intoxicating liquors" was just one of several restrictions that were outlined in the Constitution's Eighteenth Amendment. But it goes without saying that not everybody followed the letter of that particular law.

One of the flagrant flouters of Prohibition was the dapper twenty-ninth president of the United States (1921–1923), Warren Gamaliel Harding, who apparently had no reservations about transporting a bottle of whiskey (secreted away in his golf bag) around the links at Chevy Chase and pausing to enjoy an occasional pop.

Harding is often presented as one of the worst presidents in history. If it's true, it is primarily because of the Teapot Dome Scandal and the messy aftermath, which involved blackmail, bribery, perjury, suicide, whispers of murder, and prison terms. For Harding personally, the only good thing about the incident was that he'd already died (at the Palace Hotel in San Francisco on August 2, 1923, probably of heart failure, though conspiracy theories abound) when it occurred.

As a senator from Ohio, Harding at least gave the appearance of being a "dry" politician—someone opposed to the brewing, selling, and consumption of alcohol. Prohibition was solidly in place when he moved into the White House in 1920. But it would be hard to name a more hypocritical president—at least on that issue.

Socialite Evalyn McLean noted: "I knew that Warren Harding was counted as a dry senator, but that in moments of relaxation he was ready to drink.... Indeed I often heard him boast that he could make a champagne cocktail just like the Waldorf bartender."

Though Harding might have made a first-rate bartender, he was quite over his head in the White House—as he himself admitted. The corrupt circle of cronies coiling around him, and his own personal flaws, did not help much, either.

Colonel Edmund Starling, the head of Harding's Secret Service detail, remarked: "He was ruined by his friends, just as Wilson was ruined by his enemies. But the main point is, he should never have been President of the United States."

Starling issued one of history's classic understatements when he allowed that "the parapets of [Harding's] virtue were probably not insurmountable."

THE BIG FOUR

Warren G. Harding loved golfing, gambling (particularly poker), chasing women (other than his wife, Florence—"The Duchess"—Kling Harding), and drinking.

Harding used alcohol to enhance the other three activities, though his friends maintained that he rarely consumed liquor to excess.

In fact, it may have been more that Harding (like Buchanan) enjoyed incredible tolerance. Harry Daugherty, Harding's savvy campaign manager, once brought the 1920 presidential long shot to *New York Times* reporter Arthur Krock's room at Washington's Willard Hotel for a drink prior to the Gridiron Club dinner. As Krock noted in his memoirs:

I had imported a couple of bottles of rare prewar bourbon from Kentucky and, as I recall, the Senator from Ohio drank almost a pint by himself. Hangover, he showed it not at all. He held his liquor well.

Warren Harding had no qualms about drinking in the White House (especially if cards were flicking around the poker table), but he also found the golf course a convenient place to imbibe. Early in his term, President Harding liked to take a pop in between holes from a bottle stashed in his golf bag. But at some point (perhaps on the advice of his aides) he decided a little discretion was in order; the president would wait until the rounds were over, *then* have a whiskey with his cronies in the confines of the clubhouse.

As Colonel Starling remarked:

> He played most often at the Chevy Chase Club, and used the house set aside for the President. I kept the key to the desk drawer where three or four bottles of Scotch and Bourbon were stored. When we returned to the house the colored man in attendance, Taylor, brought set-ups, and while the players drank highballs I calculated the results of the bets and announced the winners. The President took a single drink, and when this was finished and the bets were settled he would say to me, "Telephone the Duchess and say I am on my way home."

If his golf scores were any indication, Harding had reason to drink. He often played twice a week, but even breaking one hundred sometimes proved a challenge for him. But nobody could doubt his love of the game—he would play even on rainy days.

While Harding enjoyed playing at Chevy Chase, he was under even less scrutiny when he golfed on the links that adjoined "Friendship"—the estate of William "Ned" McLean and his eccentric wife, Evalyn. McLean was a hard-drinking tycoon who owned the *Washington Post* and eventually became ensnared in the Teapot Dome fiasco.

In the wonderfully engaging book *First off the Tee: Presidential Hackers, Duffers, and Cheaters from Taft to Bush*, Don Van Natta Jr. relates a story from Shirley Povich, who caddied for Harding when Povich was just seventeen. Three-quarters of a century after the fact, Povich (who later became a renowned sports writer and editor at the *Post*) recounted:

> "I showed up at the first tea and McLean was glad to see me.... He turned to the man standing with him and said 'Mr. President, this is Shirley Povich, the best caddy in America,' which was untrue. 'He's going to caddie for you today'." Shortly after the introductions were made, Povich recalled that he was surprised to see butlers arrive with the afternoon's first round of drinks. And—to hell with Prohibition!— President Harding took a glass and a gulp. Imagine that.

Imagine that, indeed. Harding's love of golf also provided him an excuse to avoid (at least for several hours) the Duchess and indulge in drinking and gambling.

THE WHITE HOUSE SPEAKEASY

The Harding White House was relatively careful about alcohol in the *downstairs* floors. But it was another matter upstairs, where, if one was invited, you could count on a cocktail, a card game, or lots of both.

Alice Roosevelt Longworth—Teddy Roosevelt's eccentric daughter renowned for unleashing her barbed witticisms against those (friend or, God help them, foe) around her—gave one of the most widely circulated accounts of what the White House social life was *really* like during Harding's term. In her memoir *Crowded Hours*, so-called "Princess Alice" wrote with thinly veiled disdain:

> No rumor could have exceeded the reality; the study was filled with cronies, [U.S. Attorney General Harry] Daugherty, Jess Smith, Alex Moore, and others, the air heavy with tobacco

smoke, trays with bottles containing ever imaginable brand of whisky stood about, cards and poker chips at hand—a general atmosphere of waistcoat unbuttoned, feet on the desk, and spittoons along side.

White House staffer Elizabeth Jaffray observed similar behaviors during the Harding years, stating:

President Harding was the only man during the four administrations that I lived at the White House who drank enough to speak of. It was also [his] habit when he entertained men ... to retire after dinner to the library or study to play cards and have Scotch and soda served.

Colonel Starling claimed that Harding drank only moderately when playing. "At card games he drank one highball, then switched to ale," he said. But Starling stops short of saying how *many* ales Harding might have downed.

THE FIRST LADY AS BARMAID

First Lady Florence Harding did not appreciate a lot of her husband's habits— especially Warren's pursuit of other women but also golf and horseback riding (he sometimes used both as an excuse to skip church). But the president often let her attend some of his poker games. But the Duchess was not there solely to kibitz; she had actual duties—such as serving drinks to Harding and his Ohio Gang cohorts.

One might find it difficult to imagine other first ladies (Jacqueline Kennedy? Rosalynn Carter? Pat Nixon? Hillary Clinton? Michelle Obama?) scurrying about to fetch alcohol for their husband's cronies—hunched like trolls over a poker table, wafts of cigar smoke curling around like serpentine ghosts. But at this task the Duchess performed diligently and proficiently, even absorbing some good-natured abuse in the bargain.

As Alice Roosevelt Longworth commented:

Harding and Nick [Senator Longworth, Alice's big-boozing husband] and the others would say when they wanted another drink, "Duchess, you are lying down on your job." And Mrs. Harding, who was watching the play of hands, would obediently get up and mix a whisky and soda for them.

THE CHINA SYNDROME

Lowlights in the Harding administration compete with each other like so many fast-growing, mutant weeds vying to muck up the perceived Edenesque glory of the White House.

That Harding once lost a set of White House china in a "cold hand" of poker is not the worst of it, but it does underscore how any pretense of presidential dignity was relegated to the rumble seat of his Roaring Twenties term.

Whether Warren G. was slightly intoxicated on a highball and ale chasers, somewhat smitten with his female adversary, or both, is difficult to ascertain. But as the story goes, Harding impulsively bet attractive socialite Mrs. Louise Cromwell Brooks that he could deal a better "cold" hand than she—and offered up some fine china as his stake. Harding lost. The next day, boxes of china—stamped with an imprint from President Benjamin Harrison's term—arrived at Mrs. Brooks's Massachusetts Avenue townhouse.

TRADING SHOTS WITH THE UNIONS

When the railroad unions went on a national strike in 1922, Harding played hardball with them in a meeting at the White House. This was not Harding's preferred style—he typically attempted to be friends with everybody and not rock the political canoe.

But knowing that the clash with union leaders was likely to be no holds barred, Harding might have first resorted to some liquid courage.

Union representatives later claimed that Harding was drinking shots of whiskey straight from the bottle (though, in all fairness, this does *not* sound like Harding's suave style) and slurring his words. Rabblerousing union speakers repeated the charges at a rally in Buffalo, New York, in the days following the White House meeting.

According to a 1998 *Washington Post* article, FBI records released in the 1990s also reported that a fired-up Harding may have been intoxicated during the confrontation with union officials.

Regardless, the result was that the unions eventually caved, and the railroads were soon running again.

THE HARDING LEGACY

On June 20, 1923, Harding, the Duchess, and his entourage departed Washington, D.C., and embarked on what was dubbed "The Voyage of Understanding"—an extended trip by train and ship that would take them to the West Coast and as far north as Alaska. Supposedly there was a "no booze" rule in effect, but there was probably some bending of the rules.

The administration stated that the main purpose of the journey was to bring Harding's message directly to the citizens.

The tour also allowed Harding and company to avoid the summer heat and humidity of the capital, not to mention the "heat" of various scandals. After Harding's untimely death (he had hoped to run for reelection, and his "friends" had hoped to continue riding his wide, generous coattails), however, the game changed rapidly.

Upon returning to Washington, Mrs. Harding immediately began burning (or hiding) papers and letters that she thought might tarnish her deceased husband's legacy. That no doubt would have included anything to do with Harding's attraction to other women, alcohol, and gambling.

BABES AND BOOZE

The Harding legacy started to go to pieces just a few years after he died, when one of his former mistresses—Nan Britton—published a scandalous memoir about how the twenty-ninth president fathered a daughter out of wedlock with her. Titled *The President's Daughter*, it was considered dynamite in its day, and there were attempts to suppress it. Those attempts failed, however, and it eventually sold ninety thousand copies.

His alleged mistress recounted how she once sent him out from a hotel room in search of a bottle of champagne ("I guess I was a bit shy with him, and a glass of champagne made me a bit more talkative and revealing....")

> Of course, Prohibition had already gone into effect, but I was told it was possible still to obtain liquor or wines if one knew how to do so and evidently Mr. Harding thought he did ...

But when Harding returned, he sheepishly admitted: "No, dearie, I couldn't get it."

LAST CALL

Evalyn McLean owned a pet monkey that once snatched a bottle of lemonade at a party, scurried up ivy vines and trellises to a lofty perch on the side of the grand mansion, and then—from a great height—splashed most of its contents down on Warren G. Harding's fine-tailored suit. Perhaps it is a fitting metaphor for Harding's presidency, but one somehow wishes the mischievous monkey had been sufficiently armed with a full bottle of whiskey.

CHAPTER 29

Calvin Coolidge

(1872–1933)

*D*espite having the sobriquet of "Silent Cal," Vermont's Calvin Coolidge rose to the presidency when Warren Harding met his untimely demise in 1923. When the news reached the powerful senator Henry Cabot Lodge, he was said to have blurted out: "Good God! Coolidge is president!"

Coolidge's term (1923–1929) was largely uneventful, though he gets high marks today from those who champion less government and fiscal discipline. There were no wars to fight (other than the unpopular and clumsy one against bootleggers that the government was losing), and the Great Depression was yet to come.

If Coolidge drank in the White House, he did so rarely. Calvin was a flyweight when it came to drinking alcohol.

When it came time to commit to a second term, Coolidge said: "I choose not to run...." But there are some historians who believe Cal was simply being coy—that he really wanted the Republican Party to plead for him to run. They did not. Instead, they hitched up Herbert Hoover—

whom Coolidge sometimes facetiously referred to as "The Wonder Boy" or "The Great Engineer"—to the GOP wagon.

But when the great Wall Street Crash came in 1929, perhaps even "Cool Cal" contemplated a shot and a beer chaser—if for no other reason than to thank Fate that he was retired in New England.

JUST AN UNEXCITABLE BOY

Coolidge was, to put it mildly, not an electrifying personality. When he died, the supreme wielder of rapier witticisms—the writer Dorothy Parker—allegedly deadpanned: "How could they tell?"

Alice Roosevelt Longworth dismissively remarked that Coolidge looked like someone "sucking on a pickle."

Baltimore writer H. L. Mencken harvested great hay during the Harding-Coolidge-Hoover eras; he could not take cynical aim at the targets fast enough. Mencken described Coolidge as "a stubborn little fellow with a tight, unimaginative mind"—and that was one of his less-malicious lines.

Of course Dorothy Parker, "Princess Alice," and H. L. Mencken all liked to drink. Coolidge, apparently, could take it or leave it—leaning most decidedly toward the latter.

But did he ever?

The best answer might be: very occasionally and with minimal consumption. William Allen White, one of Coolidge's earliest biographers, wrote in 1925:

> Once every blue moon he sat down in one of the gardens of Northampton (Massachusetts, where Coolidge once served briefly as mayor), took a single, solemn glass of beer—this was, of course, before the great Volstead drought—cracked a single, solemn joke, drier than the pretzel that he munched, and felt that he had for that day and season done his full social duty to God and man.

Suffice to say, Coolidge was not a man destined to put a dent in the nation's grain production.

THE BARRISTER OF BREW

There was, however, a time in Coolidge's career when he championed those who did use up a lot of grain in their everyday production of goods: the Springfield Brewery. This was early in Coolidge's lawyering career (1909 or so), but as biographer White suggested, it most likely helped him win the mayor's race in Northampton.

> Among his other clients was the Springfield Brewery. It was his business to look after its barkeeps in the courts. Sometimes he appeared for its drunks in the police court.

Coolidge locked up the "wet" vote in Northampton, but he did his best not to antagonize the entire block of "dry" voters. And so he won the mayor's race. Not long after, he became the lieutenant governor of Massachusetts, then governor (and a tough-acting one who broke the Boston Police Strike). Then—despite it being such an obvious mismatch of personalities—Coolidge latched on as copilot on the long-shot (but ultimately winning) Harding ticket in 1920.

PECKING ORDER

Nothing lasts forever, and that, apparently, meant Teddy Roosevelt's precious bed of White House mint. In his book *42 Years in the White House*, Irwin "Ike" Hoover, the long-serving White House usher, wrote that President Coolidge once received a gift of two dozen chickens.

Coolidge turned the birds loose in TR's precious bed of mint—the very same bed that Colonel Roosevelt once plucked to make his special mint juleps after a few hotly contested sets of tennis. The chickens pecked away, and, when they were later consumed, Ike Hoover claimed the meat had a definite hint of mint to it.

"We never knew whether [Coolidge] selected the mint bed on purpose or not," mused Hoover. "If he did, it was in keeping with many other odd things the President was up to."

REASONABLE DOUBT?

Arguably one of the most bizarre stories about Coolidge involves not chickens, but whiskey.

The accomplished and prodigious presidential historian Richard Norton Smith unveiled this little gem in his 1990 book *An Uncommon Man: The Triumph of Herbert Hoover*. Smith writes that, according to some White House staffers, Coolidge—stung by the Republican Party's embracement of Hoover—trudged off to his room on the day of that announcement and had a bottle of Green River whiskey clutched in his hand.

While the drinking of whiskey seems wildly out of character for Coolidge, the fit of pouting and pique does not. And perhaps Franklin Pierce's alleged adage—that ex-presidents have nothing left to do but get drunk—resonated with a brooding (and possibly depressed) Coolidge.

THE TOKAY RUSE

After Coolidge left the White House and Hoover (Herbert, not Ike!) took over, Cal and Mrs. Coolidge traveled across the country. One special stop was the sweeping Hearst Castle in San Simeon, California.

At the majestic estates, publishing magnet William Randolph Hearst felt he should offer the ex-president a cocktail. Coolidge promptly reminded "The Chief" that he did not drink. As related in McCoy's *The Quiet President*, Hearst slyly attempted the host's equivalent of the quarterback sneak.

"Neither do I," the publisher replied. "But I find that a sip of wine is an excellent appetizer."

The former President asked: "Is it alcoholic?"

"Not perceptibly," Hearst said. "The alcohol content is slight."

Hearst finally talked Cool Cal into a small glass of Tokay wine. Coolidge drank it. Then he accepted a second (virtually binge-drinking for him) and remarked that he must remember what he drank for future reference.

THE COOLIDGE COOLER

Just a few years ago, an American maker of vodka—Vermont Spirits—suggested that imbibers could use their product to make something called a "Coolidge Cooler"—preferably to be concocted on July 4, Silent Cal's birthday. The suggested recipe (with whiskey optional) is this:

Coolidge Cooler

Ingredients:

1.5 ounces of Vermont White vodka
½ ounce of American whiskey
2 ounces of orange juice
club soda

Mix vodka, whiskey, and orange juice over ice. Top with club soda.

While it seems doubtful that Coolidge would have indulged in this libation, if the Green River whiskey story is true, then anything is possible.

LAST CALL

Proof that Prohibition was not working was highlighted by gang wars over turf and liquor distribution. The infamous St. Valentine's Day

Massacre in Chicago in 1929 took place just weeks before Coolidge's term ended—just another headache that incoming Herbert Hoover—"The Wonder Boy"—inherited.

CHAPTER 30

Herbert Hoover

(1874–1964)

*I*f timing is everything, then Herbert Hoover (1874–1964)—like a power hitter completely fooled on a fluttering knuckleball—looked totally out of synch by the end of his one, disastrous trip to the presidential plate. The Republicans had won handily in 1928, promising "a chicken in every pot and a car in every garage" and predicting that poverty was on the brink of banishment in America. But when the stock market crashed and the Great Depression struck in 1929, the euphoria evaporated with mind-boggling rapidity.

Banks folded, bread lines and "Hoovervilles" formed, and the populace could not (at least not legally) even console itself with a shot and a beer, since Prohibition was still the law of the land.

As the thirty-first U.S. president limped toward the bench at the end of his term (1929–1933), it seemed unlikely that he could beat the Democratic nominee, Franklin Delano Roosevelt. And, of course, he did not.

With just a few days left in Hoover's term, journalist Agnes Meyer wrote (on February 25, 1933) in her diary: "Hard on H. to go out of office to the sound of crashing banks. Like the tragic end of a tragic story.... The history of H's administration is Greek in its fatality."

Once billed by some as "The Wonder Boy," Hoover had become associated with a word that rhymed with "wonder"—but meant something else entirely. As Meyer admitted: "God knows I wished him well. Looking back it seems like nothing but blunder after blunder...."

GONE, BABY, GONE

A graduate of Stanford, Hoover (prior to his political career) made good money as a mining engineer in Australia and China. His successes allowed him to enjoy some of the luxuries of life. For example, when Hoover resided in California (and also London), he possessed a quality wine cellar, including some well-aged port.

But when Prohibition came into effect, his wife, Lou Henry Hoover (an abstainer of alcohol) got rid of it all—apparently without even consulting Herbert. The rules of Prohibition would have allowed Hoover to keep his liquid stash, though transporting it somewhere else was technically against the law.

But that was a moot point once Lou dumped it all. Probably less than thrilled about this radical move, Hoover nevertheless managed to mutter something like: "I don't have to live with the American people, but I do have to live with Lou."

HERBERT'S NOT-SO-FUNNY VALENTINE

Just a few weeks before he was to take office, the thirty-first president of the United States already knew of at least *one* messy problem waiting for him—the public outcry from the February 14, 1929, gangland killings that occurred in Chicago, the infamous St. Valentine's Day Massacre.

Most likely a tussle over who would control the bootlegging turf in Chicago, the news of it was just more embarrassing evidence that the federal government could not enforce the unpopular Prohibition laws and, furthermore, that gangsters like Al "Scarface" Capone were profiting from the sale of illegal hooch.

Hoover soon pressed his U.S. Treasury chief, Andrew Mellon (who himself had once purchased a distillery from business titan Henry Clay Frick), to put Capone in jail, and it was eventually accomplished when Internal Revenue Service agents busted the mobster for tax evasion in 1931. Capone's incarceration was a rare bright spot for the Hoover administration, though it did nothing to slow the popularity of the speakeasy.

GOING THROUGH THE MOTIONS

Unlike the Warren G. Harding era, there was no cheating in the Hoover White House when it came to Prohibition. Dinner guests might have had experienced a jolt of hope when they saw dinner staff circling the table with bottles wrapped in towels.

But it was not to be. The towels did not conceal a fabulous bottle of French champagne or a California red. With the ceremonial flourish suggesting something stronger, surely the majority of guests were doubly dismayed to find White Rock mineral water gurgling into their glasses.

A BRONX CHEER IN PHILLY

Hoover had once referred to Prohibition as "a noble experiment," but the president did not have to do anything more than venture out among the working-class (many of them unemployed) citizens to get the hint that the "experiment" was failing miserably.

When Hoover attended a World Series game between the St. Louis Cardinals and the hosting Philadelphia Athletics at Shibe Park in October 1931, a vocal section of the crowd—aware of the president's presence—began to jeer: "We want beer! We want beer!"

To make matters worse, Hoover received bad news during the game. He (and the first lady) got up to leave in the eighth inning, but—as he later recorded somberly in his memoirs—the crowd once again proved rudely hostile:

I was not able to work up much enthusiasm over the ball game and in the midst of it I was handed a note informing me of the sudden death of [New Jersey] Senator Dwight Morrow. He had proven a great pillar of strength in the Senate and his death was a great loss to the country and to me. I left the ballpark with the chant of the crowd ringing in my ears: "We want beer!"

H. L. MENCKEN'S BARBED-WIRE WORDS

If Hoover was unable to dodge the frustrated chants of would-be beer drinkers at a baseball game, he had even less luck in the press.

One of his chief tormentors was H. L. Mencken, the Baltimore-based columnist known for his zingers. Mencken (who frequently referred to Hoover as "Lord Herbert" or even more mean-spiritedly "Fat Herbert") made no pretense that he was against Hoover from the start, and would not concede that the Republican's embracing of Prohibition came about for any reason other than political convenience. As Mencken wrote, just prior to the 1928 election:

> Certainly no one who knows him believe that he is a Prohibitionist. He is simply a candidate for office, willing and eager to do or say anything that will get him votes, and the fortunes of war have made it more prudent for him to cultivate the drys than to cultivate the wets.

And then Mencken took Hoover to the woodshed for his see-no-evil existence in the Harding administration.

> He [Hoover] came from London, the wettest town in the world, to sit on the Harding cabinet, the wettest since the days of Noah. No one ever heard him utter a whisper against the guzzling that surrounded him. He was as silent about it as he was about the stealing.

Although typically wary of all politicians, Mencken backed Hoover's Democratic opponent Al Smith of New York City, a defiant and definite "wet" candidate if ever there was one. (When Prohibition was repealed, Budweiser sent the Budweiser wagon to Gotham to provide Smith with a ceremonial taste of the suds.) But Hoover trounced Smith in the election, and, given the Wall Street swoon looming just beyond the precarious ledge, it may have been Al's lucky day when he lost.

HERBERT'S MAIN BEEF

Long before he became president, Hoover sided with the "dry" side, whether for political convenience, as Mencken suggested, or not. According to Hoover, it was to save every bit of wheat and barley to support both the Allied war effort in Europe or to feed the innocent civilians who inadvertently found themselves displaced and hungry during the horrific and widespread hostilities.

"If I were dictator in this war I should stop brewing and distilling for beverage purposes at once," proclaimed Hoover, quoted in the *Saturday Evening Post* in 1917. "The product adds little or nothing to human nutrition—at best, it is a luxury."

Hoover himself, however, had not given up drinking at the time of his emphatic statement.

JUNIOR GETS A "PEP TALK"

When Herbert Hoover Jr. was selected to serve in John Foster Dulles's State Department (during President Eisenhower's presidency), he received perhaps some surprising advice from his aging father. According to Richard Norton Smith's in-depth biography *An Uncommon Man: The Triumph of Herbert Hoover*, the aging ex-president told his junior namesake: "Herbert, keep a bottle of whiskey in your bottom drawer and after the day is over, when you're tired and before you start home, take a swig ... and it will pep you up."

A MARTINI WITH MOTHER MAGDALENA

Hoover enjoyed relaxing and fishing in the Florida Keys during cold weather months. He picked up a case of pneumonia in March of 1953, probably after attending the Eisenhower inauguration in Washington, D.C. But Hoover—almost eighty years of age at the time—stubbornly refused to seek medical attention and went down to Key Largo to fish.

But in Key Largo, Hoover's condition seemed to get worse and the ex-president was carted off by ambulance to a nearby Catholic hospital. When Hoover was checked in, he was visited by the hospital supervisor, Mother Magdalena, whereupon the onetime Wonder Boy must have caused some wonder when he cheekily inquired: "Sister, can you make a good dry martini?"

But apparently without missing a beat, Mother Magdalena assured Hoover that she could indeed make a good dry martini—and then she proved it.

BELGIUM RELIEF

According to at least one Prohibition historian, Hoover's drink with Mother Magdalena was far from his first dry martini. In his book *Last Call*, author Daniel Okrent records that Hoover—while a cabinet member for both President Harding and President Coolidge—would swing by the Embassy of Belgium (where he was technically *not* on U.S. soil) for a martini.

Having successfully headed up the Belgian Relief Fund (based out of London, where Hoover lived for a number of years) in 1914, he could count on a warm welcome—and apparently a cold libation of choice—there.

As Hoover aptly put it later in life, a stiff cocktail could provide "the pause between the errors and trials of the day and the hopes of the night."

LAST CALL

Hoover grew up in West Branch, Iowa. He was raised as a Quaker and a Republican, recalling that one of the few Democrats in town was a notorious drunk.... Hoover had a stormy relationship with Congress and once referred to it as "that beer garden on the hill".... Hoover's press secretary, George Akerson, was dismissed in 1930, in part because his excessive boozing had become an embarrassment to the administration.... There's a bar in Seattle named "Hooverville," and its ambience on Yelp is described as "divey."

CHAPTER 31

Franklin Delano Roosevelt

(1882–1945)

*F*ranklin Delano Roosevelt is consistently ranked as one of America's greatest presidents (1933–1945). Roosevelt deserves high marks for guiding the country through World War II and digging out from the Great Depression.

FDR's first presidential election victory, in 1932, was partly the result of his belief that most voters were sick of Prohibition. Although Teddy Roosevelt's side of the family (TR and FDR were distant cousins) had experienced tragedy from alcohol-related problems, Franklin—usually a man of moderation when he imbibed—often used drinking to break the ice in social situations. On those rare occasions when FDR did charge through his typical limit of two cocktails, he held up well enough that even his enemies could not accuse him of drunkenness.

His daily drink rituals may have helped Roosevelt deal with some of the harsher realities of his life— in particular his confinement to a wheelchair due to polio and his less-than-perfect marriage with the less-than-exciting Eleanor.

FDR enjoyed mixing gin-based martinis (and occasionally whiskey-based Manhattans) for guests as much as he liked drinking them—although his tendency to dump-and-stir won him no accolades as a bartender. He is most associated with cocktails, but FDR (much like John Adams) pleasantly indulged in a variety of libations—including champagne, rum, brandy, and beer. He consistently drank in the White House, but the president sometimes upped the ante of his alcohol consumption when he (like his successor, Harry Truman) was on a sailing trip or flicking the cards around a poker table—the details of which are wonderfully chronicled in the diaries of Secretary of the Interior Harold L. Ickes.

FRANKLIN "SPIKE" ROOSEVELT

One of FDR's most outrageous stories (and one he related in detail to Ickes during his first term) involved spiking a friend's drink—in his buddy's best interest, of course. The story—which dates back to FDR's pre–World War I days and, frankly, sounds a bit embellished—goes like this:

Franklin knew a stockbroker down on his luck. After a few drinks with FDR, the hapless broker admitted that he was several thousand dollars in debt and saw no clear way out of his predicament. Later in the evening, Franklin, the broker, and a mutual friend wandered into a high-class New York City casino. The broker, who continued to drink heavily, begged FDR and the third man to each lend him twenty-five dollars to gamble on a spinning wheel game—a desperate attempt to right the shipwreck of his personal finances.

Long story short, the broker was down to his last ten dollars when Lady Luck suddenly reversed course and planted a demonstrative buss upon his alcohol-flushed cheeks. And the broker began to *win* … first five hundred dollars, and then a thousand, and then even more. That was the good news.

The bad news was that this "Wall Street Wally" also continued to drink and refused all pleas to leave the field of chance with his winnings still intact. It did not require incredible imagination to picture the boozy broker losing it all back.

So what did his friends do?

Franklin and his pal bought the already tipsy broker back-to-back drinks, spiked extra strong, and the broker finally cooperated by passing out. When the broker awoke in his hotel the next day, he had (along with a crushing hangover) all of his winnings—and only a vague memory of how he'd secured the cash.

FDR'S RUM SWIZZLE

As a young man in 1921, FDR was diagnosed with crippling polio. His doctors had no hope of a cure to offer. Roosevelt, partly in an effort to remain upbeat and partly because he half-believed tropical climates might ease the effects of his disease, embarked on sailing trips in 1923 and 1924.

And rum was a standard part of those excursions.

Before one of his voyages, a friend sent Roosevelt an ensign (a signal flag or pennant) to display on the ship, and FDR joyfully fired off a thank-you letter proclaiming that he would hoist it to the mast and "salute it with 17 rum swizzles!"

Jean Edward Smith, author of the book *FDR*, not only records that exchange but—as if to participate in the fun—felt compelled to add a popular recipe (from FDR's time) for "Bermuda Rum Swizzles" at the bottom of the page:

Bermuda Rum Swizzles

Ingredients:

2 ounces dark rum
1 ounce lime juice
1 ounce orange juice
1 generous dash of Falernum (a sweet syrup)

Shake with ice. Strain into a highball glass filled with ice. Garnish with a slice of orange and a cherry.

BEER FOR ALL

Most discussions about Franklin Delano Roosevelt and alcohol typically start with his desire to mix cocktails for his guests. That picture is accurate, but one plainly clear sentence spoken to a national radio audience might be more significant.

"I think this would be a good time for beer," an upbeat FDR announced during one of his "fireside chats" in March 1933.

One can imagine the jubilation of the man in the street at such a simple sentence. After all, less than two years before, his presidential predecessor—a subdued Herbert Hoover—had been showered with boos and sweeping chants of "We want beer! We want beer!" while attending a World Series game in Philadelphia.

And now FDR was inviting them to *have* beer.

Roosevelt's stance on alcohol was founded in principle, not political convenience. He had always been tolerant of drinking—at least in moderate amounts. He had run, unsuccessfully, as the vice-presidential candidate with Jim Cox when the Republicans rode dark-horse candidate Warren G. Harding to the White House in 1920. But Harding—a consistent drinker—hypocritically had no qualms about courting the support of the "dry" contingent.

All that said, FDR—running against the incumbent Herbert Hoover in 1932—knew the country was in need of a lift. The Great Depression was smothering the people, and he felt that moderate amounts of alcohol might help the masses to better cope with the daily struggle and also stimulate the economy.

It would be a stretch to say that FDR won the White House chiefly by rolling back Prohibition. He believed the turning point came when Hoover sent the army in to clear out the tattered Bonus Army (thousands of World War I veterans who marched on Washington demanding cash-payment redemption of service certificates), using tear gas, horses, and tanks. The brutality of that action (deemed necessary by some) was splashed across the front pages of America's newspapers.

But the idea of bringing back beer did not hurt the Democratic cause, either. Days after Prohibition was repealed, the famous Budweiser beer wagon (first marketed for this momentous occasion), arrived in the capital, its powerful Clydesdales clip-clopping down Pennsylvania Avenue with a gift of free brew for the new occupant of the White House. Yuengling—a Pottsville, Pennsylvania, operation that can trace its roots back to 1829—also sent a truckload of specially brewed "Winner's Beer" to the White House for the occasion.

That FDR liked a few beers himself is a given. As a freshman at Harvard, young Franklin eagerly attended "beer night"—a social icebreaker at the Ivy League institution. That taste for suds did not slacken over the years, as various entries in Ickes's diary attest. After the president returned from a Labor Day mini-vacation on Vincent Astor's yacht, Ickes penned:

> September 5, 1933
>
> I have never seen [FDR] looking so well.... He said he had had three days of absolute rest where no one could get at him. He said that one night he had sat up until six o'clock in the morning playing poker and drinking beer and I remarked that if it had the effect on him that it appeared to have, he had better make a practice of it.

And several years later, Ickes hosted a poker game—one with both plenty of action and booze—and then noted:

> April 16, 1938
>
> ... we played poker until well after one o'clock. It was a lively game and the money changed hands pretty rapidly. I have had a bottle of 152-year-old Scotch whisky which I opened up for the occasion. I served this as a liquor after dinner as well as some 1811 Napoleon brandy. The President

is quite fond of beer. He drank four bottles last night. The others preferred Scotch … I served Virgin Island rum cocktails before dinner and sparkling Burgundy during dinner.

Famed Broadway actress Helen Hayes Brown (a.k.a. "The First Lady of the American Theatre") could also attest to FDR's affinity for beer. Nervous to meet the president for the first time, she recalled a visit to the White House in her autobiography (*My Life in Three Acts*):

FDR was alone in the family sitting room. "I'm having a beer," he said. "What'll you have?" "The same," I answered. We sat chatting about this and that. All I remember is thinking that once I downed the beer I'd be free to disappear among the throng of foreign diplomats arriving downstairs.

When King George VI and Queen Elizabeth visited Hyde Park during their 1939 visit, much was made that hot dogs were served to the royals during a very informal picnic at the estate. FDR also offered the king and queen the perfect alcoholic beverage to accompany those hot dogs—American-brewed beer.

MIXOLOGIST-IN-CHIEF

Martha Gellhorn, a war correspondent and Ernest Hemingway's third wife, was sometimes invited to stay at the White House. Both President Roosevelt and First Lady Eleanor were fond of the globe-trotting journalist.

But imagine Gellhorn's surprise when she found FDR mixing up a batch of martinis in, of all places, the cloakroom, and giggling like a naughty schoolboy as he did it.

What could have driven FDR into the confines of the White House cloakroom? Most likely his mother's appearance for dinner and the knowledge that the matriarch of the Roosevelt clan not only disapproved of Franklin's imbibing, but also was quick to berate him for it.

Eleanor also disliked her husband's drinking habits. When FDR hosted his typical post-work, pre-dinner cocktail hour (he referred to it playfully as "The Children's Hour") straight-laced Eleanor was essentially banned—though she would occasionally attempt to disrupt the festivities under the pretense of bringing the president an important message.

But the main purpose of the Children's Hour was to unwind from work and chat about more frivolous topics. The cocktails assisted perfectly in that mission. The president loved to nudge his guests toward a refill with such playful lines as "How about another sippy?" or "How about a little dividend?"

Although he sometimes mixed up batches of Manhattans or Rum Swizzles, FDR was more noted for his gin martinis, with a little vermouth and a classic garnish of olives. Most people gave his martinis (barely) passing marks, but Hall Roosevelt (Eleanor's hard-drinking younger brother) dismissed FDR's concoctions as somewhat wimpy; Hall preferred more gin, less vermouth, and opted for what he considered a more masculine garnish—onions instead of olives.

WHEN BRANDY PROVED HANDY

FDR preferred his cocktails on a daily basis, but he knew there were occasions that called for something more traditional—brandy.

One of those bring-on-the-brandy moments occurred during his 1940 presidential campaign against Republican Thomas Dewey. To combat the constant (and not unfounded) rumors of President Roosevelt's ill health, FDR planned an open-car tour through several major cities. But when he got to New York City, the conditions deteriorated to a windy and bone-chilling rain. FDR toured through Gotham despite the weather but occasionally ducked into a garage for a change of dry clothes and—yes—a bracing glass of brandy to warm him up.

But in FDR's drinking history, brandy was not just for medicinal purposes; he also summoned it when pondering a crucial decision.

In 1939, Roosevelt received a visit from Alexander Sachs, a prominent New York businessman. Wishing to persuade FDR to pursue research on building an atomic bomb, Sachs trotted out something of a cautionary tale: he mentioned that Napoleon had once been approached with the idea of constructing a fleet of combat-ready steamships—but Napoleon (who met his Waterloo soon after) failed to explore this offer of new naval technology.

Perhaps the mention of the doomed French emperor was not lost upon FDR. He called for a well-aged bottle of Napoleon brandy (a bottle long in the Roosevelt family) and two glasses, and the men began to hash out a plan to beat Nazi Germany to the punch in acquiring what was to be, in that era, the world's most devastating weapon. One can almost smell the warm, delectable fumes wafting up from proper brandy snifters.

THE BRITISH ARE COMING!

During his three-plus terms as president, FDR had to entertain heads of state, generals, and diplomats from around the world. But three of the most important had to be the King and Queen of England (who came to visit both Washington and Hyde Park, New York) and Sir Winston Churchill, who visited Hyde Park and the White House (including right before Christmas 1941—mere weeks after the Pearl Harbor attack) on different occasions.

Roosevelt's mother, Sara, still felt she had the authority to control FDR's drinking. (The president would often retreat to his study—off-limits to any would-be spoilsports—if he wanted a second drink without a garnish of criticism.) A comical scene evolved from these differing opinions concerning alcohol when King George VI and Queen Elizabeth arrived at Hyde Park in 1939. As FDR's son James Roosevelt recalled in *My Parents*:

> Later granny served a formal dinner for the royal couple. To her horror, [FDR] had drinks brought out before dinner. He said to the King: "My mother thinks you should have a cup of tea. She doesn't approve of cocktails."
>
> The King, who had little to say, thought this over for a few minutes, then observed: "Neither does my mother."

Whereupon they grabbed their glasses, raised them to one another in an unspoken toast and downed their martinis.

Prime Minister Churchill presented a different challenge. His demands for liquor when visiting the United States were legendary. A much-circulated story involved the bulldoggish PM instructing White House staffer Alonzo Fields to his various alcohol "must haves"—a tumbler of bedside sherry in the morning, a few glasses of scotch and soda before lunchtime, and French champagne (despite his half-American heritage, Churchill had no interest in stateside bubbly) and ninety-year-old brandy before he turned in after a long day.

Speaking of long days, it was said that Churchill's visits often required FDR to stay up well past midnight, something he rarely did on his regular schedule. Since most extended stints with Sir Winston typically involved more drinking, FDR sometimes needed extra rest and recovery once his esteemed visitor returned to England.

Whether he was completely serious or not, FDR's early-in-the-war assessment of the famous British leader (according to the Ickes diaries) was that Churchill was "the best man that England had, even if he was drunk half of his time."

At Hyde Park, James Roosevelt remembered Churchill quite vividly—pinky-pale, huddled beneath an umbrella by the pool—smoking a cigar and waiting for a full bottle of brandy to arrive. And, in something of an understatement, James Roosevelt added: [Churchill] could do justice to a bottle of brandy."

LAST CALL

Once called upon to make a graduation day speech at West Point on a very sultry day, FDR was in need of something to keep his throat in working order. He opted for a libation that might have brought forth an enthusiastic "Bully for you!" from his relative Teddy Roosevelt—none other than the classic mint julep.

CHAPTER 32

Harry S. Truman

(1884–1972)

arry Truman was not given a full middle name at birth—simply the letter "S." According to some accounts, "S" was arrived at because both of his grandfathers had an "S" that figured prominently in their names—and it was left at that so as not to favor one over the other.

Those interested in what presidents like to drink might have pushed for the letter "B" given Truman's fondness for bourbon.

What's particularly interesting about Truman and bourbon is that the thirty-third president (1945–1953) seemed to enjoy a shot of the amber-colored elixir not long after the break of dawn. But by no means did he limit his intake to that morning "nip."

With or without bourbon, Truman had plenty of truly tough decisions to make, including giving final approval to drop the atom bombs on Japan and various difficult choices during the Korean War, not least of which the firing of the popular general Douglas MacArthur. The aftermath of Truman's attempt to seize control of the U.S. steel industry—a dubious move foiled by the Supreme Court—involved a peace offering of bourbon in its denouement.

If there is a lasting image of Truman it is probably the one of him holding up the *Chicago Tribune*—its front page erroneously proclaiming: "DEWEY DEFEATS TRUMAN." Consider that Harry Truman might have offered the Cheshire Cat a glass of bourbon in exchange for the feline's classic grin on this particular occasion.

WEATHER, WHISKEY, AND DIAMONDS

Born (in 1884) and raised near Independence, Missouri, young Harry Truman attempted to woo one of the town's best-known belles— Bess Wallace. He finally mustered up the right stuff and proposed to her in a letter. Relying on such diverse topics as weather and whiskey, before a smooth segue into the true aim of his letter, Harry wrote:

> The elements evidently mistook one of my wishes for dry instead of wet. I guess we'll all have to go to drinking whiskey if it doesn't rain soon. Water and potatoes will soon be as much a luxury as pineapples and diamonds. Speaking of diamonds, would you wear a solitaire on your left hand should I get it?

Ms. Wallace managed to contain her enthusiasm for this initial proposal, but she did eventually marry Harry in 1919 after the artillery captain returned from the battlefields of France.

THE FRENCH CONNECTION

Harry Truman had rarely been out of Missouri, but the Great War (as it did with many young American "doughboys") gave him a crash course in dealing with the French. Although a drink of whiskey was somewhat difficult to come by, the French soldiers and citizens had plenty of wine and brandy to offer—and the Americans had extremely parched throats to receive it.

Captain Truman commanded an artillery unit—Battery D, to be exact. On November 11, 1918—after days of rumors—the Germans signed an armistice and soldiers at the front received word to cease hostilities at 11:00 a.m. Truman's battery fired its last round about fifteen minutes before the war officially ended.

Then it got very quiet—but not for very long. As Truman later recalled:

> ... a great cheer rose all along the line. We could hear the men in the infantry a thousand meters in front raising holy hell. The French battery behind our position were dancing, shouting and waving bottles of wine.... Celebration at the front went on the rest of the day and far into the night.

No doubt Truman would have preferred a shot of bourbon, but the occasion (and availability) called for French wine—and the jubilant French soldiers were more than willing to share.

> I went to bed about 10 P.M. but the members of the French Battery insisted on marching around my cot and shaking hands. They'd shout "Vive le Capitaine Americain, vive le President Wilson," take another swig from their wine bottles and do it over. It was 2 A.M. before I could sleep at all.

Truman spent about a year in France, but that he never became a fan of French wine—or, for that matter, French food—is a matter of record. One of his handwritten letters to sweetheart Bess in January 1919 left no doubt of that, while reaffirming his appreciation of bourbon, even in the face of the recently enacted Prohibition Act. As Truman put it:

> For my part I've had enough *vin rouge* and frog-eater victuals to last me a lifetime. And anyway it looks to me like the moonshine business is going to be pretty good in the land of Liberty loans and green trading stamps, and some of us want

to get in on the ground floor. At least we want to get there in time to lay in a supply for future consumption. I think a quart of bourbon would last me about forty years.

THE BOYS FROM BATTERY D

There is no doubt that Truman loved his men from Battery D and went out of his way to help organize and attend postwar reunions with those who served with him in France. The men loved Captain Truman, too, and more than one gave him credit for saving their lives.

The men admittedly were a rough and rowdy bunch, and sometimes proved to be an embarrassment for Truman back in the States. For example, at one of the gatherings in the early 1920s, the boys of Battery D—obviously drunk (Did Prohibition apply to war veterans?)—began tossing objects (rolls, dinner plates, glasses, and even a sugar bowl) at each other at an Elks Club they had rented out for the occasion. Although Truman was not one of the main combatants, it nevertheless fell on him to pay the damages the next day—which the future president sheepishly did.

By the time Truman ran for president in 1949, most of the surviving members of Battery D would have been over fifty. After he won, Truman invited them to a breakfast in the nation's capital, just prior to his inauguration. Remembering some of their past shenanigans, Truman felt compelled to issue a plea for good behavior. As Frederick Bowman, one of the former artillery men, recalled:

> Well ... he had a breakfast for the Battery and his parting words as we left ... [it was over about 9:00 a.m.] were, "Well, I've got a very busy morning and I hope you fellows will stay sober at least until I'm inaugurated into office, then I don't care what you do."

TOASTING WITH "CACTUS JACK"

When Truman was sworn in as the new U.S. senator from Missouri in 1935, he (along with other newcomers to Congress) was marched before one of Washington's most famous political characters—John "Cactus Jack" Garner of Texas, who was then speaker of the House.

As witnessed by James Aylward, a Missouri political operator, who accompanied Truman to his swearing in:

> [Garner said] "Men, before we enter into these ceremonies, I'd like you all to join me in striking a blow for liberty." So he got a jug that looked like corn liquor and we all pertook thereof.

Garner served as FDR's vice president (1933 to 1941), though it would be an understatement to say he found the job less than satisfying. In fact, Cactus Jack (he won this moniker because he once lobbied to have the prickly pear cactus named as the Texas "state flower") once infamously said that the vice president's position was "not worth a bucket of warm piss."

A SOBERING SUMMONS

Truman was quite content to be a senator. But in 1945, President Roosevelt tapped him to be his vice president (replacing Henry Wallace, who had succeeded Garner). Truman reluctantly agreed when FDR—peeved at Truman's initial resistance—played the "party loyalty" card.

Less than three months later, Truman adjourned the Senate then headed to House Speaker Sam Rayburn's office (a typical stop for Truman) for an end-of-the-day drink. But before Truman even had his bourbon, he was told to call Stephen Early, FDR's press secretary. Early told him to head to the White House immediately for an urgent announcement. By some accounts, Truman—sensing some sort of bombshell—blurted out: "Holy General Jackson!" and then hustled off to the White House.

When he got there, Truman was brought to Eleanor Roosevelt. The first lady gently informed him, "Harry, the President is dead." Briefly stunned, Truman naturally responded by asking Eleanor if there was anything he could do? And Mrs. Roosevelt famously replied: "Is there anything *we* can do for *you*? Because you are the one in trouble now."

A MORNING WALK WITH OLD GRAND-DAD

President Truman's typical routine was to begin each day with a brisk walk, often as much as two miles. And sometime after the walk, the president enjoyed a vigorous massage.

But it was what Truman did in between his morning walk and the massage that was interesting: Truman knocked off an ounce (or so) of bourbon (typically Wild Turkey or Old Grand-Dad)—a classic "eye-opener" that the old artillery officer must have felt helped him take direct aim at the day. Truman was doubly sure to employ these daily tactics when he was off resting in one of his favorite hideaways, such as Key West, Florida—all this after a few hours of poker the previous night.

STEEL, STRIKES, AND BOURBON

On April 8, 1952, President Truman attempted to take military control of the steel industry, fearing that a threatened national strike would hinder the American war efforts in Korea.

Several months later, the Supreme Court ruled against the president. Truman was piqued that the court had defied him. Three days later, Chief Justice Hugo Black invited the still-simmering president to an outdoor steak fry in a not-so-subtle attempt to smooth things over. Bourbon was served, too.

Truman sat almost silently for a while but eventually broke the tension with: "Hugo, I don't much care for your law, but, by golly, this bourbon is good."

In a 1972 CBS News interview, Justice William O. Douglas was a little more hard-boiled about Black's get-together, noting: "We all went and poured a lot of bourbon down Harry Truman.... He didn't change his mind, but he felt better, at least for a few hours."

TRAVELS WITH WINNIE

Truman and Winston Churchill respected and understood each other. When the recently disposed British leader (stunningly, Churchill had failed in his reelection bid for prime minister in 1945) arrived for an American visit in 1946, Truman—at the request of others—was able to get Churchill to agree to a speaking engagement at tiny Westminster College in Fulton, Missouri. They headed west from Washington, D.C., but traveling with "Winnie" also meant meeting certain expectations. As General Harry Vaughn, one of the Missouri-bound members of the party, recalled:

> We got aboard the train and we'd gotten about ... to Silver Springs (MD). Mr. Churchill and his secretary ... and the President and I were sitting there in the car. The President said: "What do you have to do to get a drink on this ... thing?"
>
> So I pressed the button and a steward came in and pretty soon Mr. Churchill had a tall whiskey and soda in his hand. He held it up and let the light shine through it (it was about four o'clock in the afternoon) and he said: "You know, when I was a young subaltern in the South African War, the water was not fit to drink. To make it palatable, we had to put a bit of whiskey in it. By diligent effort I learned to like it."

When the party arrived in Fulton, Missouri, the next day, the Americans realized that they were in a "dry" town—a definite dilemma when one considered their portly, distinguished guest and his well-known indulgences. At Truman's request, Vaughn rustled up a pint bottle of spirits somewhere.

> I went out to the kitchen and got some ice and a pitcher of water and a glass and went upstairs. Mr. Churchill was sitting there with his robe on and I said: "Mr. Churchill, here, I thought you might need a little pick-me-up before we go over to the gymnasium."
>
> "Well," he said. "General, am I glad to see you. I didn't know whether I was in Fulton, Missouri, or Fulton, Sahara."

Whatever libations Churchill consumed prior to his speech, it must have been precisely the right amount of fortification. Those in the audience were treated to one of Sir Winston's most famous postwar oratory efforts—"The Sinews of Peace"—far better known as his "Iron Curtain" speech.

THIRD TIME'S THE CHARM

After serving the Roosevelts for many years, White House butler-bartender Alonzo Fields considered himself a pro. But early in Truman's administration, First Lady Bess asked for two pre-dinner cocktails—specifically, Old Fashioneds.

Fields's first effort proved too weak for Bess's taste. So Fields, his pride slightly dented, dug up an alternative recipe. This attempt, too, fell short of the mark—apparently, a bit too fruity.

With a flash of frustration, Fields put two generous pours of bourbon over ice into bar glass tumblers and added a few bitters.

This strong-on-the-bourbon, light-on-everything-else approach did the trick—and Alonzo Fields fielded compliments from the president and the first lady on his creation.

JOUSTING WITH MCCARTHY

No political history of the 1950s would be complete without mention of the anti-Communist zealot Joe McCarthy, a Republican senator from Wisconsin. It was Truman's misfortune that his second term coincided with McCarthy's brief rise to power.

Truman's controversial removal of General MacArthur from command brought out McCarthy's fangs, and he ripped the president in a speech. McCarthy labeled MacArthur's removal as a "Communist victory won with the aid of bourbon and Benedictine"—an accusation that Truman drank too much.

Truman was not amused and (in a letter to Russ Stewart, the *Chicago Sun-Times* general manager) responded curtly: "I appreciate very much your thoughtfulness in forwarding me Bill Kent's story on McCarthy's cockeyed statement. I think he will be extremely sorry about that statement before this show is entirely over."

Senator McCarthy continued to be a political abscess for Eisenhower, as well, but Ike ignored the controversial anti-Communist crusader. Eisenhower once noted (in regards to McCarthy) that he had no intentions of "getting in a pissing contest with a skunk."

The hypocrisy of McCarthy accusing Truman (a moderate, if consistent, drinker) is that there was strong evidence that it was the senator who had serious alcohol problems. McCarthy died in 1957 in Bethesda, Maryland, at just forty-eight years of age. The official cause was acute hepatitis, but most speculate that cirrhosis of the liver brought on the hepatitis.

THE TRUTH ACCORDING TO TRUMAN

On a visit to New York City, then–former president Truman ducked into the barroom—Bemelmans—at the Carlyle Hotel. Irish-born bartender Tommy Rowles was serving exactly his fourth customer of what was to be a fifty-plus-year career at that fine establishment. Nevertheless, he knew who Truman was.

"I'll tell you what he drank if you don't ask what time of day it was," Rowles joked with a *New York Times* writer in a 2012 article about the celebrated barman's retirement.

Truman ordered an Old Grand-Dad on the rocks; no big surprise. But the former leader of the free world also asked Rowles if the young publican was allowed to join him.

"I told him I could drink, but I could never drink an Old Grand-Dad," remembered Rowles. Whereupon Truman asked the Irishman to look outside and report what he saw—a noisy gaggle of reporters and photographers, Rowles observed.

Then Truman smiled and said: "Yes, and if you had to walk 15 blocks with these guys following you, you'd drink this, too."

THE MISSOURI MULE

Very few presidents can claim to have had a drink invented in their honor. Harry Truman, however, is among the chosen few. When President Truman would stay in London, he typically set up camp at the much-esteemed Savoy Hotel in Westminster, which included the famed American Bar, featuring jazz and inventive U.S.-style cocktails.

A fixture for decades at the American was Belfast-born barman Joe Gilmore. Gilmore—who rose to head barman in 1955—created commemorative cocktails to honor famous people and historical occasions. For example, Gilmore came up with the "Moonwalk" after Neil Armstrong's walk on the moon in 1969.

To honor Truman, Gilmore created the "Missouri Mule." It was a clever name choice, given that Missouri (not to mention the Democratic Party) has long been associated with this hardworking hybrid between a horse and a donkey. This drink—which suggests the potential of a mean "kick" if handled frivolously—requires bourbon as its main base, a few other liquors, and a vigorous shake or two.

Missouri Mule

Ingredients:

2 parts bourbon whiskey
2 parts Applejack
1 part Campari
1 part Cointreau

Prep: Shake ingredients together with ice, and strain into a cocktail glass.

A fine establishment such as the American Bar could never have let it go as a simple bourbon and water—but it is quite likely that Harry Truman would have indulged in a Missouri Mule only out of politeness. With a wink, he would sometimes describe his drink as "H-2-O, with a little bourbon flavoring."

LAST CALL

Truman enjoyed playing poker and sipping a few bourbons when he traveled on the presidential yachts.... A collector and seller of historical items recently featured a large sterling silver bourbon "jigger" (about two ounces) that was engraved with "HST" and the words "Only A Thimble Full." It was billed—like Harry himself—to be the real deal.

CHAPTER 33

Dwight D. Eisenhower

(1890-1969)

"The Man on Horseback"—meaning, a successful military hero—has often been an unstoppable force in the history of presidential races. Victorious generals—Andrew Jackson, Zachary Taylor, and U. S. Grant come readily to mind—often hold a competitive edge over less-decorated candidates.

So it was with Dwight D. "Ike" Eisenhower, the thirty-fourth president of the United States (1953–1961). Riding a wave of national adoration (and unlike, say, the egotistical General Douglas MacArthur, Ike knew how to play the "Ah, shucks, folks" card), Eisenhower—running on the Republican ticket—hammered the opposition in both the 1952 and 1956 elections. As Democratic foe Adlai Stevenson (a skilled and intelligent orator but twice trounced by Ike) put it: "It was like running against George Washington."

Like Washington, Eisenhower enjoyed modest amounts of alcohol and typically in social situations. Except for a few wild moments in his early years, Ike rarely over-imbibed.

In fact, if Eisenhower could be said to have had one truly bad habit, it was smoking. Against regulations, Ike began rolling and smoking his own cigarettes at West Point (in earnest, apparently, after an injury ended his football career). He was said to have smoked several packs of Camels per day during World War II. Although he allegedly went "cold turkey" after the war, it is highly likely that Ike's poor health (he had several heart attacks late in life, including one that led to his death in 1968) had much to do with years of hard smoking.

IRASCIBLE IKE?

The picture of unflappable General Eisenhower, coolly directing the Normandy invasion and other critical campaigns of World War II, is a strong one.

But those unfamiliar with the details of Dwight D. Eisenhower's young adulthood might find it hard to believe that a temper-flared (and whiskey-fueled) Ike once put his fist through a wall. The incident occurred in the months after Ike's graduation from West Point, where Eisenhower had excelled on the football field. He suffered a career-ending injury in a game versus Tufts in 1913, but Ike no doubt still carried back to Kansas some of the swagger of the gridiron.

As Eisenhower biographer Carlo D'Este detailed in his 2003 book *Eisenhower: A Soldier's Life*:

> With little else to do in Abilene ... Eisenhower could be found hunting, fishing, and occasionally drinking and playing poker. One evening he and several friends had imbibed enough bootleg whiskey to become loud and boisterous when they ambled into a local café. Eisenhower attempted to teach his friends some of his West Point songs in his dreadful singing voice ... Eisenhower defied several profane requests from the owner to stop or be tossed out, responding by angrily daring him to try; then, to make a point, he thrust his fist through the wall ... where it became stuck. A portion of the wall had

to be cut away with a kitchen knife to free a very chagrined Dwight Eisenhower.

In his later years, the five-star general and president claimed that the fist-in-the-wall incident had been dramatically embellished.

BATHTUB GIN

After World War I, Eisenhower and another West Point product—George Smith Patton—were stationed together at Fort Meade, Maryland. With Prohibition in full swing, the young officers and friends had no qualms about making their own alcohol.

Patton bottled some of his home-brewed beer. But at least one account has it that the man who would become a celebrated expert on tank warfare was reduced to a "duck and cover" response one day when some of the bottles suddenly blew their tops—the sound apparently mimicking some kind of weaponry. (Except for some good-natured ribbing from his young wife, Patton, who would one day earn the nickname "Blood and Guts," escaped the incident unscathed.)

Ike was in the game for stronger stuff, even if the production process was less hazardous. He used grain alcohol and a bathtub to mix up a reasonable facsimile for gin.

SPECIAL KAY

With World War II in full swing, Eisenhower arrived in London—a proud city still standing but also smoldering from the Luftwaffe's brutal *blitzkrieg*. It was here that the rising American general was assigned a British captain to drive him around: an attractive, Irish-born strawberry blonde by the name of Kay Summersby.

If you want to start an argument in a roomful of Eisenhower "scholars" simply ask: "Were Eisenhower and Kay Summersby wartime lovers?" The historical flak—not all necessarily facts—will fly. Diehard Eisenhower supporters (and especially family members) typically tiptoe around this subject as if it were a minefield or blatantly deny that it ever could have happened. As for Summersby, in 1973—terminally ill with cancer—she penned a book entitled *Past Forgetting: My Love Affair with Dwight D. Eisenhower.*

David Eisenhower, the president's son, weighed in with an open mind—and the possibility that alcohol might well have played a role in any of his father's indiscretions—*if*, in fact, there *were* lapses in the general's discipline. Quoted in a 1977 Associated Press story, David Eisenhower allowed:

> Nobody can bear witness that something did not happen. How can I go on the witness stand some place and swear Dad didn't get a couple of drinks of scotch in him sometime and get affection?

What we *do* know is that Ike and his driver-assistant were quite close and drinking buddies to boot, almost from day one. When Summersby initially drove Ike and General Mark Clark around England in 1942, she wrote:

> It was warm and I was parched. Without thinking how outrageous I was being, I pulled up in Beaconsfield and said, "You absolutely must visit an English pub."
>
> It was a gin and tonic kind of day. As we sat there and sipped our drinks, the late-spring afternoon slipped into evening. The nightingales were singing. It was high time for the three truants to get back to London.

Since the English are renowned for their top-shelf gin, one must assume it was better than the bathtub batches that Ike once mixed up during Prohibition. And since a lunch with wine had preceded the bouts with British gin tonics, one must picture the "three truants" feeling rather happy upon their return to the embattled capital.

CHAMPAGNE—SPARKLE AND FLAT

Legend (and it is probably only that) has it that when the monk Dom Perignon accidently "discovered" champagne, he urged his fellow theologians: "Come quick, brothers! I am drinking stars!"

Eisenhower was not drinking stars, but on some special occasions he had them pinned to his uniform—and that called for champagne. When Ike was awarded a fourth general's star (he eventually achieved five stars) in February 1943 en route to his selection as supreme commander of Allied forces, he saw fit to break out the bubbly. The end of the war was far from in sight (in fact, the Allies were still attempting to oust Axis forces from North Africa), but to hear Summersby tell it, the occasion was a rare one of splendid respite from Eisenhower's ever-increasing responsibilities:

> That night Ike broke out the champagne and we had an impromptu party just for our headquarters group. He was very, very happy that evening. I'll never forget the sheer pleasure that radiated from him. I remember thinking, There's a man who has never had very much fun in his life. The General was always very charming, always had that grin at the ready, but underneath it all he was a very serious and lonely man who worried, worried, worried.

Another champagne scenario reflected just how much spearheading the Allied High Command had wrung out of Ike; after the Germans signed the armistice in 1945, he was clearly too tired to generate much enthusiasm for a celebration.

"I suppose this calls for champagne," said an unenthusiastic Ike.

And, as if to match Eisenhower's vibe, when the champagne was poured, it happened to be disappointingly flat.

HOT DOGS AND BEER

Ike was serving as president of Columbia University in 1949 when he made a speech at an elite New York City hotel that rattled some lunch kettles in working-class America and drew fire from the Columbia student body.

Eisenhower insinuated that perhaps some Americans harbored high-roller tastes for "caviar and champagne" when "hotdogs and beer" might be a more realistic fare for the masses.

Even the student newspaper at Columbia did not let this comment slide without a well-aimed jab at the general:

> Being content with beer and hot dogs has never been a part of the American tradition we know. The one we know assures any citizen that he may some day eat champagne and caviar, and in the White House at that. We don't know, of course, but we are willing to bet that beer and hot dogs weren't on the menu at the Waldorf-Astoria last Wednesday night either.

A few days later, piqued students took it to the next level: they decorated Alexander Hamilton's statue at Columbia with an empty beer carton and a half dozen or so hot dogs and added five stars onto Hamilton's bronze derriere. The students also hung a protest sign around Hamilton's neck that read: "Ike prefers beer and franks for all." Fortunately, the famous general had not said: "Let them eat cake!"

Controversy aside, one year later Eisenhower was a serious candidate for president of the United States.

SCOTCH-LIKING IKE

Eisenhower acquired a taste for scotch whisky during his military career, and he would occasionally indulge in a glass or two during his presidential years and in retirement.

State dinners at the White House were accompanied by wine and champagne. But when President Eisenhower and the first lady entertained at their home in Gettysburg, it was standard procedure to serve cocktails—the American libation of choice in the 1950s. The Gettysburg home had all the cocktail-making equipment—ice buckets, shakers, shot glasses, and bar glasses to concoct a potent highball.

Before their falling out, Ike sent a nice bottle of scotch to then president Harry Truman (who, as is well known, preferred bourbon whiskey—but would, on occasion, settle for scotch) in 1946. Truman responded with a thank-you letter, reflecting both his sense of humor concerning alcohol and his obvious fondness for Ike. "I think I'll inhale it rather than pass it out to these 'thugs' who hang around here and drink my whiskey," joked the man from Missouri. "Maybe you and I could think up an occasion when we could share it."

But the Eisenhower-Truman relationship was destined to become as icy as any cocktail recipe that instructed its maker to serve it "on the rocks."

FIXING THE FEUD

When Dwight D. Eisenhower aligned himself with the Republicans, Truman (who had wished to entice the popular general into the Democratic camp) and Ike began to drift apart.

Their relationship was mired in its deepest muck after Eisenhower arrived at the White House on his 1953 Inauguration Day. Presidential protocol typically follows that the incoming president goes inside to be greeted by the outgoing one. But Eisenhower ignored this tradition and refused to leave the presidential limo. Eventually, a snubbed Truman was forced to come out to Ike and proceed to the inauguration ceremony in what must have been an awkward ride for all involved. (One can almost imagine the steam escaping from "Give 'Em Hell Harry's" ears and fogging up his trademark glasses.)

More than a decade passed before the two men—both ex-presidents by then—patched up their differences. Both were in Washington to attend John F. Kennedy's funeral, and a simple twist of fate (or perhaps some man's deliberate stroke of genius) happened to place Ike and Truman in the same limousine. As the *Washington Post's* White House correspondent Edward Folliard noted:

But at any rate, the limousine brought them back from Arlington on this sad day, and drew up at Blair House where Mr. Truman was staying ... Well, as Truman got out of the limousine, he turned around, and said: "Ike, how about coming in for a drink?"

And Ike looked at Mamie and she seemed to agree so they went in ... and they had a few drinks, and, oh, talked about old times, and finally when it was time to go, Mamie Eisenhower thanked Mr. Truman for something he had done just before the inauguration in 1953. Truman without consulting with Ike had arranged for John Eisenhower, their son, to be sent back from Korea. He ordered him back for the inauguration. Mamie thanked him for that and then kissed him. That was the end of the feud, and they once again were the friends they had been for many years.

MAMIE'S MANHATTANS

If the Eisenhower family was sick of dealing with the ever-present suggestion that Ike and Summersby had indulged in a wartime romance, equally tiresome were rumors that Mamie drank to excess.

When Mamie had some trouble walking straight, some gossip-mongers sniped that it was because of drinking. The whispers were persistent enough that Eisenhower supporters issued a statement that the first lady suffered from an inner-ear condition that sometimes caused havoc with her balance.

There is, however, no shortage of evidence that Mamie liked champagne and, on occasion, a cocktail or two—typically an Old Fashioned or Manhattan.

Not all of Mamie's handling of champagne involved drinking it. In 1954 the first lady was called upon to "christen" America's first nuclear submarine—busting a ceremonial bottle across the bow of the *Nautilus* in New London, Connecticut. She performed this task in high fashion—clad in a mink fur coat.

DIRTY POOL

A Midwestern preacher (and fanatical anti-Communist) named Gerald L. K. Smith—who planned to support General Douglas MacArthur for president in 1951—wanted to make Eisenhower look bad. Considering Ike was a popular war hero, that was going to take a little bit of trickery.

But Smith stooped to the dirty task of manipulating a photograph (cropping out other participants from Britain and France) from a V-E Day toast so that it looked like Ike was drinking solely with the Soviet Union's Field Marshal Georgy Zhukov. Then, in the caption, Smith poison-penned: "Zhukov, Communist General, decorates drinking partner Eisenhower...." Smith attempted to circulate what he hoped would be a picture of doom for Eisenhower's political career. But MacArthur never ran for president, and Ike skated to an easy victory over the Democrats in the November election.

DR. SNYDER AND THE SECOND SCOTCH

Being Eisenhower's physician was not without its challenges, but Dr. Howard Snyder—a friend of Ike's to boot—did his best. By some accounts, Eisenhower had four heart attacks (the first coming during his first term) and more than a dozen incidents of cardiac arrest during his seventy-nine years of life.

Dr. Snyder was vehemently supportive of Ike's golf habit, noting that the president was "like a caged lion" if he did not get to play. He also managed to get Eisenhower to cut way down on his once massive cigarette addiction.

But the former D-Day commander did not lose *every* battle. Snyder had tried to restrict Ike to a solitary glass of scotch and soda for his nightcap. When Ike asked the butler to bring him reinforcements, the doc reminded him: "I said only one, Mister President."

And Ike would pleasantly reply: "Thank you, Howard. You've done your duty."

Then he would turn to the butler, smile, and firmly state: "Bring me a second scotch."

LAST CALL

Eisenhower probably would have chosen golf over booze; he haunted the links whenever possible during his presidential terms. Any alcohol would have waited until the last round had been completed.

CHAPTER 34

John Fitzgerald Kennedy

(1917–1963)

More has been written about John Fitzgerald Kennedy than about any other American president—an estimated forty thousand books, just for starters. Some of this fascination no doubt arises from his tragic assassination on November 22, 1963.

Many Kennedy books are almost mythical in their worship and lament of the murdered president cut down near the pinnacle of his life. But other books that question and tarnish the Kennedy image and mystique also have emerged over the decades. For instance, Seymour Hersh's *The Dark Side of Camelot* alleges strong ties between patriarch Joe Kennedy and the Mafia, among other things.

Where does alcohol fit in when one talks about the Kennedys? If you believe that it is virtually impossible to run for president, let alone get elected, without truckloads of money to back up the effort, then one could speculate that without the profits from alcohol (an early cornerstone of Joe Kennedy's multi-million-dollar empire) JFK might not have ever glimpsed the White House.

On a more personal level, John Kennedy—the thirty-fifth president of the United States (1961–1963)—liked alcohol, but he did not love or need it. Alcohol was more of a prop for his other interests—politics, recreation, male camaraderie, and female companionship. That said, it is hard to envision Camelot—or at least the Jack and Jackie version of it—without daiquiris, the occasional Bloody Mary, or the finest French champagne.

HERE IN CAMELOT

Arthur Schlesinger Jr. was an astute observer of the heady days of JFK. Schlesinger's journals (which he kept from 1952 to 2000) are an invaluable source for several presidents, but particularly JFK.

Schlesinger served as an occasional speechwriter for JFK, and he sometimes spoke on behalf of the campaign.

On June 12, 1960, Schlesinger wrote about his first trip to the Kennedy compound on Cape Cod:

> We arrived about noon on a hot, overcast day. Jack and Jackie were playing croquet on the lawn with a couple of friends. They stopped and we had daiquiris on the terrace.

And, similarly, on Aug 6 of the same year, Schlesinger arrived in Hyannis Port and joined Kennedy on a boating excursion:

> Then we drank Bloody Marys, swam from the boat and finally settled down for an excellent lunch. After lunch, cigars and conversation....

With JFK's political future on the rise, it all sounds pretty relaxing. But, then again, Kennedy wasn't yet in the Oval Office or facing off with Khrushchev over missiles in Cuba. That was all yet to come.

JFK'S TRUE INTOXICANT

Journalist Joseph Alsop remembered JFK's arrival at Alsop's Georgetown apartment a few hours after midnight—snow drifting down in flakes as if heaven-sent confetti—following his inauguration ceremony. The good host offered the new president a bowl of Maryland terrapin (a much-coveted dish in George Washington's era) and, of course, a glass of champagne.

> He took the wine but needed no more than a glance to reject what had formerly been the greatest delicacy of the United States.
>
> It hardly mattered. I soon observed that what he really wanted was one last cup of unadulterated admiration, and the people crowded around gave him that cup freely, filled to the brim.

NOT YOUR AVERAGE JOE

Kennedy patriarch Joseph Kennedy was worth millions, and much of that fortune was the result of shrewd setups he arranged on the eve of FDR's move to end Prohibition.

Joe Kennedy (who also made money in other ways, including in banking, on Wall Street, and in the film industry) was appointed by FDR to be U.S. ambassador to England in 1933. Kennedy used some of his connections—including FDR's son, James Roosevelt—to line up contracts and warehousing for massive amounts of high-quality scotch and gin in Great Britain. When liquor was once again legal in the United States, few people were in a better position to capitalize on that change of events than Joe Kennedy.

It would be an understatement to say that not everybody was a Joe Kennedy fan. (As ambassador to England, for example, he predicted that Hitler and the Nazis would prevail over the British.)

One non-fan was Harry Truman. Truman preferred bourbon and would always choose that drink over scotch whisky. Once asked why, Truman quipped something like: "You know, every time you drink a glass of scotch you put another quarter in Joe Kennedy's pocket!"

THE JFK BEER TAX

Although he had access to millions (and, as president, could direct billions with a stroke of a pen), some staffers in JFK's inner circle were sometimes perplexed that the president often had no money in his pocket. In fact, he sometimes would borrow ten dollars from White House staffers if he needed a haircut.

And there was never any change. JFK justified this by joking that it would even out the score for all the times his entourage had raided the president's beer supply.

A STAKE THROUGH THE "DRY" HEART

Although the Kennedy White House had sophisticated tastes—with French cuisine and French wine often front and center—advocates of temperance tried to make a "last stand" of sorts. They wanted to at least keep hard liquor out of the equation for White House events. As the late journalist Helen Thomas wrote in her autobiography *Front Row at the White House*:

> It was held in the State Dining Room where open bars had been set up. In addition, butlers circulated through the rooms with trays of champagne and mixed drinks.
>
> The stories that appeared about the open bar unleashed a furor as certain parts of the country and one group in particular, the Women's Christian Temperance Union (WCTU) weighed in with their outrage. The first couple abandoned the practice, but later on it was quietly resumed, and during such functions, one could walk up to a strategically placed bar for a drink. It's hard to believe in this day and age that something like an open bar would prompt

such a backlash—and the practice became White House routine over time.

One thing was apparent: The old-fashioned frumpiness of the Woman's Christian Temperance Union was no match for the youthful, dashing elegance of the Kennedy White House.

JFK SHAKES IT UP: THE CHAMPAGNE TWIST

The former *Washington Post* managing editor Ben Bradlee had a close-but-sometimes-awkward relationship with JFK. On one hand, Bradlee and the president often attended the same dinners and cocktail parties; but JFK (despite the fact that the *Post* had endorsed him over Nixon) was nevertheless wary about what Bradlee printed, or might print. As far as JFK's drinking, Bradlee waited until 1975 when he published *Conversations with Kennedy* to mention much about it, noting that he really only saw JFK "tight" one time and that was after a very small dinner (sans Jackie, but with her younger socialite sister Lee Radziwill) at the White House.

> … after dinner Lee Radziwill put Chubby Checker's records on and gave all the men lessons. The champagne was flowing like the Potomac in flood, and the president himself was opening bottle after bottle in a manner that sent the foam flying over the furniture, shouting "Look at Bill go" to Walton, or "Look at Benji go" to me, as we practiced with "the princess."

Bradlee, however, admitted that the "champagne twist" incident was an unusual "one off" for the president. More typically, JFK nursed a scotch and water, sipped his wine at dinner, and rarely indulged in a drink during the day.

FLYING HIGH ON AIR FORCE ONE

Since Kennedy had an easygoing personality (particularly compared to his brother, Attorney General Robert Kennedy), it is not that surprising that he allowed his White House staff to imbibe when traveling. The food on Air Force One even had a regional slant in that New England clam chowder was often on hand.

Drinks onboard included gin, scotch whisky, beer (JFK enjoyed Heinekens), wine, and the ever-present daiquiris. The president himself—true to form—rarely drank more than one or two. He did not chide others for drinking more, but sometimes just the hint of a disapproving look might bring an overly festive passenger to back off slightly.

As noted in Kenneth T. Walsh's book *Air Force One*, Robert Kennedy also brought his rambunctious black Labrador onboard. One can picture the Lab causing a commotion by prancing round the cabin, whipping his tail about, and poking his nose wherever he pleased. The flight staff solved this problem by treating the canine to a martini, and he soon curled up for a nap.

Air Force One, of course, would become the backdrop for the terrible aftermath of JFK's assassination in Dallas. In a futile attempt to dull the shock and pain, aides of the slain president (his casket onboard and Vice President Johnson waiting to be sworn in) broke out the scotch whisky. But as one of them said, even several glasses could not budge them from stone-cold soberness and the horrible reality—Jack Kennedy was dead.

It was hardly much better for those close to Kennedy who learned of it secondhand. As Schlesinger recorded in his November 23, 1963, journal entry:

> I heard the terrible news as I was sipping cocktails with Kay Graham, Ken Galbraith and the editors of *Newsweek*.... A man entered in his shirtsleeves and said, a little tentatively, "I think you should know that the President has been shot in the head in Texas." It took a few seconds for this to register. Then we all rushed for the radio.

THE KENNEDY CURSE

The assassination of Jack and, later, Robert Kennedy, prompted the notion of the so-called "Kennedy Curse." Edward "Ted" Kennedy's 1969

Chappaquiddick car crash (which resulted in the drowning death of Mary Jo Kopechne and was rumored to have been alcohol-fueled) only reinforced the theory.

As a senator, Ted Kennedy had a reputation for heavy drinking. A *Washington Post* feature in 1990 portrayed the Massachusetts senator like this:

> Tales of his drinking and raffish behavior have become part of his public persona, often lumped under a vaster damnation known as "the character issue."

JACKIE'S DAIQUIRIS

Keeping in mind that Jacqueline Kennedy's favorite drink was French champagne—and not just *any* champagne but Veuve Clicquot (with historical hindsight, something of a morbid irony since this premium vintage from Reims is named for a nineteenth-century French widow) served in an elegant flute glass, she also would occasionally kick back with a daiquiri. The Kennedys particularly liked to serve daiquiris during summer get-togethers at their Cape Cod compound.

Here is a surprisingly simple recipe that Jackie Kennedy reportedly posted for her kitchen staffers to follow:

Jackie's Daiquiri

Ingredients:

2 parts rum
2 parts frozen limeade
1 part fresh lime juice
    dash of Falernum (a sweet syrup, 2 or 3 drops max, depending on how "tart" you want them)

Blend all the ingredients together and enjoy!

LAST CALL

The Kennedy White House was a "happening" place, and countless celebrities were invited to dinners there. Schlesinger relates the funny story of the famed composer Igor Stravinsky, who was invited to a White House dinner in his honor.

Schlesinger went over to talk to him, and Stravinsky implored him to lean closer so that he could whisper in Schlesinger's ear. "When I did," Schlesinger wrote, "he said, with a smile of great content on his face, 'I am drunk.'"

CHAPTER 35

Lyndon Baines Johnson

(1908–1973)

yndon Baines Johnson loyalists will point to the tall (six feet three inches or so, second only to Honest Abe in presidential height) Texan's efforts to advance civil rights and the enactment of the Great Society and the War on Poverty as his greatest achievements. The Vietnam War, inherited from John F. Kennedy and expanded by the thirty-sixth president (1963–1969), led to LBJ's personal and political downfall and certainly played a major role in his decision not to seek a second term in 1968. "That bitch of a war...." was how he occasionally referred to it.

Regardless of his standing in history, it would be extremely difficult to defend LBJ's personal conduct. LBJ could turn on the Texas charm when necessary, but it did not take much to flip his switch. As one newsman put it: "He'd call you in, give you whiskey, and joke with you. But he was a mean SOB, too."

Lyndon Baines Johnson, in fact, is arguably the crudest U.S. president in history, and probably by a wide margin. To take just one example, he had no qualms about urinating in front of others when nature called. That alcohol served as an accelerant to some of LBJ's gross and belligerent endeavors is without question.

DRINKIN' AND DRIVIN' IS SO MUCH FUN

LBJ was long deceased when the British rock band The Business came out with the outrageously inappropriate tune: "Drinking and Driving"—but he might have smiled at the title.

Johnson died in 1973, a victim of the "Four Horsemen" of horrendous health habits—drinking (scotch and beer, primarily), smoking (although he sometimes quit for long stretches, LBJ loved smoking so much that he once told a doctor he would rather "have my pecker cut off" than quit), far too much food (often wolfed down so he could get back to work), and virtually no exercise of value (some occasional rounds of golf played poorly). After at least his third heart attack, the former president died at the relatively young age of sixty-four—but he looked at least a decade older.

Nevertheless, Johnson would have understood what The Business was ... well ... *driving* at. Johnson apparently loved to drink and drive (at high speeds, too) and obviously relished terrorizing anybody unsuspecting enough to jump into his Lincoln Continental and tour his "spread"—the president's sprawling Texas ranch near Stonewall.

Time magazine ran a story in April 1964 (titled: "The Presidency: Mr. President, You're Fun") that documented one such episode. Johnson loaded four journalists (LBJ biographer Robert Dalleck referred to it as treating the Washington press corps to some "Texas-style drinking and driving") into his Lincoln—under the usual pretense of touring the ranch—and soon had the Lincoln blasting away at full throttle. As the *Time* story told it:

> A cream-colored Lincoln Continental driven by the President of the United States flashed up a long Texas hill, swung into the left lane to pass two cars poking along under 85 miles per hour, and thundered on over the crest of the hill—squarely

into the path of an oncoming car. The President charged on, his cup of Pearl beer within easy sipping distance. The other motorist veered off the paved surface to safety on the road's shoulder. Groaned a passenger in the President's car when the ride was over: "That's the closest John McCormack has come to the White House yet."

McCormack was speaker of the House and thus second in line to the presidency had LBJ rolled his barreling Lincoln—spilling both Pearl beer and Texas blood in the process. The idea of a fatal crash did not seem entirely far-fetched. When Johnson finished his own beer, he helped himself to some of a female reporter's (Marinna Means, who gushed: "Mister President, you're fun!"—thus providing the title for the piece) and then took off at high speeds to go get more.

At one point, one of the "lucky" press corps passengers along for this grand adventure glanced over at the speedometer and noticed that the needle was flirting with ninety miles per hour. LBJ—like the master magician he could be in the political arena—responded by placing his cowboy hat over the speedometer so nobody could see how fast they were rollicking around the ranch roads.

Perhaps the riders in LBJ's Lincoln displayed needless apprehension: Johnson was an old hand at drinkin' and drivin', dating back to his pre-presidential days. According to Robert Caro—Johnson's most prolific biographer—LBJ drove a flashy yellow Buick in 1932, when he was a congressional secretary. According to Caro's *The Path to Power*, Johnson enjoyed driving people around in it, providing refreshment:

> Loading them into the Buick, he drove them around, pulled out a bottle of whiskey, bragging about famous people that he knew.

Another trick LBJ sometimes enjoyed in his later years was driving unsuspecting passengers right into a lake on his ranch. As the vehicle careened downhill toward the body of water, LBJ would bellow that the brakes weren't working! But Johnson—as he had often done as a highly skilled politician—had access to the "inside" information; in this case, that the car was a specialized amphibious vehicle.

STEP IT UP

Being on LBJ's Secret Service detail was no easy task and required at least one duty that the agents had not previously trained for: "running bartender."

When Johnson would tour his ranch, he would sometimes drive his Lincoln while the agents charged with his protection trailed a little bit behind in a station wagon. Since LBJ occasionally enjoyed a scotch or two on these tours—and would sometimes require a refill—it was the additional duty of the Secret Service men to see that he got it.

LBJ would cut off the agents by stopping his Lincoln, putting his arm out the window, and rattling the diminishing ice cubes in his plastic foam cup. An agent would then scurry up from the trail car, trot back to the car, make the president another scotch, soda, and ice, then hasten it back to the thirsty commander in chief.

THE THREE-SAM SLAM

Three men named Sam played key roles in Lyndon Johnson's life— and all three were well acquainted with alcohol.

Lyndon's father—Sam Ealy Johnson Junior—was a colorful politician from the Texas Hill Country (a large expanse of land rolling west of Austin). He bucked the forces of Prohibition in the 1920s—a stand that proved as popular as beer and pretzels with the German-American and Czech-American constituents in his district.

But Sam Johnson failed to make any lasting mark in the political rodeo ring, and, later in life, he overindulged in drinking and displayed periodic bouts of drunkenness. Sam Johnson also lost the family farm after cotton prices tumbled in the early 1920s. That experience seems to have left LBJ with some lasting empathy for the poor and disenfranchised.

A second "Sam"—Sam Rayburn—also helped guide Lyndon's career. Rayburn was famous for his "Board of Education" room at the

Capitol where members of Congress (even some opposition Republicans) gathered for a belt or two after a long day at the political grindstone.

Rayburn, the speaker of the House, allegedly pressured a freshman congressman to vote along with the Democrats. The political newbie squirmed and mumbled something about not wishing to disappoint his major contributors, who wanted him to vote the other way. "Son," Rayburn supposedly pontificated, "if you can't take their money, drink their whiskey, screw their women, and then vote against 'em, you don't deserve to be here."

Rayburn did not immediately admit LBJ—despite the fact he was a fellow Texan—into his sanctuary. But once he did, the two men became close—almost like father and son, according to various Johnson aides. In addition to an ample supply of whiskey and "branch water," the "Board of Education" room had history. It was here that then vice president Harry S. Truman mixed an afternoon drink and then—before he could even enjoy it—got the call that summoned him to the White House, where he received the stunning news that Franklin Delano Roosevelt was dead and *he* would ascend to the presidency.

The third "Sam" was Sam Houston Johnson—LBJ's younger brother. It may have been a jinxed name choice from the get-go, since the original Sam Houston—the hero of the Battle of San Jacinto and the first president of the Republic of Texas—brawled with John Barleycorn for much of his life. (The Indians sometimes called Houston "Big Drunk"—the latter referring to both his size and the amount of alcohol he could consume.)

Sam Houston Johnson also had alcohol problems, and they tended to sabotage his fragile relationship with Lyndon and his wife, Lady Bird. When LBJ was a fast-rising congressman, Sam would crash at their Washington, D.C., apartment. Both Lady Bird Johnson and SHJ himself (in his book *My Brother Lyndon*) documented an uncomfortable incident involving the two men. LBJ apparently drank too much at a rain-soaked golf outing and arrived home (soaked, in all meanings of that word) to find Sam (once again) asleep on his apartment couch. LBJ then proceeded to—in today's parlance—"get in his face." As Jan J. Russell noted in her biography *Lady Bird*:

> Lady Bird woke up to the sound of Lyndon yelling at his brother. "I want Sam Houston to look at me," he told her. "Yes, by God, I want you to take a damned good look at me. I'm drunk, and I want you to see how you look to me, Sam Houston, when you come home drunk."

Although she was far from a Sam Houston fan, Lady Bird eventually had to step in and calm down her irate husband.

ALCOHOL AS A VOTING LUBRICANT

Like George Washington, Andrew Jackson, and William Henry Harrison—to name just a few—Johnson had no qualms about dispensing alcohol on the campaign trail. While running for Congress in 1937, Johnson rolled out the barrel—beer, to be exact—to quench the thirst of potential voters, particularly in some counties of his district where there were significant numbers of voters of German and Czech ancestry.

While young George Washington paid a rather hefty sum for the alcohol he supplied to ply voters in his House of Burgesses election, Johnson went the father of our country one better. According to Randall Woods (author of *LBJ: Architect of American Ambition*), the wily Texan somehow got Anheuser-Busch to provide *free* beer for his campaign. Anheuser-Busch (the company that makes Budweiser) already had a solid connection to the Democratic Party, since the brewers sent Franklin Delano Roosevelt some free Bud for his role in repealing Prohibition—pulled down Pennsylvania Avenue by hardworking Clydesdales nonetheless.

JOHNSON IN CONTROL

Johnson was famous for drinking the soft drink Fresca in the White House during working hours, but LBJ did not hesitate to bring out the hard stuff (typically, Cutty Sark scotch for himself) when he was attempting to rally support for a bill he wanted passed.

Johnson sometimes walked around with a scotch and soda in his hand, but his staff was under strict orders to keep his on the weak side. Not so with other guests, and it did not take long for the president to work this to his political advantage.

A prime example was presented in Joseph Califano Jr.'s book *The Triumph and Tragedy of Lyndon Johnson*, as the author (special assistant to Johnson starting in 1965) revealed that LBJ might have a very weak scotch, while Republican Senator Everett Dirksen would be treated to his favorite—Jack Daniel's bourbon—but with perhaps three times as much whiskey. A visitor, then, might be under the false assumption that he was matching LBJ drink for drink but was, in fact, consuming three times as much as his bigger—and craftier—host.

DR. LBJ: BOOZE, BEEFSTEAK, AND BABES

Everett Dirksen was a powerful Republican senator from Illinois, but Johnson—both as a fellow congressman and later as president— sometimes teamed up with him for bipartisan causes. For example, LBJ was able to convince Dirksen that he should support civil rights legislation, reminding Dirksen that the senator was from the Great Emancipator's home state.

Not surprisingly, some of these deals and compromises were hashed out over a bottle of bourbon or scotch.

When Dirksen (who supposedly once quipped that "champagne was his vegetable") was hospitalized with a bleeding ulcer in February of 1964, LBJ was quick to phone in some humorous support and some Texas-styled medical advice. Thanks to taped White House telephone conversations (released in the 1990s), we know the conversation flowed exactly like this:

> LBJ: How're you feelin'?
> Dirksen: Well, I'm doing pretty good. That ulcer hit me last night about midnight.
> LBJ: You quit drinking that damned Sanka and get on a good Scotch whiskey [sic] once in a while!

Dirksen: You got a point there.

LBJ: ... What you need to do is go out and get you about three half glasses of Bourbon whiskey. Then go down to the Occidental (a Washington, D.C., restaurant) and buy a red beefsteak, and then get you a woman. So maybe that's what you need. Instead of drinking Sanka.

Dirksen: (chuckles) You've got an idea.

THE JOHNSON TREATMENT

Avid readers of LBJ biographies or articles have probably encountered the phrase "The Johnson Treatment."

For those unacquainted with the term, the Johnson Treatment occurred when LBJ approached someone, got disconcertingly close to his face (regardless of lunch, cigarettes, scotch, or whatever else might have been lingering on LBJ's breath), and then "persuaded" (profanely, if necessary) him to his own way of thinking.

As Hubert Humphrey noted in his oral history for the LBJ Presidential Library:

> Johnson got votes by whispering in ears and pulling lapels, and nose to nose.... He'd just lean right in on you, you know.... He was so big and tall he'd be kind of looking down on you ... pulling on your lapels and he'd be grabbing you.... Even if he wasn't asking you to vote for something, he'd be talking about the bill in such a way that you knew what he had in mind.

And keep in mind that Humphrey (who became LBJ's vice-presidential candidate in 1964) was almost always on Johnson's side. One can only imagine the full brunt of the Johnson Treatment concentrated upon a perceived enemy.

WOULD YOU LAHK TA DANCE?

The Johnson Treatment became even weirder when LBJ happened to have knocked down a few drinks.

The journalist Robert Novak was once treated (if that is the right word) to just such a strange spectacle. Back in early 1960, when Johnson was still a U.S. senator, Novak and fellow journalist Bob Jensen of the *Buffalo Evening News* were enjoying a drink at the National Press Club bar. The men were (if journalists in the capital ever really can be) "off duty." But their R&R was soon interrupted when someone barged into the bar and announced that Lyndon Johnson was in the adjacent ballroom and apparently "drunk as a loon."

The lure of this possibility was too much, and Novak hustled next door, where he found LBJ exuberantly intoxicated. As Novak related in his book *The Prince of Darkness*:

> The report was not exaggerated. Johnson was attending the 70th birthday party of Bascom Timmons, a famous Texas journalist who headed his own Washington news bureau. To my surprise, I found the majority leader without aides or limo. LBJ, until then, had shown little interest in me and absolutely no affection, spotted me and wrapped one of his long arms around me. "Bob, I like ("lahk" was the Texas pronunciation) you," he drawled drunkenly, "but you don't like me." He chanted it over and over, embracing me and swirling me in a little dance.

Novak observed that the rest of the revelers at the party seemed equally incapacitated by drink. So the journalists felt compelled to assist LBJ and—not without effort or charity—guided the big Texan down to the street and dumped him into a homeward-bound taxi.

LBJ'S SWITCHEROO

Did the future president thank Novak the next time he saw him? He did not. But he did mention the incident.

Novak was among reporters who approached "a cool immaculately groomed" Senator Johnson the next day, hoping to get a few minutes of Q&A before the Senate kicked off official business. Johnson looked up, perhaps feigning surprise at the reporters around him, but quickly singled out Novak and, as the journalist later wrote, said:

> "Well, Novak, saw you at the Press Club last night. Got a little drunk out, didn't it?"
>
> The other reporters chuckled appreciatively, thinking it was I who had been "a little drunk," as LBJ intended.

LAST CALL

LBJ had surprising success with getting most of his favorite legislation through Congress. The key, according to LBJ, was to gradually introduce bills. He once explained it like this to Joseph Califano:

"Congress is like a whiskey drinker. You can put an awful lot of whiskey into a man if you just let him sip it. But if you try to force the whole bottle down his throat at one time, he'll throw it up."

CHAPTER 36

Richard Milhous Nixon

(1913–1994)

*I*n November 1962, Richard Nixon—having been soundly thrashed in the race for the California governorship—delivered one of his most famous lines. Insinuating that a predatory press was at least partly responsible for his defeat, Nixon addressed reporters through a tight smile and ended with a promise: "You won't have Nixon to kick around anymore, because, gentlemen, this is my last press conference...."

As fate would have it, Nixon was wrong on both counts. It was far from Nixon's last press conference. And, five decades later, Nixon continues to be "kicked around"—if anything, with increased vigor. David Fulsom's 2012 book *Nixon's Darkest Secrets* is particularly brutal and includes a chapter titled: "The World's Most Powerful Drunk."

Alcohol certainly played a role in Nixon's worst moments—especially during the 1972 Watergate scandal and his eventual resignation (the only president to resign from office) in 1974. But alcohol also was hoisted on those rare triumphant occasions—such as Nixon's trip to China.

The stresses of being president (1969–1974) in general, and the added burden of Watergate in particular, plus the fact that Nixon reached a state of intoxication quite rapidly, combined to produce some interesting—some might even say scary—anecdotes involving Richard M. Nixon and Demon Alcohol.

THIS WINE IS MINE

Nixon lived up to his nickname, "Tricky Dick," when serving wine at his White House dinners.

The thirty-seventh president of the United States certainly knew—and relished—wines from the world's most renowned cellars. In fact, Nixon often had his wine glass filled with a fine French vintage, a 1957 Château Lafite Rothschild.

His guests, however, were typically given a decent (but far less expensive) wine—and the waiters were instructed to serve it with a towel wrapped around the bottle so as to hide the label.

In some circles, this sly practice—serving a mediocre brand of booze to others while saving the top-shelf stuff for oneself—has been dubbed "pulling a Nixon."

MAOTAI MOMENTS

From World War II on, virtually all U.S. presidents had to—at one point or another—deal with either Russian vodka or the potent Chinese liquor called *maotai*. It would not be inaccurate to say that drinking these powerful alcohols "came with the territory" because international protocol often mandated partaking in toasts, even if they amounted to little more than "sorority sips."

Richard Nixon drank vodka with the Russian leaders and, more famously, maotai with the Chinese. Maotai is an extremely potent (typically about 110 proof) alcohol, distilled from sorghum. TV journalist Dan Rather—with maybe only slight exaggeration—once compared the consumption of this traditional Chinese libation to "drinking liquid razor blades."

Perhaps the major triumph of the Nixon White House occurred in February 1972 when the administration visited the People's Republic of China. One of the strategic goals of this historic tour to Peking (particularly surprising from Nixon, who—in his younger days postulated on the great evils of communism) was to keep the Soviets "honest" by, at least in appearance, cozying up to the Chinese. As Dr. Henry Kissinger—Nixon's secretary of state—tellingly put it, the U.S. might be able to "have its Russian vodka and its *maotai*, too." (In less cryptic language, Kissinger allowed that a friendly visit to China might establish more "equilibrium" in the world.)

Knowing that there was bound to be some toasting between U.S. officials (and accompanying journalists) and their Chinese counterparts, General Alexander Haig (Nixon's chief of staff) sent forth a cable warning against the mind-numbing properties of the infamous maotai. (Haig knew of what he spoke because he had jousted with the formidable liquid on an advance trip to the Chinese capital just the month before.) Haig's memo all but came with a blinking red light and beeping warning signal—and the gist of it no doubt took into account that Nixon was a notorious lightweight when it came to handling much more modest amounts of alcohol than the legendary maotai would bring to the table.

Haig's cable read: "UNDER NO ... REPEAT ... NO CIRCUM-STANCES SHOULD THE PRESIDENT ACTUALLY DRINK FROM HIS GLASS IN RESPONSE TO BANQUET TOAST.

Nixon rose to the occasion. After toasts with Chinese premier Chou En-lai, the president approached each table and (taking small sips!) toasted all of the important banquet participants. Somewhat surprisingly, the chief executive managed to stay—or at least appear to stay—sober throughout the festivities.

As a bonus, Chou En-lai playfully demonstrated just how powerful maotai could be. Chou put a match to a cup of the volatile liquid and announced: "Mr. Nixon, please take a look. It can indeed catch fire!"

BURNING DOWN THE HOUSE

The band Talking Heads formed just about the same time Nixon was drummed out of the White House. But perhaps the band's hit song "Burning Down the House" (which was released in the 1980s) conjured up a smile among those privy to one particular Nixon episode.

The story, once again, involves maotai. According to some accounts, Nixon attempted to duplicate Chou En-lai's fight-fire-with-fire demonstration at the Peking banquet—only this time in the White House dining room.

Although it seems wise to allow some leeway for embellishment, Henry Kissinger recounted the incident in a welcoming toast to Vice Premier Deng Xiaoping, when the Chinese leader visited the United States on April 14, 1974. The toast was offered at a dinner held at New York City's swanky Waldorf-Astoria and unfolded like this:

> Henry Kissinger: I think if we drink enough *maotai* we can solve anything.
>
> Deng Xiaoping: Then when I go back to China, I must increase production of it.
>
> HK: You know, when the President came back from China, he wanted to show his daughter how potent *maotai* was. So he took out a bottle and poured it into a saucer and lit it, but the glass bowl broke and the *maotai* ran over the table and the table began to burn! So you nearly burned down the White House!

Whereupon, Kissinger lifted his glass to all the guests and they drank to Nixon's alleged mishap.

DRUNK DIALING

If the tale of Nixon and an almost-flaming White House was fueled by good-natured exaggeration, the fact that his administration was—at least in the figurative sense—about to implode was not; the Watergate scandal was about to take him—and many of his top men—down.

As federal investigators began to close in, the president weirdly indulged in some "drunk-dialing" incidents.

Nixon's slurred speech is quite apparent on the Watergate-era tapes. But the president's strange actions are also well documented by some of his trusted inner circle—including John Ehrlichman (domestic council chief), who witnessed an intoxicated Nixon's late-night rambling over the phone lines. Apparently, the beleaguered president stooped to such actions in an attempt to measure the levels of loyalty of others or to have them understand the weight of his Watergate woes.

One frequent late night target was the lawyer Leonard Garment, who served as White House counsel and as a special consultant on various projects. Concerning Nixon's late night phone calls, Ehrlichman would recall:

> He (Nixon) would talk to political people. Then for the last call, he'd say: "Get me Len." By that time we would have given him his Seconal (a sleeping pill) and a good stiff single malt scotch. And he'd get on the phone with [Garment] until the phone dropped from his fingers and he fell asleep. Then I'd pick up the phone very quietly, and hang up.

LONDON CALLING

If Nixon was guilty of sometimes phoning others while under the influence, on at least one important occasion he also was incapacitated to an extent that he wasn't able (at least in the opinion of his staff) to field an important call from British prime minister Edward Heath.

On October 11, 1973, Heath attempted to contact Nixon to discuss the outbreak of hostilities between Israel and the Arabs—but the talk had to be postponed. When Brent Scowcroft (Henry Kissinger's assistant) called to alert the White House that Heath was eager to discuss the situation, a hesitant Kissinger replied: "Can we tell them no? When I talked to the president, he was loaded."

Did Scowcroft answer: "What! The president's loaded?!"?

No, he did not.

Seemingly unsurprised, Scowcroft, rather nonchalantly, answered: "Right. OK. I will say the president won't be available until the first thing in the morning. . . ."

THE CHINA TOAST

Not all of Nixon's drinking stories are negative ones. After successfully reestablishing ties with China and gaining the go-ahead to visit that country with an official message from Chou En-lai, Nixon was understandably quite jubilant. Nixon proudly included this one (toasting his then chief of staff Henry Kissinger in the Lincoln Sitting Room at the White House) in his memoirs:

> In one of the cabinets I found an unopened bottle of very old Courvosier [sic] brandy that someone had given us for Christmas. I tucked it under my arm and took two large snifters from the glass cupboard. As we raised our glasses, I said: "Henry, we are drinking a toast not to ourselves personally or to our success, or to our administration's policies which have made this message and made tonight possible. Let us drink to generations to come who may have a better chance to live in peace because of what we have done."

As it turned out, some three years later, the same bottle of brandy was called upon. Nixon asked Kissinger (his recently named secretary of state in 1973) to have a drink with him (and then to join him in prayer) on a dramatically more somber occasion: Richard Milhous Nixon's resignation.

THE CHINA (SLOSHED) SYNDROME

While Nixon was relatively well behaved at official banquets during the China visit, he apparently went over the edge at a plush high-rise hotel in Shanghai on his last night in the country. As the historian Robert

Dalleck related in a 2007 interview with PBS (in regards to his book, *Partners in Power: Nixon and Kissinger*):

> Nixon was drinking all afternoon, Mao-ties, and he was pretty well sloshed.... At 2:00 in the morning, he called [Bob] Haldeman and Kissinger to his suite and he almost begs them to assure him that this is going to be a great success, that the press isn't going to blight this achievement. And Kissinger writes later in his memoirs about this lonely, almost desperate man. And there's something very sad about him.

The press, for the most part, applauded Nixon's diplomatic trip to China. But the Watergate break-in was just a few months away, and Nixon's finest hour was fading fast.

THE ELUSIVE DR. K

It is difficult to pin down *exactly* how the brilliant Dr. Henry Kissinger (named Nixon's security advisor in 1969 and, by the time of Nixon's resignation, his secretary of state) felt about Nixon and, for that matter, the extent of Nixon's drinking.

Kissinger is on the record as saying stories of Nixon drinking himself into a useless stupor were "absurd." But he also notes that two glasses of wine might result in Nixon slurring his words or becoming either overly sentimental or, conversely, combative or vulgar. In fact, behind the president's back, Kissinger sometimes referred to Nixon as "our drunken friend" to other staff members.

Then again, Nixon was not always polite to Kissinger. He sometimes made snide, anti-Semitic remarks in front of Kissinger and behind his back to others.

GOOD QUESTION

Just ten months after his resignation, Nixon was brought before a grand jury and made to listen to a slew of tapes from the Watergate days.

On more than a couple of tapes, it is quite obvious that Nixon was slurring his words. To which the former president could not help muttering: "I wonder what I had to drink that day?"

A good question indeed! (And "how much"?)

Like James Buchanan, Nixon liked many kinds of alcohol, though he was very much lacking in Old Buck's much-vaunted tolerance.

Nixon certainly drank various rum concoctions (particularly when he hobnobbed with tycoon Bebe Rebozo in Florida), top-shelf wines and champagnes, dry martinis, vodka, scotch, brandy, and, of course, the famous Chinese maotai.

MIXIN' A NIXON

Belfast-born Joe Gilmore, the highly touted (and creative) mixologist at the American Bar in London's Savoy Hotel, made many a cocktail in honor of celebrities. Keep in mind that Nixon was coming off his 1968 election victory over Hubert Humphrey and third-party "Deep South" candidate George Wallace. Watergate was far in the future, and Nixon was riding high. In honor of the president's 1969 visit to Britain, Gilmore whipped up this concoction dubbed:

The Nixon

Ingredients:

1 part bourbon whiskey
1 part sloe gin
2 dashes of peach bitters

Stir and then serve "on the rocks" with a garnish.

Going with the "If Mohammed won't come to the mountain, move the mountain to Mohammed" theory, Gilmore mixed the drink at the American Bar but then sent it over to the Claridge Hotel, where the president and his entourage were staying. There is no proof that Nixon actually drank "The Nixon"—but how many people can claim that the famous bartender Gilmore created a drink in their honor?

LAST CALL

Richard Nixon may have displayed alcohol issues as early as 1959. On a trip to Moscow for the so-called "Kitchen Debates," then vice president Nixon reportedly downed half a dozen vodka martinis and uttered some vulgarities.

A California Angels fan, Nixon was invited into the clubhouse after that team won its first divisional playoff title in 1979. The Angels were in the full flight of festivities when second baseman Bobby Grich famously poured a full beer on the former president's head.

CHAPTER 37

Gerald Ford

(1913–2006)

*Y*ou could argue that Gerald "Jerry" Ford was dealt less than an ideal hand when he was called upon by bizarre circumstances to replace a disgraced Spiro Agnew as vice president and then to finish out Richard Nixon's disastrous Watergate-shortened term as the thirty-eighth president of the United States (1974–1977). Some felt Ford wasn't intelligent enough to be president. Lyndon Johnson claimed—with typical mean-spiritedness—that Ford must have played too much football without a helmet. But perhaps a modest mind is precisely what those troubled times called for.

Born Leslie King Jr., the future president changed to his stepfather's name of Ford when he was still a boy. His biological father was an alcoholic who physically abused Ford's mother—the primary reason she divorced King and remarried.

Like most U.S. congressmen, Jerry Ford found daily drinks just part of the Washington terrain—no big deal. When he stepped up to the White House after Nixon's resignation, however, Ford suddenly needed to downshift to a slightly less liquid routine—a change that took longer than expected and was not without a few amusing miscues.

That Betty Ford, the first lady, had serious issues with alcohol and drug abuse is widely documented. By most accounts she is given high marks for not only facing up to her own demons and conversing candidly about them, but also helping others in similar predicaments through the renowned efforts of the Betty Ford Center.

THE MIGHTY MARTINI

Jerry Ford was a tenacious football letter–winner at Michigan in the 1930s and helped take the Wolverines to two national titles. In an era when the best athletes on the field still played "both ways," Ford starred at center and also performed at linebacker. He knocked heads with some of the best collegiate players of his era.

Ford the politician, however, had trouble holding his own when he went head-to-head with the small-but-mighty martini. Already accused of being clumsy (his occasional trips and tumbles drew attention from *Saturday Night Live*, providing ample fodder for comedian Chevy Chase) and as a terror to a cringing gallery when he whacked golf balls into the crowd, these tongue-tying concoctions (of which he was admittedly quite fond) did nothing to dispel accusations that Ford was less than articulate.

But to give Ford the benefit of the doubt, there is no proof that these clumsy-oafish incidents were alcohol-related—though both he and the first lady drank routinely on Air Force One, and some of his untimely trips *did* occur while getting on and off the aircraft.

And on at least one occasion alcohol was identified as the culprit behind a less than stellar speech. As veteran journalist Bob Woodward chronicled in *Shadow: Five Presidents and the Legacy of Watergate*.

> Ford was unaccustomed to the high level of scrutiny. He was used to the Congressional lifestyle, which often included alcohol at lunch. This habit proved particularly embarrassing for Ford when he gave a luncheon speech. Once, in Denver, he skipped several dozen pages of his remarks because he had

what his aides called a few "marts" (for martinis), before speaking.

WHAT'S UP, DOC?

To diffuse the ongoing issue of the proper roll of the martini in the chief executive's daily routine, William Lukash—the White House physician and a navy admiral— confronted Ford with some blunt advice. In Woodward's account, Lukash firmly stated: "You're President of the United States. Stop drinking. Especially stop drinking martinis at lunch."

Ford had his own special "humor writer"—a man by the name of Don Penny. Penny's job was to help Ford weave some jokes into his speeches, but he, too, felt the president's fondness for a potent martini or two at midday was no laughing matter. After Ford mispronounced some words in a speech, Penny—after confirming that martinis were part of the problem—also approached Ford about it.

Ford eventually heard from enough advisors, got the message, and cut back on his lunchtime libations. But it did not stop Ford from vigorously defending that fine drink when President Carter later tried to tax the well-entrenched "three-martini lunch."

PARDONS AND PEANUTS

Can anyone blame Jerry Ford if he downed a few stiff ones before (and after) he made the decision to pardon Richard Milhous Nixon?

Ford called the controversial pardon "the end of our national nightmare," but there are those who also believe it seriously hurt his election chances against Jimmy Carter in 1976. Certainly ultra-conservative Joseph Coors—owner of the esteemed Coors brewery in Colorado—thought so, and put his support and money behind Ronald Reagan, albeit unsuccessfully, in the Republican primaries.

The Democrats made the Nixon pardon part of their attack plan, of course, and Jimmy Carter prevailed. Martinis, once again, emerged as a gremlin in the Ford campaign. Ford—trying to suggest that Carter would diminish America's military might—liked to riff off the famous and much-quoted Teddy Roosevelt catchphrase of "Speak softly, and carry a big stick." He would then follow TR's line with: "Jimmy Carter says, 'Speak softly, and carry a flyswatter....'"

But as Thomas DeFrank (a Ford aide and eventual biographer) noted in his book *Write It When I'm Gone*:

> At one torchlight rally at the end of a long day and after a couple of martinis, it took Ford three times to nail the punch line: "Speak softly, and carry a flywasher ... flyspotter ... flyswatter."

MISTER PEANUT PREVAILS

Ford—former star athlete and congressional heavyweight—had trouble accepting that the American people had chosen the former peanut farmer over him. (According to one story, a frustrated Ford once blurted out that Carter was an "SOB.") Along the same lines, Ford's outgoing staff (having served less than three years in the White House) also proved to be less than good sports. The fact that some of Carter's advance staffers began to move into the White House early drove home the point of the political sword. Ford had lost—and they were out of a job in arguably the most important city in the world. As Ford's press secretary Ron Nessen later admitted:

> On Ford's last night in the White House, I and my press office staff, all feeling sad, gave ourselves a farewell party. First we downed several bottles of champagne purchased for the occasion. When that was gone, we drank all the liquor we could find in cabinets and closets. And when that was gone, we even consumed an old bottle of fizzy white wine brought home from a Ford visit to Romania. We dimmed the lights to match our mood.

When some members of the Ford team (including the former president and Betty) left the White House for California the next day, it was said that everyone onboard a backup plane (Carter did not grant permission for them to use Air Force One) refused to eat the peanuts from an offering of mixed nuts—and then, in a fit of political pique (reinforced, perhaps by semi-serious hangovers or still slightly inebriated embers of the previous night's ceremonial drowning of sorrows), purposely tossed the peanuts around the aircraft.

DON'T SHOOT ME, I'M ONLY JERRY FORD

Gerald Ford managed to survive *two* assassination attempts (both by women), despite serving less than a full term in the White House.

The first bungled attempt was by Charles Manson devotee Lynnette "Squeaky" Fromme (she failed to have a bullet in the firing chamber) in Sacramento on September 5, 1975. A few weeks later, as Ford left the St. Francis Hotel in San Francisco, Sara Jane Moore took an unsuccessful pop (she accidently winged a cab driver) at the president. After Moore was subdued, the Secret Service rushed Ford to the airport, onto Air Force One, and roared off to the presumed safety of Washington.

Having been off doing her own thing during the day and not having heard any radio reports, Betty Ford innocently inquired of her husband, something like: "How did your day go, dear?"

According to Nessen: "I think it was [Secretary of State Donald] Rumsfeld who finally told her that someone took a shot at the president.... We took off and what had happened sunk in. I can tell you quite a few martinis were consumed on the flight back."

In addition, Nessen observed: "The booze and black humor flowed. Someone asked if legislation granting equal rights to women included equal rights to take a shot at the President...."

Supporting Nessen's scenario, Kenneth T. Walsh wrote in his book *Air Force One*:

> More than anything, there was the consumption of a considerable amount of alcohol, to the point where some staffers got tipsy. Ford had a couple of martinis, extra dry, and Mrs. Ford had vodka tonic on ice, as everyone tried to relax and count their blessings.

Ford, apparently, was far less shaken than his martinis. He rather casually phoned his children to let them know he was fine. In addition to his post–assassination attempt libations, the former gridiron star wolfed down a sizeable beefsteak before nodding off to sleep.

Ford lived to ninety-three—still a presidential record. He died in December 2006.

As for Sara Jane Moore, she served thirty-two years in prison. A few years after she was released, Moore agreed to an interview with Matt Lauer on NBC News. She appeared more like somebody's grandmother enthusiastically poised to share a gingerbread recipe than a crazed political assassin.

During her time in prison, Moore had managed to escape (climbing over a razor-wire wall) for about half a day. One of Moore's regrets was that, during her brief interval of freedom, she had not downed a drink or two in a bar she had passed by.

BETTY FORD: TRIALS AND TRIBULATIONS

Betty Ford certainly was not the only first lady with substance abuse problems, but she was probably the most forthright in later acknowledging them. (Mrs. Ford was similarly open about her mastectomy for breast cancer.)

Betty Ford began problem drinking while her husband was away in Washington during his days in Congress. Her drinking became even more problematic and accelerated by an addiction to painkillers that occurred after she pinched a nerve in her neck.

Attempts at moderation did not work. As Betty noted: "Jerry would hand me a mild vodka and tonic and I'd sigh, 'Why don't you give me a *normal* drink?'"

Betty Ford's addiction to painkillers and alcohol seemingly increased after the former president and she moved back to California, eventually settling in Rancho Mirage in 1977.

On April Fools' Day, 1978, the family (including Jerry Ford) confronted Betty in an "intervention," with daughter Susan Ford spearheading the effort. "I saw a very sluggish person," Susan later remarked in a PBS special. "It was like watching a robot in slow motion."

After initial tears and anger (Betty accused her family of being unfeeling "monsters") of denial, the intervention resulted in the former first lady checking into the Long Beach Naval Hospital in California. Betty's experience there planted the seeds for establishing what would become the Betty Ford Center—a detox program known for attracting famous cliental, such as Liz Taylor, Liza Minnelli, baseball stars Darryl Strawberry and Dwight Gooden, and—more recently—Lindsay Lohan.

Once she confronted her addiction, Ford spoke bluntly about the power it held over her. "I liked alcohol," she wrote in 1987. "It made me feel warm. And I loved pills. They took away my tension and pain."

Her announcement gave others the courage to be open about their substance abuse issues, too. The public and most of her friends were sympathetic to her struggle and complimentary of her courageous response to her problems.

When Elizabeth "Betty" Ford died in July, 2011, the *New York Times* obituary stated: "Few first ladies have been as popular as Betty Ford, and it took her frankness and lack of pretense that made her so."

TABLE DANCER

If there is one signature photograph from the presidential years that best reflects Betty Ford's free-spiritedness, that photo is arguably David Hume Kennerly's classic of the first lady dancing barefoot on the White House table.

There were some initial concerns that some people—given Betty's history—might assume she'd been intoxicated at the time. But apparently the first lady was simply feeling impish and wanted to punctuate her departure from the White House with a bit of unpretentious fun.

LAST CALL

Presidential son Jack Ford apparently liked to have some fun, too. He invited Bianca Jagger—then wife of Mick, of Rolling Stones fame—

to the White House for a drink. Allegedly it led to some kind of romantic encounter, possibly referred to in the Stones's song "Respectable." Former president Ford also gave up drinking late in life, primarily, he said, because (after Betty quit) he had no interest in drinking alone.

CHAPTER 38

James Earl "Jimmy" Carter

(1924–)

*J*ames Earl "Jimmy" Carter—a graduate of the U.S. Naval Academy and a Democratic governor of Georgia—typically gets low marks as a president. But whatever Carter's shortcomings, it is safe to say that they cannot be blamed on his own consumption of alcohol, since he rarely—and then very sparingly—imbibed. (If one believes that habitual drinking is sometimes a reaction to stress, then Carter, like most presidents, certainly had reason to hoist a few.)

Carter's brother Billy, however, drank enough for the two of them— and then some. Billy's various shenanigans—no doubt most of which were in part influenced by alcohol—proved embarrassing to his presidential older brother. But Billy was not completely alone; others from Carter's "inner circle" caused him alcohol-related problems, too.

WAR ON THE MARTINI LUNCH

Jimmy Carter, the thirty-ninth president of the United States (1977–1981), became unpopular in his one term for lots of reasons—the boycott of the Moscow Olympic Games, long gas lines, the Iranian hostage crisis, and, yes, his war on the "three-martini lunch."

Carter felt that hotshot business executives should not be allowed to write-off elaborate, booze-blasted lunches on their expenses accounts—while the working class guys could not do the same for their bologna sandwiches or hot dogs served up by a street vendor.

An unexpected side effect of Carter's attack on the three-martini lunch was that it moved both Gerald Ford and Barry Goldwater to erupt with humorous declarations—something neither of these Republican stalwarts were typically identified with.

Ford—who enjoyed martinis—said: "The three-martini-lunch is the epitome of American efficiency. Where else can you get an earful, a bellyful, and a snootful at the same time?"

Not to be overshadowed, Goldwater (who often unabashedly broke out a bottle of Old Crow bourbon in his Senate office at the end a hard day) quipped: "None of us had a three-martini-lunch until Carter was elected."

CRAFT BREWERS ROCK

Lest one believe that President Carter's attack on martinis proves that he was an ultra-religious fun-sucker, it warrants noting that in 1979 he deregulated the American beer industry. It was the first time since Prohibition (1920–1933) that it was once again legal to sell hops, malt, and brewer's yeast to homebrew aficionados in the States. So, if you recently cooked up a batch of home brew and are lifting a mug of fresh India pale ale to your lips, take time to toast James Earl Carter.

ROSALYNN'S RULES

The Carter White House years were far from a freewheeling time for diplomats or press corps members who liked to drink hard stuff.

Official dinners or receptions were not exactly a throwback to the days of Lucy Hayes, but the situation and general vibe would have caused some consternation for whiskey or vodka drinkers or even those inclined to look for rapid refills.

The prim and proper Rosalynn Carter (her mother once said she was the kind of girl who could put on a white dress and keep it clean all day) admittedly had a dislike for hard alcohol—to the point that she found the mere appearance of it to be distasteful.

As the former first lady once stated to a *Vanity Fair* writer:

> We served wine, punch, and cordials. That was what was served at the White House before John Kennedy. I had been to one dinner at the Nixon White House, when Jimmy was governor. It was so beautiful and so elegant and I was so impressed. Then here comes a waiter carrying a tray with bottles of liquor on it. I just did not like that. Everybody thought it was because we were Baptists, but it was not. I just thought it distracted from the elegance of the evening. And Jimmy agreed.

BILLY BEER

It is safe to assume that "Billy Beer" was not on Rosalynn's list of drinks considered classy enough to be served in the White House. It is also possible that she would have considered Billy Carter as not classy enough to be allowed in the White House, too—something akin to serving fried catfish and unshelled peanuts for a state dinner.

In fact, Billy Carter—the president's younger brother—was a stark reminder of that old phrase: "You can choose your friends, but not your relatives."

Once Jimmy Carter was in the national spotlight, it did not take very long for the press to figure out that Billy—a gas-pumping, beer-guzzling good ol' boy from Plains, Georgia, could create some copy on a slow news day. Billy once proudly told reporters: "Yes, I'm a real southern boy. I got a red neck, white socks, and Blue Ribbon beer."

But Billy's quips and hee-haw mannerisms took him beyond Blue Ribbon beer—he promoted his own brew called "Billy Beer." The first batches were brewed in July 1977 by the Falls City Brewing Company. The cans were labeled with a quote attributed to Billy: "I had this beer brewed up just for me. I think it's the best I've ever tasted. And I've tasted a lot. I think you'll like it, too."

The beer turned out to be a fad, then a complete flop; it is almost impossible to find anyone who will claim it tasted good. By 1978 (according to the *New York Times*), Reynolds Metals purchased close to nine million empty "Billy" cans (ones that never had beer in them, *not* ones emptied by thirsty aficionados of hops and malted beverages) and melted them down. But you can still buy a can of Billy Beer (a full one or an empty) on eBay or similar sites.

Just months after Reynolds melted down the Billy Beer cans, Billy himself had something of a meltdown. In March 1979 the president's brother—who sometimes drank beer for breakfast—entered the Long Beach Naval Hospital in California (former first lady Betty Ford also sought help at the hospital for drug and alcohol abuse) in an effort to "dry out." (There is strong evidence that Billy never had another drink after he left rehab.)

Billy's escapades resulted in occasional bursts of both entertainment and embarrassment (more of the latter if one was high up in the Carter White House). But the embarrassment factor actually soared to the next level when Billy visited Libya in 1978 and 1979 and cozied up to the notorious dictator Muammar Gaddafi, coming away with a reported $220,000 loan. The scandal—which became known as "Billygate"—attracted the attention of both the Senate (which launched an investigation) and the Justice Department. Billy was forced to register as a "foreign agent," and President Carter had to vehemently declare that his beer-swilling sibling had no influence on White House foreign policy decisions.

Billy Carter died of pancreatic cancer at just fifty-one years old. Jimmy Carter has been quoted as saying: "The only one of our family who really suffered because of [his presidency] was my brother Billy."

A "ROAD-IE" WITH MISS LILLIAN

Carter's mother—Lillian Carter (a.k.a. Miss Lillian)—occasionally liked to drink bourbon. In Robert Scheer's book *Playing President: My Close Encounters with Nixon, Carter, Bush I, Reagan, and Clinton—and How They Did Not Prepare Me for George W. Bush*, he writes that he was invited to a fish fry in Plains, Georgia, where Jimmy Carter "looked about as relaxed as one of the flapping fish in the drained pond."

But Scheer found Miss Lillian and Carter's sister, Gloria, much more fun:

> But Carter does come from a delightfully informal family. On one earlier occasion, Gloria and Miss Lillian had invited me to go along for supper at a local diner. Gloria had carefully prepared two jars of liquid refreshment—one filled with Early Times bourbon and the other with water—so I "wouldn't get thirsty" on the way to the dinner. While we were there, they playfully felt under my coat to see if I was wired for sound and became totally relaxed as they sipped on the bourbon and talked irreverently about the foibles of people in Plains.

Miss Lillian was once quoted to the tune of: "I know folks all have a tizzy about it, but I like a little bourbon.... It helps me sleep. I don't care much what they say about it."

Apparently, one guy who saw things Miss Lillian's way was Hubert Humphrey. In the late 1960s, Humphrey (then vice president under LBJ) visited Georgia and met a young Jimmy Carter, who was not yet in the political game. Humphrey learned that Miss Lillian was then working in the Peace Corps in a rather remote village in India. Through his Peace Corps connections, the vice president saw to it that Miss Lillian received a fifth of better-than-your-average bourbon.

THE RUSSIAN FACTOR

In 1979, Jimmy Carter met with Soviet president Leonoid Brezhnev at the American Embassy in Vienna, Austria, for talks on limiting the deployment of nuclear weapons. As was typical with Russian leaders and diplomats, some drinking of toasts inevitably came into play. Needless to say, this was not Carter's strong suit, and—with proper supervision—might have been a place for Brother Billy to have "pinch-hit." In his book *Keeping the Faith: Memoirs of a President*, Jimmy Carter admits Brezhnev sensed his weakness in this particular arena.

> We served them (the Russians) a drink, and Brezhnev immediately asked for supper. He was only half joking. Brezhnev and I discussed wine, grandchildren, the shortage of gasoline in both countries.... The meal was served as soon as it was ready, because Brezhnev clearly wanted to retire early. During supper we offered several toasts, and he bottomed up his glass of vodka each time, teasing me when I failed to do the same.

At a follow-up meeting at the Soviet Embassy, the peanut farmer from Plains figured out how to keep up with Brezhnev—without suffering great consequences during the event or, for that matter, the next day.

> Again Brezhnev offered frequent toasts. I arranged with the waiter for a tiny glass, shifted to a somewhat milder drink, and joined in the "bottoms up" ceremonies along with everyone else. There was a lot of jovial banter....

Always playing his cards tight to the vest, Carter does not tell us *exactly* what this "milder drink" was ... white wine? Perrier? Atlanta, Georgia's own Coca Cola? We just don't know.

LAST CALL

According to the Secret Service agents in Ronald Kessler's book *In the President's Secret Service: Behind the Scenes with Agents in the Line of Fire and the Presidents They Protect*, the Carters asked for (and got) Bloody Marys before attending church on their first Sunday in the White

House.... One agent claimed that—contrary to their teetotaler reputations—Jimmy would occasionally have a martini or a light beer, and Rosalynn would have a very occasional screwdriver. The agents also reported that Miss Lillian once appeared at the White House door with two six-packs of beer in a paper bag intended for them. They appreciated the gesture but allegedly declined the gift.

CHAPTER 39

Ronald Reagan

(1911–2004)

onald Reagan is regarded as a founding father of modern conser-
vatism. But Republicans aren't the only ones who unabashedly
wax nostalgic for the Reagan days. Many Democrats quote him,
as if to preemptively steal the Reagan rhetorical thunder.

Regardless of how you view the Reagan era, his election record
shows that he hammered Jimmy Carter in 1980 (taking forty-four states)
and obliterated Walter Mondale in an even larger landslide in 1984. And
when he left office, Reagan had the loftiest approval rating of any president since FDR.

The fortieth president (1981–1989) also had a sense of humor and
deployed it often, no matter how dire the moment might have appeared.
When he was wheeled into the hospital after an assassin's bullet collapsed
his lung on March 30, 1981, he managed to quip to the medical person-
nel: "I hope you're all Republicans!"

The future president grew up enduring some family dysfunction: his
father, Jack Reagan, was an alcoholic. Understandably, the son never

underestimated the damage that alcohol was capable of inflicting. That traumatic experience helped Ronald Reagan form his moderate drinking habits.

THE GHOSTBUSTER BLUSH

Michael K. Deaver, one of Ronald Reagan's most trusted advisors, expertly staged some of the president's "photo ops" (on the D-Day beaches of Normandy for the fortieth anniversary of that battle, atop the Great Wall of China, and loading up sandbags in flood-ravished Mississippi, for example) and helped his boss "look good" for public-speaking engagements.

Despite his Hollywood background (or perhaps because of it), Reagan resisted any attempts to get him into a makeup room prior to appearances. But Deaver learned early on that there was one trick that gave Reagan a bit of color in his otherwise ghostly pale face: a glass of red wine.

"Well, he could not resist a good French wine, and I figured if I put the bottle on the table, and he could see the vintage and the label, he'd have to have a taste," Deaver recalled in 2004. "And of course it brought all the capillaries out in his cheeks ... and it worked."

Both California guys, Reagan and Deaver knew a lot about the best U.S. vintages, too. So even for simple cosmetic purposes, the president never drank mediocre wine—be those vintages from France, or the so-called "Left Coast."

SINS OF THE FATHER

Jack Reagan, the future president's father and a man who barely subsisted during the Great Depression by selling shoes, suffered from alcoholism. Eleven-year-old Ronnie once found his father passed-out drunk near their house. He managed to help his father inside and put him to bed. It was not an isolated incident. Jack's bouts with the bottle plagued the family as Reagan and his older brother, Neil, grew up in small-town Illinois.

Despite the trauma of these childhood experiences, Reagan often said he loved his father and learned some life lessons from him—beyond the obvious one of alcohol's potential for destruction. Reagan's mother, Nelle, told her sons that their father's inability to handle drinking was "a sickness."

THE SODA POP LESSON

Even after witnessing his father's alcohol woes, young Ronald—on one memorable occasion—obtained some firsthand knowledge on the subject when he downed too much liquor during his student days at Eureka College.

Claiming "curiosity" led him to over-imbibe with a couple of more experienced fraternity brothers, Reagan confessed in his autobiography:

> It was during Prohibition and a lot of movies depicted illicit drinking as "collegiate" … I'd take a big drink, as if it was a bottle of soda pop.…

And the result, if not pretty (Reagan described himself as "blind drunk"), provided an indelible lesson.

> … they brought me back to the frat house and threw me in a shower. They had to smuggle me in, because everyone was in bed asleep. I woke up the next day with a terrible hangover. That was it for me. Although in later years I might have a cocktail before dinner, or a glass of wine with dinner, I'd been taught a lesson. I decided if that's what you get for drinking— a sense of helplessness—I didn't want any part of it.

HAVE PUB, WILL TRAVEL

Like most U.S. presidents with roots "across the pond," Ronald Reagan made it a point to visit the village of his Irish ancestors (in

Ballyporeen, County Tipperary) when he traveled to the Emerald Isle in June 1984.

The traveling party spent the first night at the lavish Ashford Castle in Galway. Reagan and his wife, Nancy—jet-lagged from the flight—turned in early. But the staffs—both visiting Yanks and hosting Irish—stayed on script and soon turned aggressively festive.

As one remembrance (printed in the *Irish Voice*, decades later) put it:

> It was the night that Secretary of State George Shultz sang "Galway Bay" and Michael Deaver, special assistant to the president, sang "Danny Boy."
>
> Then Irish Minister for Foreign Affairs Peter Barry sang, as befitting a Cork man, "The Banks of My Own Lovely Lee," and then Secretary of the Department of Foreign Affairs Sean Donlon manned the piano all evening. It got so loud that they were warned they might wake the president up.

President Reagan and Nancy slept through all this moonlit malarkey (the most committed revelers, in fact, partied until the sun rose and splashed some sense on the survivors), though as Irish-American journalist Niall O'Dowd unflinchingly put it: "There were certainly many sore heads on both sides the next morning."

THE RONALD REAGAN LOUNGE

Once in the village of Ballyporeen, Reagan received a few gifts from the locals and spoke briefly to them. This was after he had visited O'Farrell's, the local pub—later renamed "The Ronald Reagan Lounge."

Reagan barely sampled a pint of Guinness in the pub (then switched to Smithwicks, which he also did not finish) and then only after Secret Service agents had sampled the mug first.

When the Ronald Reagan Lounge/O'Farrell's closed in 2004, the wooden bar and most of the establishment's barroom paraphernalia were purchased by the Reagan Library and Museum and shipped to Simi

Valley, California, and its new home in an old aircraft hanger—alongside Air Force One.

THE PUB PHOTO OP

The Reagan team realized early on that an occasional photo of their man hoisting a brew with the average guy in a pub helped balance out any "fat cat" accusations. Never mind that the president rarely swallowed more than a few swigs.

In January 1983, Reagan was on a rather routine tour of some tech facilities in Boston when his entourage took a detour for a late lunch at the Eire Pub in blue-collar Dorchester. Apparently, two of Reagan's Secret Service agents were from the area and knew the pub well. Political cynics said the stop may have been, in part, to counterbalance a recent TV appearance at the fictional *Cheers* bar by Democratic heavy weight (and House Speaker) Thomas "Tip" O'Neill—in essence, to show that President Reagan was capable of hoisting a brew with working-class men, in *real* time.

Similarly, revelers at Pat Troy's Ireland's Own pub in Alexandria, Virginia, were astounded to see Ronald Reagan saunter through the doors on St. Patrick's Day 1988. (Some of the president's advance men had been there before and thoroughly scouted out the tavern.)

Reagan (accompanied by journalist James Kilpatrick) had a few sips of beer (Harp, an Irish lager, Troy later said) and dined on traditional corn beef and cabbage. Troy robustly led his loyal patrons in the various enactments of the "Unicorn Song"—a St. Paddy's Day ritual (typically booze-propelled) that the amused president apparently had not previously witnessed. Now retired from the bar business, the Irish-born Troy often describes the Reagan appearance as "awesome."

RUSSIANS AND VODKA

Like most American leaders from FDR on, President Reagan had to deal with the Russians, which meant vodka (its literal translation meaning "little water") would always be close at hand for any summit meetings—despite that Soviet president Mikhail Gorbachev, during Reagan's time, was futilely attempting to wean his countrymen from guzzling the clear-but-powerful elixir.

At a 1985 arms summit in Europe, George P. Shultz—Reagan's secretary of state—found himself seated next to Andrei Gromyko, the Soviet ambassador to the United States. Gromyko droned on about how alcoholism was a major problem in Russia and how Gorbachev's stern message to the people to cut back on their massive consumption of vodka was a courageous edict.

Shultz apparently felt compelled to acknowledge his Russian counterpart's burden in some fashion:

> I told him that we, too, were trying to curb excessive drinking, especially by drivers, but I reminded him of our disastrous experience with Prohibition. I told him rather spontaneously a joke that was going around:
>
> Two guys were in a long line waiting to buy vodka. An hour went by, then two. One said to the other: "I'm fed up. I'm going over to the Kremlin to shoot Gorbachev." He left, and when he came back, his buddy asked him, "Well, did you shoot him?" "Hell, no," he responded. "The line there was even longer than this one." Gromyko's face was motionless.

And although the Russians were trying to downshift on vodka consumption back at home, they obviously had no problem obliterating bottles of booze abroad. As Shultz noted:

> At the first day's session at the Soviet embassy, nice motherly Russian ladies pushed vodka on our security people and pushed it hard. The Americans all declined, but the Russians partook enthusiastically. In the afternoon session at the American mission, bottles of Jack Daniel's and Johnnie Walker Black Label had been set on a table outside the meeting room; Soviet security guards drained them all.

No doubt President Reagan was pleased by this steadfast show of American restraint in the face of Russian temptation.

The Orange Blossom Special

If the president was not a big beer drinker, he did occasionally indulge in an Orange Blossom, which typically consists of:

1 ounce (or slightly less in Reagan's case) vodka
1 ounce of either grenadine or sweet vermouth
2 ounces fresh orange juice
All brought together in a barroom glass filled with ice

Though Orange Blossoms often are made with gin, Reagan would have substituted vodka because, by some accounts, he did not react well to gin (he perhaps had an allergy to it). President Reagan also enjoyed an occasional screwdriver (vodka and orange juice).

REALLY SOURED ON THE IDEA

Not all of Ronald Reagan's political moves were brilliant. While jousting for the 1976 Republican nomination, Reagan named Pennsylvania senator Richard Schweiker as his vice-presidential candidate. Some Republican supporters were underwhelmed by this choice. Deaver (in an interview with the Miller Center) recalled one particularly bumpy day on the campaign trail:

> This man from Alabama stands up. He's got a bow tie on, perfectly dressed. "Governor," he said. "I am not a drinking man. But when I heard that you picked Dick Schweiker to be your running mate, I went home and drank a pitcher of whiskey sours." And then he said, "I would rather have had my doctor call me at home and tell me my wife had a venereal disease."

The GOP tapped Gerald Ford that year and Jimmy Carter—initially a Democratic dark horse—won the White House. As for Reagan, history shows he made a better VP draft pick when he brought George H. W. Bush onboard in 1980.

TWENTY-ONE: IT'S NOT JUST FOR BLACKJACK ANYMORE

If you are nineteen or twenty and disappointed that you cannot sip a legal drink in the USA, then you might want to wing darts at Reagan's portrait. Reagan pushed hard to obtain an across-the-nation uniform age—twenty-one—for the legal consumption of alcohol.

The stats suggest that raising the drinking age to twenty-one saved lives. Reagan's comments and letters absolutely reflect his sincerity on the controversial issue.

"We know that drinking plus driving spell death and disaster," Reagan said upon signing the National Minimum Drinking Age Act on July 17, 1984. "We know that people in the 18–20 age group are more likely to be in alcohol-related accidents...."

GREAT SCOTT! DEBATING REAGAN ON THE DRINKING AGE

About six months after Reagan signed the National Minimum Drinking Age Act, he received a letter from a young Californian—Scott Osborne (whose mother, Kathy, was Reagan's secretary at the White House)—writing of his goals to study architecture in college. But young Osborne could not resist adding a P.S.: "I'd just like to say one thing. If at age 18 we're old enough to vote and to fight for our country ... we should be able to drink."

Reagan responded thoughtfully:

> Scott I shouldn't do this but I have to argue with you a bit on your postscript about age 18 and the right to drink.... Now don't think I'm a hypocrite, I enjoy a cocktail now and then before dinner and have a taste for a good dinner wine. I also

recall feeling exactly as you do now and looking back I realize the good Lord must have been watching over me. At that age (about 18) getting drunk seemed like the thing to do, the point of drinking. Then before something too awful happened (although there were a few near scrapes) I realized that I was abusing the machinery, this body, we only get one you know. But more than that I had an example to look at. My father was an alcoholic, I loved him and I love him still but he died at age 58 and had suffered from heart disease for a number of years before his death. He was a victim of a habit he couldn't break."

And then Reagan—who was always an expert at poking fun at himself if it helped his cause—closed with:

Forgive me for playing grandpa—but think about it a little. Become an architect or if you change your mind—whatever and we'll celebrate your graduation with a champagne toast and I'll furnish the wine.

Whether he was dealing with a Russian leader on nuclear arms control or a teenager lamenting the seemingly lofty drinking age of twenty-one, Ronald Reagan—sometimes called "The Great Communicator"—was usually skilled at making his case.

TEARY-EYED TIP

"Herbert Hoover with a smile" was the way Democratic House Speaker Thomas "Tip" O'Neill Jr. sometimes referred to Ronald Reagan, but the two men also could often talk out the issues over an afternoon drink. (As his moniker implied, Tip certainly held the superior credentials when it came to hoisting a few and did his more serious imbibing with Ted Kennedy.)

The tumultuous division between parties in more recent times perhaps provides a sentimental nostalgia for one to view the O'Neill-Reagan years as more cooperative than they actually were, but, nonetheless, the term "Frenimies" does not seem too far-fetched when discussing Tip and Ronnie.

Speaking of sentiments, Reagan invited O'Neill to the White Hosue for the Speaker's sixty-ninth birthday and broke out some celebratory champagne to toast the occasion. The chief exectuvie then burst forth with an old Irish proverb worthy of the fine wine. Lifting his glass to the Democratic warhouse, President Reagan proclaimed:

> "Tip, if I had a ticket to heaven and you didn't have one, I would give mine away and go to hell with you."

It might have been a bit of blarney (from one Irish-American to another) but the toast brought tears to Tip O'Neill's eyes.

LAST CALL

In his Hollywood days, Reagan owned a pair of Scottish terriers that he named "Scotch" and "Soda".... The swashbuckling film star Errol Flynn once allegedly told Reagan to go "f***" himself because the young American actor had sidestepped a bourbon-drinking stint (by secretively pouring the whiskey into a spittoon) with Flynn prior to shooting a movie scene.... When Gorbachev visited Washington in 1987, the White House staff served him American wine—but they made sure he knew the vintage was from California's Russian River region.

CHAPTER 40

George H. W. Bush

(1924–)

George Herbert Walker Bush was a war hero and an outstanding baseball player, two accomplishments that most American voters admire.

Bush became the youngest navy pilot in World War II, tallying nearly sixty combat missions and surviving being shot down over the Pacific. The future president was a recipient of the Distinguished Flying Cross.

After the war, Bush entered Yale University, where he became a member of the Skull and Bones secret society and a team captain of the Bulldog baseball team.

By the mid-1950s, Poppy Bush was solidly established in Texas (though he later admitted that initially he hadn't really been sure what a "chicken-fried steak" might be), made money in oil, and eventually moved into politics. He won a congressional seat but lost a key Senate race to Lloyd Bentsen in 1970.

President Nixon appointed Bush to be the U.S. ambassador to the United Nations. And after Nixon resigned, President Ford offered Bush the post of envoy to China in 1974.

Throughout his career, the elder Bush proved himself to be a savvy social drinker. He exhibited tolerance and—perhaps more importantly—a sense of when to stop. In short, "41"—unlike his son "43"—never had to "surrender his guns" (so to speak) when it came to handling alcohol. To steal a line from an old beer commercial, Poppy knew "when to say when."

DRINKING IN CHINA

George Herbert Walker Bush kept a diary in China and later elevated it to book form (naturally called *The China Diary*). The writings document political and diplomatic happenings, but Bush also provides some interesting insights into the cultural life of his time there—including drinking and eating.

A typical example is an entry in which the future president talks about a picnic (washed down with tasty—but warm—beer) on the Great Wall of China:

> We climbed to the top of the left side of the wall. A real workout, tough on the legs, but exhilarating when one gets through.... It is hard to describe the spectacle of the wall ... We then drove down and had a picnic.... The sun was out. I sat in my shirt-sleeves and we ate a delicious picnic. A kind of sweet and sour fish. Excellent fried chicken. Lots of hard boiled eggs. The inevitable tasty soup. The only thing we forgot was ice so the beer was warm, but we had worked hard enough walking up to the top so that we devoured about six bottles of it. It's a heavy beer and I find it makes me sleepy but it's awful good.

When Bush returned home from his Great Wall excursion, he indulged in a hot bath and a long nap—but awoke for an 8:00 p.m. dinner consisting of caviar and a vodka martini.

Although China does not readily come to mind when beer brewing is discussed, Bush nonetheless gave it high marks in his diary:

> China goes about [brewing beer] in the same old way with excess labor and nevertheless their beer is considered very very good. We enjoy it. It seems lower in carbonation. It's more like draft beer here and it's excellent.

With the cheap Chinese prices, a typical Bush entry beams about a feast that cost less than five dollars per person:

> Peking duck dinner with a standard of 8 yuan per person. There were twelve of us—the total bill was a 119 yuan including two wines, maotai, and plenty of beer. Not bad for Peking duck.

MAOTAI MOMENTS

Needless to say, Bush (like Nixon and most other visiting Westerners) sampled some *maotai*—the powerful Chinese liquor of about 110 proof. He mentions (not without a tinge of respect) this libation of hefty clout several times in his diary and, in fact, once speculates that the ultra-strong alcohol might be the cause of some disturbed sleep patterns. ("Bed at ten. Couldn't sleep at all. Maybe it's the maotai. Strong stuff.")

Sometimes maotai caused liaison Bush some political consternation, too. When the U.S. Olympic Track and Field team visited Peking in the spring of 1975, they mopped up the host squad in competition but then became a tad rowdy at a farewell banquet several days later. One can almost picture Poppy Bush wincing as he wrote:

> Return to banquet for the Chinese, give by the AAU (Amateur Athletic Union) side for the Chinese on May 29 at the International Club. Went well. [Bob] Giegengack [U.S. track coach] funny as hell. Talked as he would in an American banquet. It got out of hand, in that some of our kids got drinking too much and showing a not particularly good side.

We cut off the maotai and that calmed things down. The banquet was not unruly in an American sense, but the Chinese are so proper and so precise that I hope they were not offended by this. That maotai really does hit a lick. A great big mustached pole vaulter was the only one that really got out of hand.

COLD BEER AND NICE BUNS

Despite giving relatively high marks to Chinese beer, George H. W. Bush did not want anything to do with the native brew when it came to celebrating the Fourth of July 1975 in Peking. In fact, he wanted the mainstays of the picnic festivities to be as American as possible. He brought in not only Miller beer, but also American cigarettes, Coca Cola, and—even though he reportedly had to bring them in from Japan—American-style hot dog rolls.

At any rate, in his diary, the future president proclaimed his Fourth of July celebration in China "a tremendous success." (He even tried to get John Denver "live"—but settled for blasting Denver's records.)

Bush must have been something of a "Miller Time" man back in the 1970s. Later in the summer, he visited a Chinese brewery and brought a case of Miller with him for the brewers there to sample. Bush and his party very graciously sampled the five kinds of beers the brewery was making, too.

Bush—finding the diplomatic experience with the Chinese somewhat frustrating—returned to Washington in 1976 when President Ford named him director of the Central Intelligence Agency.

QUAYLE HUNTING

There is one political theory that suggests that vice presidents make good lightning rods—meaning, they're good at drawing fire away from the president. If that is truly an asset, then James Danforth Quayle was probably a great pick as Bush's running mate in 1988.

When George H. W. Bush chose Dan Quayle, a young senator from Indiana, the reasoning behind the move was that Quayle was good looking (i.e. he might appeal to women voters) and that his politics might attract support from the conservative base of the Republican Party. (Bush was seen as somewhat moderate by some in the GOP, despite having served as Ronald Reagan's vice president for two terms.)

Today we tend to remember Quayle as the guy who instructed a schoolboy to tag an unnecessary "e" on the end of the word "potato" after the kid had spelled it correctly. But before that legacy-defining gaffe, there was James Quayle, the candidate's father, quoted in the *New York Daily News* (during the campaign) that his son's main interests in college had been "broads and booze."

Several days after that appeared in print, the elder Quayle attempted to backpedal (not so deftly, it should be noted), claiming that he meant to say: "If he's anything like his old man, it probably was broads and booze.... He's not like that."

All that said, quotes from former college classmates who knew Dan Quayle from his DePauw University days inevitably made references to girls, golf (Dan was a three-time letter-winner on the links), and, yes—drinking.

THE *BUSHU-SURU* INCIDENT

In January 1992, President George H. W. Bush paid a visit to Japan. The sixty-seven-year-old chief executive played tennis in the afternoon. Apparently not feeling terribly well, he still had a banquet to get through that evening—and not just any banquet, but one with more than one hundred guests at the estate of Japanese prime minister Kiichi Miyazawa.

The banquet did not go exactly as planned. In fact, President Bush became suddenly nauseous and, by most accounts, promptly threw up in the lap of the Japanese prime minister, who was sitting next to him. First Lady Barbara Bush rushed in with her napkin to clean up her husband (who had fainted), and Miyazawa held Bush's head in his hands. The Secret Service agents rushed to the president's side. Bush recovered quite quickly but was taken back to his room at Akasaka Palace and missed the rest of the evening.

Needless to say, President Bush was not available to participate in the usual rounds of toasts. But Mrs. Bush remained and participated, while National Security Advisor Brent Scowcroft proved to be an able pinch hitter when it came time for the Americans to propose a toast to their Japanese hosts.

Only the most cynical foes of the president could have believed President Bush had drunk too much. (That would not have been in character for him.) White House press secretary Marlin Fitzwater, attributing the illness to a twenty-four-hour bug, simply stated: "The President is human.... Sometimes he gets sick."

Nevertheless, the incident apparently has resulted in a Japanese slang term for upchucking, or puking. Consider, say, a dozen young businessmen are out on the town in Tokyo, celebrating some major deal. One of them drinks too much and (to his embarrassment) gets physically ill. His friends might say that he demonstrated *Bushu-suru*—or "to do the Bush thing."

The incident also proved to be comic fodder for *Saturday Night Live* and *The Simpsons*.

LAST CALL

The White House served American wines at state dinners during President George H. W. Bush's term (1989–1993). At a state dinner for the Australian prime minister in 1989, for example, the staff served a merlot reserve, a brut rose, and a chardonnay—all recent vintages from California—although supposedly there still was some high-priced French wines from the Nixon era down in the cellar. But as First Lady Barbara Bush proudly stated: "It's our job to be selling America...."

CHAPTER 41

William Jefferson "Bill" Clinton

(1946–)

*A*s a teenager, Bill Clinton traveled to Washington, D.C., with a student group from his home state of Arkansas. The main event was a meet-and-greet at the White House Rose Garden, where young Clinton shook hands with then president John Fitzgerald Kennedy. It is not a stretch to suggest that that handshake helped illuminate the political path for Clinton.

Imagine crossing a swiftly moving river, but hopping from one inviting stone to another. That's sort of what Clinton did—he hopped from Georgetown University to Oxford as a Rhodes Scholar, to Yale Law School, to governor of Arkansas, and, eventually, in 1992, into the White House.

Not that there weren't occasional slipups during his otherwise successful term as the forty-second president (1993–2001). Clinton was accused of numerous extramarital affairs; then there were the "Whitewater" scandal and a messy impeachment for perjury and obstruction of justice.

But Clinton—with great oratory skills, a top-rate intellect, and some luck—survived it all. In 2012, the former president still had enough star power to stump for Barack Obama's reelection.

Whatever Bill Clinton's personal flaws, drinking to excess is never mentioned among them. As he wrote in his autobiography: "A few times in my twenties and early thirties I might have had too much to drink.... But fortunately, liquor never did that much for me.... I'm relieved that I never had a craving for it. I have enough problems without that one."

ROUGH START

Bill Clinton's biological father—William Jefferson Blythe—died in a car crash three months before his son was even born. His mother, Virginia, remarried, and the future president grew up with Roger Clinton as his stepfather.

One explanation for Clinton's go-easy attitude when it comes to drinking is that Roger Clinton was an alcoholic, with violent tendencies when he drank too much. As Clinton recalled in his autobiography *My Life*:

> One night his [Clinton's stepfather] drunken self-destructiveness came to a head in a fight with my mother I can't ever forget.... They were screaming at each other in their bedroom in the back of the house. For some reason, I walked out into the hall to the doorway of the bedroom.
>
> Just as I did, Daddy pulled a gun from behind his back and fired in Mother's direction....

Young Clinton and his mother literally dodged a bullet, fled to a neighbor's house, and called the police. Clinton's stepfather was carted off in handcuffs in front of young Bill and his mother.

Roger Clinton did come back and stayed sober for some time, but his relapses eventually drove Clinton's mother to flee with her boys (Bill and younger half-brother, little Roger) and file for divorce. President

Clinton and his stepfather reconciled somewhat later in their lives. Bill learned from his stepfather's struggles. "I hated what liquor had done to Roger Clinton" Clinton once wrote, "and I was afraid that it might have the same effect on me."

MY THREE BUDS

The actions (and antics) of staff or family members might drive a president to drink, but the reverse can sometimes be true as well. Dealing with the drama in Bill Clinton's political career, for example, certainly would have tested the true grit of his staffers.

Clinton was building political momentum prior to the 1992 presidential election when the Gennifer Flowers allegations (she claimed Clinton had carried on a twelve-year affair with her) broke. In something of a gamble, Clinton agreed to a *60 Minutes* interview in late January—knowing full well that he would be grilled on the latest accusations. Somehow candidate Clinton (with wife Hillary Rodham Clinton by his side) managed to escape with limited damage (and without giving a "yes" answer in regards to Flowers's charges). He went on to gain the Democratic nomination that summer and then defeat President George H. W. Bush in November.

James Carville, Clinton's chief strategist, was perhaps as nervous as the governor and Mrs. Clinton through the grueling ordeal of the *60 Minutes* interview.

As Carville relates in an insightful book called *All's Fair: Love, War and Running for President*:

> I had said, "Man, whatever you do, tell them to put about three cold Budweisers on ice." And when we got to the governor's suite I chug-a-lugged them. I know it sounds ridiculous, but that damn ordinary mass-produced Budweiser tasted better than the best glass of Chateau Margaux anybody ever had. I will never forget how good that beer tasted.
>
> Then I went back to being a political professional.

One can only speculate that Governor Clinton and Hillary may have indulged in a drink or two after the *60 Minutes* interview was over, too.

PHOTO OPS

Although Bill Clinton was a very moderate drinker, a quick cruise around the internet will produce some pictures of him engaged in various toasts (with various kinds of alcohol) with a variety of world leaders. Like Reagan before him—and Obama after him—President Clinton certainly understood the value of the "drinking photo op."

Of course, some photo ops are more noteworthy than others. For example, former president Clinton met with Peru's Alan Garcia in 2009 as part of the Clinton Global Initiative program, and there is a photo of them drinking a Pisco Sour toast. (A Pisco Sour is made from Pisco, a powerful grape brandy native to Peru and Chile.)

In 1994, Bill Clinton traveled to Prague to meet with Czech president Vaclav Havel, and the former playwright knew just where to take his American visitor in the historic city. Havel took Clinton to a wood-paneled, working-class drinking spot called *U Zlateho Tygra* ("The Golden Tiger") and knocked back a few pints of the authentic Czech pilsner. One story has it that Clinton enjoyed three pints at the Golden Tiger and then opted to give his daily jog a skip the next morning.

On the same trip, Havel took Clinton to Prague's prestigious Reduta Jazz Club, where the president was presented with a Czech saxophone. Clinton (who had a lifelong interest in music and once played his sax on *Arsenio Hall Show*) responded by playing a few tunes, including Elvis Presley's "Heartbreak Hotel"—Elvis being one of his late mother's favorite artists.

The Prague excursion was one of Clinton's most memorable. When Havel died, the president reminisced about the days he spent there in 1994 and about the famous Czech who sacrificed so much of his life to bring democracy to his country. He was, Clinton emphasized, "a big personality." Coming from the gregarious Bill Clinton—a man who scores large on the "likeability" scale—that's quite a compliment.

SNAKEBITE WILLIE

When former president Clinton arrived in Great Britain for the Yorkshire International Business Convention in the spring of 2001, he eventually found himself (and his entourage) in a Harrogate (North Yorkshire) establishment called the Old Bell Pub. A widely circulated story claims that Clinton requested a Snakebite—a half hard cider/half beer drink that he remembered trying from his student days at Oxford.

The publican supposedly turned down Clinton's request, claiming that the establishment was not allowed to serve that particular drink. To which Clinton was said to have replied: "Well, that's too bad then, because you won't get to see my true personality."

The pub's special guest then sampled a few kinds of British ale, but—according to some versions—settled on a Coke to go with his steak and ale pie.

The Snakebite
(a.k.a. Bill Clinton's Lament)

Many of the stories surrounding Bill Clinton's alleged (the Old Bell Tavern landlord Jamie Allen has been quoted in the British press about President Clinton's request and Allen's refusal) attempt to order a "Snakebite" are often followed by an explanation of what actually comprises such a concoction. With that in mind, here we go:

Ingredients:

Hard cider
Lager beer

Pour 8 oz. of hard cider into a chilled glass. Float 8 oz. of chilled lager beer on top of the hard cider. (Pour over the back of a spoon to do this delicately.)

(*Add a ¼ oz. of black currant liqueur for a Snakebite variation the Brits call "Diesel")

I SAW THE SIGN

At least two pubs in the United Kingdom have signs claiming that Bill Clinton once visited.

At the Old Bell Pub (Harrogate, Yorkshire)—scene of the alleged Snakebite request—a sign claims:

> This plaque commemorates the visit to Old Bell Tavern on Friday, 8th June 2001 of **William Jefferson Clinton** sometimes President of the United States of America, charismatic leader of the free world and (alleged) philander [sic]. He sat adjacent to this spot and enjoyed an Old Bell Steak & Ale pie!

An even more "cheeky" sign has been displayed at the Turf Tavern, an establishment that claims (among other things) to date back to the thirteenth century. The sign reads:

> IT IS ALLEGED THAT IT WAS HERE AT THE TURF TAVERN THAT BILL CLINTON WHILE AT UNIVERSITY HERE IN OXFORD, DURING THE SIXTIES "DID NOT INHALE" WHILST SMOKING AN ILLEGAL SUBSTANCE

And then, in a thinly veiled reference to the Lewinsky episode, the sign adds on:

> (WHAT HE DOES WITH CIGARS IN HIS OWN HOME IS HIS BUSINESS)

BILL BOLTS BILL?

What is it with Bill Clinton and British pubs? In December 2000, President Clinton, while accompanying Hillary and daughter Chelsea on a London shopping trip, opted for the classic male "I-think-I-need-a-beer" detour. (The Clinton women kept shopping.)

With the Secret Service (think *Men in Black*) checking out the place in advance, Clinton sauntered into the Portobello Gold Pub in Notting Hill. He grabbed a quick lunch and chased it down with a half-pint of Pittsfield's organic lager.

What happened next is, as the Brits might put it, a bit "dodgy."

Simply stated, "Slick Willie" and his bodyguards left the pub without paying—the lingering tab just over thirty-six dollars.

Pub proprietor Michael Bell was quick to say that he did not believe that the president purposely did what the Brits are fond of calling "a runner" (i.e., eat, drink, don't pay, take off with pre-planned haste); he was fairly certain that Clinton simply forgot.

When word leaked out about the incident, the British tabloid the *Mirror* could not help giving President Clinton (what we Yanks would say) "the business." They slapped "We Pay Bill's Bill" on page one after paying the president's tab for him; but then the U.S. Embassy felt obligated to cough up the sum to the tabloid.

Publican Michael Bell ran with the joke and claimed he also received reimbursement from "Socks"—"Socks" being the Clinton family cat. Bell told a British newspaper that a note came with the fee, and it read: "Please forgive me. I thought I trained my human better but every now and again I catch him going on the carpet. Hope this settles the tab."

BORIS GETS HIS PIZZA

FDR and Truman may have had their hands full when Sir Winston Churchill came to visit, but Bill Clinton had to deal with Russian president Boris Yeltsin.

Yeltsin was a notorious drinker, even by Russian standards, but Clinton liked dealing with him. "Yeltsin drunk," Clinton once quipped, "is better than most of the alternatives sober."

But even Clinton's patience was tested when Yeltsin visited Washington, D.C., in 1995. Apparently the Russian leader drank the better part of the day, continued on through dinner, and well into the night. Clinton went to bed sometime before midnight, but in the early morning hours an apologetic Secret Service agent rang him awake with a "problem."

The "problem" was this: a boisterous Boris was out on Pennsylvania Avenue, clad only in his boxers, and drunkenly attempting to flag down a cab. It seems that Boris desired a pizza. When the ruddy-faced Russian leader ignored the suggestion that he should go back inside Blair House (his guest quarters for the visit), the agents reluctantly called a bleary-eyed President Clinton.

The Yeltsin incident only came to light when an oral history of Clinton's White House years was published in 2009 (*The Clinton Tapes: Wrestling History with the President* by Taylor Branch). The agents eventually coaxed the belligerent Boris back inside, and, as Clinton later sighed, "Well, he got his pizza."

LAST CALL

Roger Clinton Jr., the president's half-brother, was a loose cannon (the Secret Service's code name for him was "Headache"), with substance abuse issues that landed him in jail. President Clinton pardoned his half-brother in 2001, thereby clearing Roger's criminal record.

More proof that Bill is smart: President Clinton opted to drink red wine—rather than the extremely potent *maotai*—when toasting with Chinese officials.

CHAPTER 42

George W. Bush

(1946–)

eorge W. Bush was the second son of a president to become president. And like the first, John Quincy Adams, "W" learned about hangovers the hard way.

As president (2001–2009), the former Texas governor did not have an easy first year; there was the aftermath of the "tech bubble" and, of course, the 9/11 terrorist attacks. If he did not drink during those crises, President Bush indeed deserves much credit for his steadfast resolve.

By his own admission, Bush was "a drinker" from at least his late teens to age forty. As he wrote in his autobiography: "By my mid-thirties, I was drinking routinely, with an occasional bender thrown in." He embraced what he called the "three B's"—beer, bourbon, and B&B, a sweet, after-dinner digestive.

But Bush experienced something of an epiphany after a rough night of boozing on his fortieth birthday and—perhaps nudged in that direction by a drumming headache and a case of dry mouth that might have rivaled conditions in the Kalahari—vowed to stop. Although his detractors speculated that Bush may have backslid once or twice, there is no proof that "Dubya" did not live up to his no-alcohol pledge during his White House years. He readily gives credit to a bit of R&R—running and religion—for his successes against alcohol and smoking.

Nevertheless, Bush's "Bluto-esque" drinking escapades prior to his political ascension certainly place him firmly in the "heavyweight" category of imbibing presidents. Truth be told, had the fictional frat brothers of *Animal House* sniffed George W. Bush during his drinking heyday, they would have immediately recognized him as one of their own.

BULLDOG WHISKEY?

Not surprisingly, some of George W. Bush's early brushes with alcohol occurred when he was a fraternity man (Delta Kappa Epsilon— DKE) at Yale. Bush's prime-time collegiate drinking moment unfolded at the prestigious Yale-Princeton football game in 1967.

Consider that it is highly unlikely that any future U.S. president has ever sat upon the top of a football goalpost in an inebriated state while attempting to collapse that structure. But George W. Bush did just that— and on the esteemed campus of Princeton University, no less.

The actions of Bush the Younger might have interested the late Woodrow Wilson—who served as the president of Princeton before ascending to the New Jersey governor's mansion (and, eventually, of course, the White House.)

Why? Because Wilson was fond of telling a story about "squirrel" whiskey—the accelerant of that tale being that there was a moonshine whiskey so powerful that those who dared drink it had a tendency to climb trees.

The frat boy version of George W. Bush was no squirrel. But, by his own admission, he *was* a diehard Yale Bulldog. (His favorite fight song was: "Bulldog, Bulldog! Bow-Wow-Wow!"—a chant that, unless inebriated, one might find difficult to engage in with any rousing enthusiasm.) But whatever he drank at the Yale-Princeton game that fall afternoon helped the future "Decider" decide that scaling the goalpost—

with gleeful intent to tear it down—was a brilliant idea. As Bush wrote in his autobiography *Decision Points*:

> ... The Princeton faithful were not amused. I was sitting atop the crossbar when a security guard pulled me down. I was then marched the length of the field and placed in a police car. Yale friends started rocking the car and shouting, "Free Bush!"

But the campus cops did not free Bush. One friend—Roy Austin, captain of the Yale soccer squad and DKE brother—jumped into the backseat of the police car to give Bush some company on the way to the station. It proved to be a good show of loyalty on Austin's part. Forty years later, President George W. Bush appointed Austin ambassador to Trinidad and Tobago.

In exchange for his freedom, the authorities insisted that the rambunctious Bulldog Bush leave Princeton and promise to never return. It seemed like a square deal, and the future president readily complied.

THE "BUSH BASH" BACKFIRE

Alcohol is never too far from the campaign trail, and Team Bush attempted to use it to attract voters during Bush's out-of-the-blue U.S. congressional bid in 1978.

This political stumble occurred when an overzealous campaign volunteer placed an advertisement in the Texas Tech student newspaper that promised free beer to anyone who attended a "Bush Bash" rally.

Kent Hance—George W.'s Democratic foe—counterattacked by sending a letter concerning the "Bush Bash" (and its offer of free brew) to several thousand members of the Church of Christ, claiming that the Bush campaign tactics did not exemplify good character.

Among other misgivings, the letter noted: "Mr. Bush has used some of his vast sums of money in an attempt, evidently, to persuade young college students to vote for him by offering free alcohol to them."

Hance also found a way to tie the "Bush Bash" to what his detractors saw as George W.'s elitist (and non-Texan) roots, telling a reporter: "Maybe it's a cool thing to do at Harvard and Yale...."

Bush lost the race, with Hance securing 53 percent of the vote. But he must have learned some lessons: Bush never lost another election.

TIE ME KANGAROO DOWN

"His first mistake was he thought he could drink with an Aussie."

That was how John Newcombe, tennis titan and quaff-master from down under, later summed up the unfolding of events that led to Bush Junior's arrest on DUI charges in Kennebunkport, Maine, in 1976.

It was Labor Day weekend and "Newk"—a friend of then CIA director George H. W. Bush—was visiting the Bush family compound on Maine's picturesque coast. The affable Aussie and the younger Bush eventually felt the magnetic pull of a local watering hole and spent several hours there. Newcombe's wife Angie, Bush's sister "Doro" (a mere seventeen), and Peter Roussel (a trusted aide to Poppy Bush) were also along for the festivities.

Bush the Elder was well aware that Newcombe was not just world class on the tennis court; he also had, according to Papa Bush, a "black belt" in drinking. The son was soon to learn that this was not an exaggeration.

Years later, George W. Bush would confess: "It was all a lot of fun— until the ride home."

LOOK, MOM! NO HANDS!

Since George H. W. Bush was a tennis enthusiast and an athlete of some merit (a standout baseball player at Yale), it stands to reason that Newcombe probably shared a few tips of the trade with his host— overhead smashes, drop shots, spin shots, and the like.

And Newk was no less generous when it came to sharing his barroom tricks (it seems a reach to call them "skills") with the young George. According to Barbara Bush, this demonstration probably took place at the House-on-the-Hill—an inn less than a mile from the Bush compound at Walker's Point.

Said Bush: "He [Newcombe] showed me how to pick up a glass, with my teeth, and—without using my hands—chug the beer down."

When the DUI story eventually came to light—and it took its good old sweet time in doing so—Bush claimed he could not remember how many beers were consumed.

Newcombe put the number at a modest half dozen (presumably per participant) or so—adding with a dash of Aussie bravado: "So ... not that many."

WHEN ENOUGH IS ENOUGH

"Not that many," perhaps, but enough that when Bush Junior (he was not technically a "Jr.," but some referred to him as such) insisted on driving back to the compound, he swerved over the line on Ocean Drive. This did not go unnoticed by Officer Calvin Bridges, who had just gotten off his shift and was on his way home when he spied a slow-moving vehicle with two wheels over the shoulder line.

A subsequent "balloon test" soon confirmed the obvious—that the driver was over the legal limit for operating a motor vehicle in the Pine Tree State. No doubt in an effort to be helpful to all concerned, Roussel blurted out the predictable "Do you know who his father is?" to Officer Bridges—but this pronouncement failed to sway the patrolman from performing his duty.

A trip to the local police station—and eventually the leveling of some modest fines—followed. Bush was banned from driving in Maine for two years. Poppy Bush subjected his thirty-year-old son to the standard "take your punishment like a man" spiel.

Given that he was not yet married, George W. at least was spared a scathing lecture from his wife. But some such scenarios were certainly in his future. As Laura Bush noted in her memoir *Spoken from the Heart*: "Maybe it's funny when other people's husbands had too much to drink at a party, but I didn't think it was funny when mine did. And I told him so. But I never said the line 'It's either Jim Beam or me.'"

There did not appear to be any real or lasting consequences from the DUI—and Bush probably assumed there never would be.

NEVER SAY NEVER

Flash forward twenty-four years. George W. Bush is just days away from what looks to be a close presidential election against Democratic foe Al Gore.

Calvin Bridges—now retired—responds to a ring. It is Erin Fehlau, a reporter from Fox News. "Did you ever arrest George W. Bush for driving under the influence?"

"Ah, yup."

Bridges was quick to say that George W. Bush was "very cooperative" (one assumes this demands the caveat: especially for a guy who had been drinking beer no-hands-Newcombe-style for several hours....)

Unlike George W. Bush, Calvin Bridges always suspected that one day his phone *would* ring concerning his strange-but-true Labor Day weekend traffic stop. If he was surprised, it probably had more to do with how long it took to happen.

Both candidate Bush and his running mate, Dick Cheney (who had two DUIs of his own), groused about the timing of the revelation—just days before the nation went to the polls. They found it difficult to believe that it wasn't some kind of "October Surprise"—a well-concealed ace—that the Dems were waiting to play at precisely the right time. Nevertheless, the Bush-Cheney ticket prevailed in a closely contested election.

How many votes it cost Bush—famed political consultant Karl Rove claims that the untimely story may have cost Bush four or five states in the 2000 election—is a matter of speculation. But if one is to believe the candidate's mother Barbara, the DUI tempest definitely did cause the future president to toss and turn. "My George," bristled Barbara Bush, "could barely sleep worrying about this."

TOTALLY TRASHED

One of George W.'s less-than-stellar moments happened when he smashed his car into Poppy Bush's neighbor's trashcan in Washington, D.C., after a night out drinking over the Christmas holidays. (His sixteen-year-old brother, Marvin, was onboard for this incident.) The rubbish bin trapped beneath his vehicle apparently wasn't the only cause of subsequent sparks—George H. W. Bush demanded an explanation.

But the intoxicated Dubya was far from apologetic and—according to many reports—challenged his father to go mano a mano to settle the issue. Younger brother Jeb reportedly stepped in (and by some accounts, Barbara Bush, too) with the timely news that George had recently received word of his acceptance at the Harvard Business School—and the situation was defused.

As far as the father-son confrontation, it was obviously an alcohol-inflamed blip on the screen, as, these days, George W. unfailingly refers to "41" with great affection and admiration.

THE EPIPHANY

Twenty years after he'd scaled the goalpost at Princeton and ten years after the Labor Day weekend screw-up in Kennebunkport, George W. Bush said: *"No mas."*

To paraphrase writer Pete Hamel in his memoir *A Drinking Life* on why *he* had quit, Hamel finally concluded: "I just don't have a talent for it." Bush presumably came to a similar conclusion, and, in his case, it would have been a difficult one to argue against.

Bush's revelation happened the day after his fortieth birthday. He had been celebrating enthusiastically with some close friends at the beautiful Broadmoor resort in Colorado Springs. Since Colorado Springs is at relatively high altitude, it is somewhat easier to reach a state of intoxication than at sea level, but one suspects that Mr. Bush ignored this peril (or—like drinking head-to-head with Newcombe—wrongly assumed that any red-blooded Texan was up to the challenge) and overindulged. Silver Oak wine at sixty dollars per bottle was the libation of choice, and Bush remembers the bar tab as "colossal."

So was the headache. The next day, Mr. Bush attempted to go for a run—his go-to activity when it came to counterattacking a morning hangover. He could barely shuffle along. The future leader of the free world suddenly arrived at a moment of clarity—if he was to honor his family, reach his potential, and serve God, then Demon Alcohol needed to be banished.

> Faith showed me a way out. I knew I could count on the grace of God to help me change. It would not be easy, but by the end of the run, I had made up my mind; I was done drinking.

RUNNING FROM THE DEVIL

George W. Bush credits running with an assist in his ability to quit both drinking and smoking. He first started running (on a dare from a friend) in 1972, when, as he puts it, "I was a man who was known to drink a beer or two." Bush actually became a semi-competitive runner with a 5K time of sub-twenty minutes. As Bush related to *Runner's World* editor Bob "Wish" Wischnia in a 2002 interview:

> As a runner, I quickly realized what it felt like to be healthy, and I already knew what it felt like to be unhealthy. If you're drinking too much, and you're running to cure a hangover, pretty soon you have to make a choice. Do you want to keep getting a hangover, or do you want to feel the way you do after a run? Running is a way to heal people. Running is something that just makes you feel fantastic.

BAD KARMA

George W. Bush occasionally joked that his antics (many of them alcohol-inspired) most likely contributed to his mother's trademark gray hair. But when his twin teenaged daughters—Jenna and Barbara—had run-ins with the law in regards to underage drinking in early 2001, it was the president's turn to undergo some parental stress.

Speaking to a Junior League gathering in Indianapolis at about the time the story concerning the twins' minor missteps broke in the mainstream press, Barbara Pierce Bush could not help but raise her eyebrows and quip: "He's getting some of his own...."

The Bush twins certainly were not in the same league as, say, Billy Carter or Roger Clinton when it came to the "family embarrassment factor"—far from it. Jenna merely attempted to purchase alcohol with a fake ID at a Tex-Mex place in Austin, and Barbara (Yale student like dad) tried to bamboozle an experienced bouncer at a New Haven club and had her fake ID confiscated when this ruse went awry. The incidents were typical teenage transgressions, but—given that they were President Bush's daughters—the public spotlight found them far too interesting to pass over.

Not long after her troubles in Austin, Jenna Bush apparently arranged for a party tour to some dance clubs in Mexico (where she was of legal age), but enterprising journalists were ready to pounce with a story—the gist of which was about the resources and manpower hours of Secret Service agents in both countries that were required to make this frivolous endeavor come to fruition. One publication had planned to run the story on September 12, 2001. But the 9/11 terrorist attacks quickly relegated any such "news" to the slagheap. Suddenly, teenage girls trying to cadge a few drinks did not seem especially newsworthy.

Speaking of karma, when George Bush was drinking with some dedication, he once blurted out at a Kennebunkport dinner party (hosted by his parents) to an older (but attractive) woman: "So.... How *is* sex after fifty?" This comment resulted in a suffocating silence around the table and perhaps some pretense of scrutinizing the intricate patterns on the china dinnerware.

To his credit, Bush later apologized.

But the incident was not *completely* forgotten. When Bush (then the governor of Texas) turned fifty, a note arrived at the Governor's Mansion. It was from the supposedly offended female guest from his parents' dinner party from years before. "Well, George," read the message, "how is it?"

Whoever she was, she had a good sense of humor.

LAST CALL

On his mother's side (Barbara Bush's maiden name was "Pierce") George W. was distantly related to President Franklin Pierce, who had serious issues with alcohol.... As a brazen adolescent, George once poured vodka in the fishbowl and thereby terminated little sister Doro's pet goldfish ... Appearing at a state dinner with the Queen of England, the president noticed there were seven wine goblets at his place setting. "Apparently the Royal Pantry had not gotten the word that I no longer drank," Bush later joked.

CHAPTER 43

Barack Obama

(1961–)

A t the risk of provoking an elephant charge from the GOP mascot or a swift kick in the face from the democratic mule one can argue that Barack Hussein Obama and Ronald Reagan have some similarities, at least when it comes to—for lack of a better phrase —"the drinking photo op."

For example, consider that both Reagan and Obama traveled to Ireland and visited a pub in the respective villages in which some of their ancestors once resided. In addition, both presidents knew that it doesn't hurt one's image to be seen sipping a beer—the blue-collar man's drink— in relaxed settings such as a barbecue (Ronnie) or while watching a basketball game (Barry).

Of course, as the former governor of California, Reagan prided himself on knowing some fine wines from that state. But Obama is no stranger to excellent vintages from Napa Valley, either.

NO ILLUSIONS

In his book *Dreams from My Father*, Obama discusses how alcohol plagued his Kenyan-born father and how his white grandfather would sometimes sneak him into a dive bar in Hawaii when he was ten or eleven. "Gramps" would have a whiskey, and young Barack would settle for a soda and perhaps a chance to smack some billiard balls around on the green felt.

As a teenager, Obama drank alcohol and experimented with drugs. By college, however, Obama became more focused on his academic career.

THE BEER SUMMIT

President Obama (2009–) had resided in the White House only a few months when he became mired in a national controversy and decided that he might have a way to, if not solve, at least *soothe* the heated issue. The solution? In a word, it was beer.

On July 16, 2009, Cambridge, Massachusetts, police arrested Henry Louis Gates Jr. during a 911 call concerning an alleged break-in at a residence. (The residence happened to be where Gates—a black Harvard University professor—lived, and the "break-in" turned out to be him simply trying to get into his own house after returning from a long trip.)

The incident became a national story when Obama questioned the validity of the arrest on racial grounds. He later admitted that he had not worded his response in the best way.

In an attempt to bring all parties together for a dialogue, and in an effort to move past the inflammatory incident, the president invited Dr. Gates and Sergeant James Crowley (the arresting officer) to the White House to talk things out over a couple of beers.

The former antagonists, President Obama, and Vice President Joe Biden all gathered near the White House Rose Garden on July 30. Beers were poured (Biden's a "near-beer," as he no longer drank alcohol), and the meeting (whatever the actual significance concerning the original incident) entered the historical record forever known as—"The Beer Summit."

A PUB AND A PRESIDENT

Obama, the son of a white woman (the late Ann Dunham) and a Kenyan student named Barack Obama, traced his ancestry on his mother's side back to Ireland. One Falmouth Kearney, a cobbler, reportedly was the first Irishman (related to the president's mother) to immigrate to the States during the Irish Potato Famine in 1850.

In 2011, President Obama traveled to the Emerald Isle, to a tiny village (population, about three hundred) called Moneygall in Offlay County.

As expected, Obama's arrival set the village and surrounding area into a beehive of activity. And since this was Ireland, a sampling of Guinness at the village local—in this case the Hayes Pub—was on the agenda.

ADVANCE WORK, INDEED!

We tend (usually) to view the Secret Service agents as hardworking, diligent, always-on-alert kind of guys. But it is not always slog and drudge, with the occasional dose of danger thrown in. Sometimes the job can be, well, refreshing!

In Moneygall, the Secret Service men checked out the Hayes Pub quite thoroughly (and that meant diligently sampling the beer) before the president and First Lady Michelle Obama entered the cozy establishment. In fact, the presidential couple joked about it:

"How often has our staff been in here?" smiled Michelle.

"Yeah, how much advance work did they do?" the president chimed in.

BUILDING A PINT

Obama showed his knowledge of Irish pub culture by patiently waiting for the barkeep to "build" his pint of Guinness—which basically means the publican *slowly* adds more stout to the glass, then lets it rest, then *slowly* adds some more—the purpose being not to have too much foam in the pour. All this is allegedly in search of the elusive "perfect pint."

"You tell me when it's properly settled," said the president, displaying his knowledge of pub ritual. "I don't want to mess this up!"

WRECKING A PINT

This is where Obama and Reagan diverge. When Reagan visited Ireland, he barely tried one sip of his Guinness, then switched to a red-amber Smithwicks and also failed to finish that. Fair enough, Ronald Reagan never claimed to be a big beer drinker.

Barack Obama, however, promptly destroyed his pint. He drank a healthy slug of the stout to start off (after some spirited exchanges of the Irish toast "*Slainte!*" around the pub) and essentially took it down in a half dozen pulls or so. (Michelle also sampled the renowned Dublin-brewed stout, if at a more measured pace.)

As one enthused Irishman who viewed the festivities on television later put it: "The president actually killed his pint! He gets my vote."

OBAMA PAYS UP

Quite complimentary of his Guinness, Obama admitted that this was not his first round of stout on Irish soil. The president had savored one at Shannon Airport on a previous trip through Ireland (en route to Afghanistan).

"It tastes better here than it does … in the States," Obama remarked. "What I realized was, is that you guys are—you're keeping all the best stuff here!"

That observation drew lots of laughter, as did Obama's next move: he slapped down some money on the bar and announced: "And by the way … I just want you to know that the president pays his bar tab!"

THE HOME-BREWER IN CHIEF

2011 was also the year that something called "White House Honey Ale" (and "White House Honey Porter" and "White House Honey Blonde") made its first appearance.

The president—using his own money—purchased some home-brewing equipment and the ingredients. Some White House staff members with home-brewing expertise then passed along their knowledge to White House kitchen staffers. Some recipes from a local brew shop were collected and tweaked slightly. The kitchen then brewed up a few tasty beers that suddenly the public had great interest in.

"To be honest, we were surprised that the beer turned out so well, since none of us had brewed beer before," admitted Sam Kass, assistant White House chef, on a whitehouse.gov blog. (There are on-line videos of Kass and fellow staffer Tafari Campbell going through the brewing process, step by step.)

One interesting ingredient is the honey—which comes from a beehive on the South Lawn of the White House, quite close to the first lady's kitchen garden. The honey is primarily enlisted to add smoothness to the brew, rather than to provide sweetness.

THE KICKOFF

White House home brew debuted at the 2011 Super Bowl. Since the Packers and Steelers knocked helmets in that one, there were also some supportive beers from Wisconsin and Pottsville, Pennsylvania's famous Yuengling lager (Yuengling lays claim to being the oldest continuous brewery in America). The beers—both White House brewed and invited "guest" beers—were called upon to wash down food from both states, too, such as bratwurst from Wisconsin and potato chips from the Keystone State.

But it did not take long for word to leak out that the White House was brewing its own beer. And then everybody wanted some. The outcry prompted the White House to release the recipes on September 1, 2012. Just a few days before, President Obama announced: "It will be out soon! I can tell you from first hand experience it is tasty."

White House beers, however, are hard to come by for Joe Six-Pack. Typical batches (which take nearly a month to make from start to finish) yield fewer than one hundred bottles. The honey ales are more apt to appear on special occasions, such as Super Bowls and Saint Patrick's Day.

But special guests can sometimes find one of the much-vaunted brews in their hand, too. When decorated war hero Dakota Meyer visited the White House in 2011, he asked if he could have one of the special beers with Obama. He got his wish.

HAVE BEER, WILL TRAVEL

President Obama has been known to take some of the special White House beer on Air Force One, or—when he ran for reelection in 2012 against Republican Mitt Romney—on his campaign tour bus. Sometimes a lucky citizen was "gifted" a White House brew during these travels.

Obama's opponents were not completely beer-less during the 2012 presidential election. While former Massachusetts governor Romney was not a drinker of alcohol due to his Mormon faith, Romney's running mate, Representative Paul Ryan (true to his Wisconsin roots), made mention of his favorite foods—and brews—in his vice-presidential acceptance speech, proudly proclaiming:

"My veins run with cheese, bratwurst, a Leine's [Leinenkugel's beer from Chippewa Falls], a little Spotted Cow [a microbrew from Wisconsin], and some Miller."

All of which reminds us: never underestimate the role of beer in politics.

All that said, here are the recipes for intrepid home-brewers!

White House Honey Ale

Ingredients:

2 (3.3 lb) cans light malt extract
1 lb light dried malt extract
12 ounces crushed amber crystal malt
8 ounces Biscuit Malt
1 lb White House Honey
1 ½ ounces Kent Goldings hop pellets
1 ½ oz Fuggles hop pellets

2 tsp gypsum

1 pkg Windsor dry ale yeast

¾ cup corn sugar for priming

Directions:

1. In a 12 qt pot, steep the grains in a hop bag in 1 ½ gallons of sterile water at 155 degrees for half an hour. Remove the grains.
2. Add the 2 cans of the malt extract and the dried extract and bring to a boil.
3. For the first flavoring, add the 1½ ounces Kent Goldings and 2 tsp of gypsum. Boil for 45 minutes.
4. For the second flavoring, add the 1½ oz Fuggles hop pellets at the last minute of the boil.
5. Add the honey and boil for 5 more minutes.
6. Add 2 gallons chilled sterile water into the primary fermenter and add the hot wort into it. Top with more water to total 5 gallons. There is no need to strain.
7. Pitch yeast when wort temperature is between 70–80°. Fill airlock halfway with water.
8. Ferment at 68–72° for about seven days.
9. Rack to a secondary fermenter after five days and ferment for 14 more days.
10. To bottle, dissolve the corn sugar into 2 pints of boiling water for 15 minutes. Pour the mixture into an empty bottling bucket. Siphon the beer from the fermenter over it. Distribute priming sugar evenly. Siphon into bottles and cap. Let sit for 2 to 3 weeks at 75°.

White House Honey Porter

Ingredients:

2 (3.3 lb) cans light unhopped malt extract

¾ lb Munich malt (cracked)
1 lb crystal 20 malt (cracked)
6 ounces black malt (cracked)
3 ounces chocolate malt (cracked)
1 lb White House Honey
10 HBUs bittering hops
½ oz Hallertaur Aroma hops
1 pkg Nottingham dry yeast
¾ cup corn sugar for bottling

Directions:

1. In a 6 qt pot, add grains to 2.25 qts of 168° water. Mix well to bring temp down to 155°. Steep on stovetop at 155° for 45 minutes. Meanwhile, bring 2 gallons of water to 165° in a 12 qt pot. Place strainer over, then pour and spoon all the grains and liquid in. Rinse with 2 gallons of 165° water. Let liquid drain through. Discard the grains and bring the liquid to a boil. Set aside.
2. Add the 2 cans of malt extract and honey into the pot. Stir well.
3. Boil for an hour. Add half of the bittering hops at the 15-minute mark, the other half at 30-minute mark, then the aroma hops at the 60-minute mark.
4. Set aside and let stand for 15 minutes.
5. Place 2 gallons of chilled water into the primary fermenter and add the hot wort into it. Top with more water to total 5 gallons if necessary. Place into an ice bath to cool down to 70–80°.
6. Activate dry yeast in 1 cup of sterilized water at 75–90° for fifteen minutes. Pitch yeast into the fermenter. Fill airlock halfway with water. Ferment at room temp (64–68°) for 3-4 days.
7. Siphon over to a secondary glass fermenter for another 4–7 days.

8. To bottle, make a priming syrup on the stove with 1 cup sterile water and 3/4 cup priming sugar, bring to a boil for five minutes. Pour the mixture into an empty bottling bucket. Siphon the beer from the fermenter over it. Distribute priming sugar evenly. Siphon into bottles and cap. Let sit for 1–2 weeks at 75°.

THE NIGHT-OWL MARTINI MAN

Although it is well established that Obama enjoys an occasional beer and likes fine wine (plus a margarita once in a while), a 2014 feature in the *New Yorker* ("Going the Distance" by David Remnick) observed that the president drinks an old FDR favorite, too. According to Remnick:

> ... the Obamas have taken to hosting occasional off-the-record dinners in the residence upstairs at the White House. The guests ordinarily include a friendly political figure, a business leader, a journalist. Obama drinks a Martini or two ... and he and the First Lady are welcoming, funny, and warm. The dinners start at six. At around ten-thirty at one dinner last spring, the guests assumed the evening was winding down. But when Obama was asked if they should leave, he laughed and said, "Hey, don't go! I'm a night owl! Have another drink." The party went on past 1 A.M.

FDR would have been proud, both of the offer *and* the drink of choice.

LAST CALL

American leaders typically expect to be treated—or subjected—to the infamous *maotai* when they visit China. But Chinese president Xi Jinping brought a surprise "roadie" of the potent sorghum-based liquor to Palm Springs, California, for a 2013 summit. Since Xi opened the bottle especially to toast Obama, one assumes the chief executive at least paid "lip service" to the Chinese liquid equivalent of dragon-fire.

Maotai aside, Obama has not missed out on fine wines. A typical lineup of top vintages was served at a dinner held at Harlem's trendy Red Rooster restaurant (where donors plunked down thirty thousand dollars to dine with the president prior to the 2012 campaign). A lobster salad was accompanied by a Riesling "semi-dry" (Hermann J. Weiner, 2000) from New York's Finger Lakes region; with braised short ribs coupled with the likes of Ridge Geyserville "Essence" from Sonoma County and Brown Estate "Chaos Theory," a 2009 vintage from the African American–owned winery in Napa Valley.

Acknowledgments

"**I** feel every day a greater disposition to drop this nonsense," John Quincy Adams groused in his diary on New Year's Day, 1788. "It takes up a great deal of my time...and was it not for the pleasure of complaining to myself, I believe I should have done long ago."

Had Adams acted on his impulse, history would have been much the worse for it.

Diligent diarists, such as John Adams and John Quincy Adams, provide wonderful nuggets—some humorous, some serious—on drinking in the early American era. Letters were equally bountiful, and without such lodes of precious material this book would have fallen short of its original aim—to both inform and entertain.

So—in addition to John Adams and son—the first wave of acknowledgments must go out, across the decades, to the dedicated diarists, such as Margaret Bayard Smith, John Hay, Gideon Welles, Colonel William Crook, Thomas Donaldson, Colonel Archibald Butt, Colonel Edmund Starling,

Harold Ickes, and Arthur Schlesinger Jr., just to name a few of the more prominent featured in this book.

Closer to home, a special nod to my tolerant family: wife Sally, daughter Jordan, and West Highland terrier Andy—who would interrupt my work by demanding his daily walk or pile onto my lap if I failed to comply with his tail-wagging wishes.

From the publishing world, heartfelt appreciation to my agent Zach Schisgal, who believed in this project from its conception, dreamed up its title, and brought the book to Alex Novak at Salem-Regnery in Washington, D.C.

In addition to Alex, thanks to all of the Regnery team who have worked on this project with equal measures of patience and passion. Any "gremlins" that have crept onto the page are certainly my fault and not theirs.

A special thanks to the staff at the Rutherford B. Hayes Presidential Center in Fremont, Ohio, for allowing the use of selected entries from the Thomas Donaldson diaries—which are appearing for the first time in a widely distributed book.

While these friends hardly deserve to be lumped into a heap under "others"—here you, nonetheless, are: Philip Greene, Patrick Egan, Mark Harris, Marty Desilets, C. Mauro Goffi, Steve Midway, Brandon Claycomb, Adam Carpenter, Vrinda Jagota, Pete and Emily Heesen, Don Wuenschel, James Lutz, Bob Cohen, my mother Trudy Weber (a voracious reader who discovered at least two "nuggets" used in this book), and the various characters who hold court at the agent provocateur's preferred hideout known as the Wise Bean Café in Bethlehem, Pennsylvania.

Lastly, a heartfelt thanks to my friend Patrick McGeehan, who several years ago said to me: "Somebody should write a book about the drinking habits of the presidents…You're a writer…Why don't *you* do it?" And so I finally gave in and plunged into what proved to be (at least for this writer) a rich and riveting subject.

Bibliography

CHAPTER 1: GEORGE WASHINGTON

Chernow, Ron. *Washington: A Life*. New York: Penguin Group US, 2010.

Fisher, David Hackett. *Washington's Crossing*. Oxford & New York: Oxford University Press, 2004.

Letters and Recollections of George Washington. Mount Vernon, VA: Archibald Constable and Company Limited, 1906.

Niemcewicz, Julian. *Under Their Vine and Fig Tree*. Translated by M. J. E. Budka. Newark, NJ: The Grassman Publishing Company, Inc., 1965.

The Writings of George Washington. Edited by Worthington Chauncey Ford. New York & London: G. P. Putnam's Sons, 1890.

CHAPTER 2: JOHN ADAMS

Adams, Abigail, and John Adams. *My Dearest Friend: Letters of Abigail and John Adams*. Edited by Margaret Hogan and C. James Taylor. Boston: Belknap Press of Harvard Univ. Press, 2007.

Adams Family Correspondence. 2 vols. Edited by Lyman Butterfield. Cambridge, MA: Harvard University Press, 1963.

Adams, John. *Diary and Autobiography*. 4 vols. Edited by Lyman Butterfield. Boston, 1961.

McCullough, David. *John Adams*. New York: Simon & Schuster, 2001.

CHAPTER 3: THOMAS JEFFERSON

Crawford, Alan Pell. *Twilight at Monticello: The Final Years of Thomas Jefferson*. New York: Random House, 2008.

Ellis, Joseph J. *American Sphinx: The Character of Thomas Jefferson*. New York: Alfred A. Knopf, 1998.

Grabler, James M. *Passions: The Wines and Travels of Thomas Jefferson*. Baltimore, MD: The Bacchus Press Ltd., 1995.

Jefferson, Thomas. *Memoirs, Correspondence, and Private Papers of Thomas Jefferson*. Edited by Thomas Jefferson Randolph. London: Colburn and Bentley, 1829.

Kranish, Michael. *Flight from Monticello: Thomas Jefferson at War*. New York: Oxford University Press, 2010.

Thomas Jefferson's Farm Book. Edited by Edwin Morris Betts. Charlottesville, VA: The Thomas Jefferson Memorial Foundation, 1999.

Wallace, Benjamin. *The Billionaire's Vinegar: The Mystery of the World's Most Expensive Bottle of Wine*. New York: Random House LLC, 2008.

CHAPTER 4: JAMES MADISON

Anthony, Katharine S. *Dolly Madison: Her Life and Times*. New York: Doubleday, 1949.

Hickey, Donald R. *The War of 1812: A Forgotten Conflict*. Champaign, IL: University of Illinois Press, 1989.

Ketcham, Ralph. *James Madison: A Biography*. Charlottesville, VA: University Press of Virginia, 1990.

Madison, James. *The Papers of James Madison*. 15 vols. Edited by William T. Hutchinson and William M. E. Rachal. Chicago: University of Chicago Press, 1962.

Smith, Margaret Bayard. *The First Forty Years of Washington Society*. Washington, D.C.: Scribner, 1906.

CHAPTER 5: JAMES MONROE

Ammon, Harry. *James Monroe: The Quest for National Identity*. Charlottesville, VA: University of Virginia Press, 1990.

Monroe, James. *The Writings of James Monroe*. Edited by Stanislaus Murray Hamilton. New York: G. P. Putnam Sons, 1900.

Styron, Arthur. *The Last of the Cocked Hats: James Monroe and the Virginia Dynasty*. Norman, OK: University of Oklahoma Press, 1945.

Unger, Harlow G. *The Last Founding Father: James Monroe and a Nation's Call to Greatness*. Cambridge, MA: Da Capo Press, 2009.

CHAPTER 6: JOHN QUINCY ADAMS

Adams, John Quincy. *Memoirs of John Quincy Adams*. 12 vol. Edited by Charles Francis Adams. Philadelphia: J.B. Lippincott & Company, 1874–1877.

Morse, John T. *John Quincy Adams*. Boston and New York: Houghton, Mifflin, 1882.

Nagel, Paul C. *John Quincy Adams: A Public Life, A Private Life*. New York: Random House LLC, 2012.

Unger, Harlow G. *John Quincy Adams: A Life*. Cambridge, MA: De Capo Press, 2012.

CHAPTER 7: ANDREW JACKSON

Jackson, Andrew. *The Papers of Andrew Jackson*. Knoxville: University of Tennessee Press, 1980.

Marszalek, John F. *The Petticoat Affair: Manners, Mutiny, and Sex in Andrew Jackson's White House*. New York: Free Press, 1997.

Meacham, John. *American Lion: Andrew Jackson in the White House*. New York: Random House, 2008.

Parton, James. *Life of Andrew Jackson*. 3 vols. New York: Johnson Reprint Corp., 1967.

CHAPTER 8: MARTIN VAN BUREN

Alexander, Holmes M. *The American Talleyrand: The Career and Contemporaries of Martin Van Buren*. New York: Harper, 1935

Marszalek, John F. *The Petticoat Affair: Manners, Mutiny, and Sex in Andrew Jackson's White House*. New York: Free Press, 1997.

Shepard, Edward M. *Martin Van Buren*. Boston and New York: Houghton, Mifflin & Co., 1888.

Van Buren, Marin. *The Autobiography of Martin Van Buren*. Edited by John C. Fitzgerald. Washington, D.C.: The American Historical Association, 1920.

CHAPTER 9: WILLIAM HENRY HARRISON

Green, James. *William Henry Harrison: His Life and Times*. Richmond, VA: Garrett and Massie, 1941.

Gunderson, Robert Gray. *The Log Cabin Campaign*. Westport, CT: Greenwood Publishing Group, Inc., 1977.

Hone, Philip. *The Diary of Philip Hone*. Edited by Bayard Tuckerman. New York: Dodd, Mead & Company, 1889.

Sugden, John. *Tecumseh: A Life*. New York: Henry Holt and Co., 1998.

CHAPTER 10: JOHN TYLER

Chitwood, Oliver Perry. *John Tyler: Champion of the Old South*. New York: Russell & Russell, 1964.

Hone, Philip. *The Diary of Philip Hone*. Edited by Bayard Tuckerman. New York: Dodd, Mead & Company, 1889.

Kirwan, Albert D. *John J. Crittenden: The Struggle for the Union*. Lexington, KY: University of Kentucky Press, 1962.

Tyler, Lyon G. *The Letters and Times of the Tylers*. 3 vol. Richmond, VA: Whittet & Shepperson, 1885.

Wise, John S. *Recollections of Thirteen Presidents*. New York: Doubleday, 1906.

CHAPTER 11: JAMES K. POLK

Borneman, Walter H. Polk: *The Man Who Transformed the Presidency and America*. New York: Random House, 2008.

Byrnes, Mark E. *James K. Polk: A Biographical Companion*. Santa Barbara, CA: ABC-CLIO, 2001.

James, Marquis. *The Raven: A Biography of Sam Houston*. Norwalk, CT: Easton Press, 1988.

Polk, James K. *Correspondence of James K. Polk*. 6 vols. Edited by Herbert Weaver. Nashville: Vanderbilt University Press, 1969.

Sellers, Charles Grier. *James K. Polk: The Jacksonian, 1795–1843*. Princeton, NJ: Princeton University Press, 1957.

CHAPTER 12: ZACHARY TAYLOR

Bauer, Jack K. *Zachery Taylor: Soldier, Planter, Statesman of the Old Southwest.* Baton Rouge, LA: Louisiana State University Press, 1993.

Hamilton, Holman. *Zachery Taylor.* Hamden, CT: Archon Books, 1966.

Hoffman, Charles F. *A Winter in the Far West.* London: Richard Bentley, 1835.

Meade, George Gordon. *The Life and Letters of George Gordon Meade.* New York: Charles Scribner's Sons, 1913.

Taylor, Zachary. *Letters of Zachary Taylor: From the Battlefields of the Mexican War.* Edited by William Bixby and William H. Samson. Auburn, NY: The Genesee Press, 1908.

CHAPTER 13: MILLARD FILLMORE

Fillmore, Millard. *Millard Fillmore Papers.* 2 vols. Buffalo, NY: The Buffalo Historical Society, 1907.

Rayback, Robert J. *Millard Fillmore: A Biography of a President.* Norwalk, CT: Easton Press, 1972.

Scarry, Robert J. *Millard Fillmore.* Jefferson, NC: McFarland & Co., Publishing, 2001.

CHAPTER 14: FRANKLIN PIERCE

Forney, John W. *Anecdotes of Public Men (Vol. 1 & 2).* New York: Harper & Brothers, 1873.

Nichols, Roy F. *Franklin Pierce, Young Hickory of the Granite Hills.* 2nd ed. Philadelphia: University of Pennsylvania Press, 1958.

Pierce, Franklin. *Franklin Pierce Papers.* Washington, D.C.: Library of Congress, 1959.

Wallner, Peter A. *Franklin Pierce.* Concord, NH: Plaidswede Publishing, 2007.

CHAPTER 15: JAMES BUCHANAN

Buchanan, James, and William Frederic Worner. *Letters of James Buchanan.* Lancaster, PA: Lancaster County Historical Society, 1932.

Forney, John W. *Anecdotes of Public Men (Vol. 1 & 2).* New York: Harper & Brothers, 1873.

Klein, Philip Shriver. *President James Buchanan, a Biography.* University Park: Pennsylvania State University Press, 1962.

Smith, Elbert B. *The Presidency of James Buchanan*. Lawrence: University Press of
   Kansas, 1975.

CHAPTER 16: ABRAHAM LINCOLN

Brooks, Noah. *Washington in Lincoln's Time*. Washington, D.C.: Century Co., 1895.
Crook, William H. *Through Five Administrations: Reminiscences of William H.
   Crook, Body-guard to President Lincoln*. New York: Harper and Brothers, 1910.
Emerson, Jason. *Giant in the Shadows: The Life of Robert T. Lincoln*. Carbondale,
   IL: Southern Illinois University Press, 2012.
Goodwin, Doris Kearns. *Team of Rivals: The Political Genius of Abraham Lincoln*.
   New York: Simon & Schuster, 2005.
Hay, John. *Inside Lincoln's White House: The Complete Civil War Diary of John
   Hay*. Edited by Michael Burlingame and John R. Turner Ettlinger. Carbondale,
   IL: Southern Illinois University Press, 1999.
Porter, Horace. *Campaigning with Grant*. New York: Century Company, 1897.
Stoddard, William Osborn. *Inside the White House in War Times*. New York: C. L.
   Webster & Company, 1890.
Welles, Gideon. *Diary of Gideon Welles (Vol. 1–3)*. Boston & New York: Houghton
   Mifflin, Riverside Press, 1911.

CHAPTER 17: ANDREW JOHNSON

Boulard, Garry. *The Swing around the Circle: Andrew Johnson and the Train Ride
   That Destroyed a Presidency*. New York: iUniverse, Inc., 2008.
Crook, William H. *Through Five Administrations: Reminiscences of William H.
   Crook, Body-guard to President Lincoln*. New York: Harper and Brothers, 1910.
Welles, Gideon. *Diary of Gideon Welles (Vol. 1–3)*. Boston & New York: Houghton
   Mifflin, Riverside Press, 1911.
Wise, John S. *Recollections of Thirteen Presidents*. Freeport, NY: Books for Librar-
   ies Press, 1968.

CHAPTER 18: ULYSSES S. GRANT

Boulard, Garry. *The Swing around the Circle: Andrew Johnson and the Train Ride
   That Destroyed a Presidency*. New York: iUniverse, Inc., 2008.
Catton, Bruce. Grant Takes Command. Edison, NJ: Castle Books, 2000.
Crook, William H. *Through Five Administrations: Reminiscences of William H.
   Crook, Body-guard to President Lincoln*. New York: Harper and Brothers, 1910.

Porter, Horace. *Campaigning with Grant*. New York: Century Company, 1897.

Smith, Jean Edward. *Grant*. New York: Simon & Schuster, 2002.

Welles, Gideon. *Diary of Gideon Welles (Vol. 1–3)*. Boston & New York: Houghton Mifflin, Riverside Press, 1911.

CHAPTER 19: RUTHERFORD B. HAYES

Hayes, Rutherford B., and Charles Richard Williams. *Diary and Letters of Rutherford Birchard Hayes, Nineteenth President of the United States*. Columbus, OH: Ohio State Archæological and Historical Society, 1922.

Hoogenboom, Ari Arthur. *Rutherford B. Hayes: Warrior and President*. Lawrence, KS: U of Kansas, 1995.

Mahan, Russell L. *Lucy Webb Hayes: A First Lady by Example*. Hauppauge, NY: Nova Science, 2010.

Wise, John S. *Recollections of Thirteen Presidents*. Freeport, NY: Books for Libraries Press, 1968.

CHAPTER 20: JAMES GARFIELD

Garfield, James A., and B. A. Hinsdale. *The Works of James Abram Garfield*. Boston: J.R. Osgood, 1882.

Millard, Candice. *The Destiny of the Republic: A Tale of Madness, Medicine and the Murder of a President*. New York: Doubleday, 2011.

Peskin, Allan. *Garfield: A Biography*. Kent, OH: Kent State UP, 1978.

Wise, John S. *Recollections of Thirteen Presidents*. Freeport, NY: Books for Libraries Press, 1968.

CHAPTER 21: CHESTER A. ARTHUR

Morgan, James. *Our Presidents: Brief Biographies of Our Chief Magistrates from Washington to Truman, 1789–1949*. Revised/expanded ed. New York: Macmillan, 1949.

Reeves, Thomas C. *Gentleman Boss: The Life of Chester Alan Arthur*. Revised/expanded ed. New York: Knopf; distributed by Random House, 1975.

Wise, John S. *Recollections of Thirteen Presidents*. Freeport, NY: Books for Libraries Press, 1968.

CHAPTER 22: GROVER A. CLEVELAND

Algeo, Matthew. *The President Is a Sick Man: Wherein the Supposedly Virtuous Grover Cleveland Survives a Secret Surgery at Sea and Vilifies the Courageous Newspaperman Who Dared Expose the Truth.* Chicago: Chicago Review Press, 2011.

Cleveland, Grover, and Allan Nevins. *Letters of Grover Cleveland, 1850–1908.* Boston: Houghton Mifflin Co., 1933.

Lachman, Charles. *A Secret Life: The Sex, Lies and Scandals of President Grover Cleveland.* New York: Skyhorse Pub., 2011.

Nevins, Allan. *Grover Cleveland: A Study in Courage.* New York: Dodd, Mead, 1941.

Wise, John S. *Recollections of Thirteen Presidents.* Freeport, NY: Books for Libraries Press, 1968.

CHAPTER 23: BENJAMIN HARRISON

Dewar, Thomas R. *A Ramble round the Globe.* London: Chatto and Windus, 1894.

Sievers, Harry Joseph. *Benjamin Harrison, Hoosier President: The White House and After.* Indianapolis: Bobbs-Merrill Co., 1968.

———. *Benjamin Harrison: Hoosier Warrior, 1833–1865.* Chicago: H. Regnery, 1952.

Wise, John S. *Recollections of Thirteen Presidents.* Freeport, NY: Books for Libraries Press, 1968.

CHAPTER 24: WILLIAM McKINLEY

Hayes, Rutherford B., and Charles Richard Williams. *Diary and Letters of Rutherford Birchard Hayes, Nineteenth President of the United States.* Columbus, OH: Ohio State Archæological and Historical Society, 1922.

Marsh, Daniel L. *The Challenge of Pittsburgh.* New York: Missionary Education Movement of the United States and Canada, 1917.

Miller, Scott. *The President and the Assassin: McKinley, Terror, and Empire at the Dawn of the American Century.* New York: Random House, 2011.

Morgan, H. Wayne. *William McKinley and His America.* Syracuse, NY: Syracuse UP, 1963.

Olcott, Charles S. *The Life of William McKinley.* Boston: Houghton Mifflin, 1916.

CHAPTER 25: THEODORE ROOSEVELT

Butt, Archibald Willingham, and Lawrence F. Abbott. *The Letters of Archie Butt, Personal Aide to President Roosevelt.* Garden City, NY: Doubleday, Page, 1924.

Dunn, Arthur Wallace. *Gridiron Nights: Humorous and Satirical Views of Politics and Statesmen as Presented by the Famous Dining Club.* New York: Frederick A. Stokes Company, 1915.

Goodwin, Doris Kearns. *The Bully Pulpit: Theodore Roosevelt, William Howard Taft and the Golden Age of Journalism.* New York: Simon & Schuster, 2013.

Millard, Candice. *River of Doubt: Theodore Roosevelt's Darkest Journey.* New York: Doubleday, 2005.

Morris, Edmund, and Edmund Morris. *Theodore Rex.* New York: Random House, 2001.

Roosevelt, Theodore. *African Game Trails: An Account of the African Wanderings of an American Hunter-Naturalist.* New York: Scribner, 1910.

———. *Theodore Roosevelt: An Autobiography.* New York: The Macmillan Company, 1913.

CHAPTER 26: WILLIAM HOWARD TAFT

Butt, Archibald Willingham. *Taft and Roosevelt: The Intimate Letters of Archie Butt.* Garden City, NY: Doubleday, Doran & Co., 1930.

Goodwin, Doris Kearns. *The Bully Pulpit: Theodore Roosevelt, William Howard Taft and the Golden Age of Journalism.* New York: Simon & Schuster, 2013.

Pringle, Henry F. *The Life and Times of William Howard Taft.* New York; Toronto: Farrar & Rinehart, 1939.

Thompson, Willis. *Presidents I've Known and Two Near Presidents.* Indianapolis: Bobbs-Merrill, 1929.

CHAPTER 27: WOODROW WILSON

Cooper, John M. *Woodrow Wilson.* New York: Knopf Doubleday, 2009.

Daniels, Josephus. *The Life of Woodrow Wilson.* Whitefish, MT: Kessinger Publishing, 2004.

Lee, Annibel. *Little Stories by Big Men.* New York: G.P. Putnam's Sons, 1913.

Smith, Gene. *When the Cheering Stopped: The Last Years of Woodrow Wilson.* New York: Morrow, 1964.

Wood, William A. *After Dinner Speeches and How to Make Them*. Chicago: T. H. Flood, 1914.

CHAPTER 28: WARREN G. HARDING

Anthony, Carl Sferrazza. *Florence Harding: The First Lady, the Jazz Age, and the Death of America's Most Scandalous President*. New York: W. Morrow, 1998.

Jaffray, Elizabeth. *Secrets of the White House*. New York: Cosmopolitan Book, 1927.

Krock, Arthur. *Memoirs: Sixty Years on the Firing Line*. New York: Funk & Wagnalls, 1968.

Longworth, Alice Roosevelt. *Crowded Hours: Reminiscences of Alice Roosevelt Longworth*. New York: C. Scribner's Sons, 1933.

McLean, Evalyn Walsh, and Boyden Sparkes. *Father Struck It Rich*. Boston: Little, Brown, 1936.

Mencken, H. L. *The Vintage Mencken*. New York: Vintage Books, 1955.

Natta, Don. *First off the Tee: Presidential Hackers, Duffers, and Cheaters, from Taft to Bush*. New York: Public Affairs, 2003.

Russell, Francis. *The Shadow of Blooming Grove: Warren G. Harding in His times*. New York: McGraw-Hill, 1968.

Starling, Edmund W., and Thomas Sugrue. *Starling of the White House: The Story of the Man Whose Secret Service Detail Guarded Five Presidents from Woodrow Wilson to Franklin D. Roosevelt*. Chicago: Peoples Book Club, 1916.

CHAPTER 29: CALVIN COOLIDGE

Hoover, Irwin Hood. *Forty-Two Years in the White House*. Boston: Houghton Mifflin Company, 1934.

McCoy, Donald R. *Calvin Coolidge: The Quiet President*. New York: Macmillan, 1967.

Mencken, H. L. *The Vintage Mencken*. New York: Vintage Books, 1955.

Smith, Richard Norton. *An Uncommon Man: The Triumph of Herbert Hoover*. New York: Simon and Schuster, 1984.

White, William Allen. *Calvin Coolidge, The Man Who Is President*. New York: The Macmillan Company, 1925.

CHAPTER 30: HERBERT HOOVER

Hoover, Herbert. *The Memoirs of Herbert Hoover.* New York: Macmillan, 1951.

Mencken, H. L. *The Vintage Mencken.* New York: Vintage Books, 1955.

Meyer, Agnes Elizabeth Ernst. *Out of These Roots: The Autobiography of an American Woman.* Revised/expanded ed. Boston: Little, Brown, 1953.

Okrent, Daniel. *Last Call: The Rise and Fall of Prohibition.* New York: Simon and Schuster, 2010.

Smith, Richard Norton. *An Uncommon Man: The Triumph of Herbert Hoover.* New York: Simon and Schuster, 1984.

CHAPTER 31: FRANKLIN DELANO ROOSEVELT

Hayes, Helen, and Katherine Hatch. *My Life in Three Acts.* San Diego: Harcourt Brace Jovanovich, 1990.

Ickes, Harold L. *The Secret Diary of Harold L. Ickes.* New York: Simon and Schuster, 1953.

Meacham, Jon. *Franklin and Winston: An Intimate Portrait of an Epic Friendship.* New York: Random House, 2003.

Moorehead, Caroline. *Gellhorn: A Twentieth-Century Life.* New York: H. Holt, 2003.

Rhodes, Richard. *The Making of the Atomic Bomb.* New York: Simon & Schuster, 1986.

Roosevelt, James, and Bill Libby. *My Parents: A Differing View.* Chicago: Playboy Press, 1976.

Smith, Jean Edward. *FDR.* New York: Random House, 2007.

CHAPTER 32: HARRY S. TRUMAN

Algeo, Matthew. *Harry Truman's Excellent Adventure: The True Story of a Great American Road Trip.* Chicago: Chicago Review, 2009.

McCullough, David. *Truman.* New York: Simon & Schuster, 2003.

Steinberg, Alfred. *The Man from Missouri: The Life and Times of Harry S. Truman.* New York: Putnam, 1962.

Truman, Harry S., and Mark Goodman. *Give 'em Hell, Harry!.* New York: Award Books, 1974.

Truman, Harry S., and Monte M. Poen. *Letters Home.* New York: Putnam, 1984.

CHAPTER 33: DWIGHT D. EISENHOWER

D'Este, Carlo. *Eisenhower: A Soldier's Life*. New York: Henry Holt, 2003.

Gray, Robert Keith. *Eighteen Acres under Glass*. Garden City, NY: Doubleday, 1962.

Krock, Arthur. *Memoirs: Sixty Years on the Firing Line*. New York: Funk & Wagnalls, 1968.

Morgan, Kay Summersby. *Eisenhower Was My Boss*. New York: Dell, 1948.

———. *Past Forgetting*. New York: Simon Schuster, 1973.

Smith, Jean Edward. *Eisenhower in War and Peace*. New York: Random House LLC, 2012.

CHAPTER 34: JOHN FITZGERALD KENNEDY

Alsop, Joseph. *I've Seen the Best of It: Memoirs*. New York: Norton, 1992.

Bradlee, Benjamin. *Conversations with Kennedy*. New York: Norton, 1975.

Graham, Katharine. *Personal History*. New York: Knopf, 1997.

Hersh, Seymour. *The Dark Side of Camelot*. New York: Harper Collins Publishers Limited, 1998.

Schlesinger, Arthur M., Jr. *Journals, 1952–2000*. New York: Penguin Press, 2007.

———. *A Thousand Days*. New York: Houghton Mifflin, 1965.

Thomas, Helen. *Front Row at the White House*. New York: Simon Schuster, 1999.

Walsh, Kenneth T. *Air Force One: A History of the Presidents and Their Planes*. New York: Hyperion, 2003.

CHAPTER 35: LYNDON BAINES JOHNSON

Califano, Joseph A. *The Triumph and Tragedy of Lyndon Johnson: The White House Years*. New York: Simon & Schuster, 1991.

Caro, Robert A. *The Passage of Power*. New York: Alfred A. Knopf, 2012.

———. *The Years of Lyndon Johnson: The Path to Power*. New York: Knopf, 1982.

Dallek, Robert. *Flawed Giant: Lyndon Johnson and His Times, 1961–1973*. New York: Oxford University Press, 1998.

Johnson, Sam Houston. *My Brother, Lyndon*. 1st ed. New York: Cowles Book Co., 1970.

Novak, Robert D. *The Prince of Darkness: 50 Years Reporting in Washington*. New York: Crown Forum, 2007.

Russell, Jan Jarboe. *Lady Bird: A Biography of Mrs. Johnson*. New York: Scribner, 1999.

Woods, Randall Bennett. *LBJ: Architect of American Ambition*. New York: Free Press, 2006.

CHAPTER 36: RICHARD MILHOUS NIXON

Dallek, Robert. *Nixon and Kissinger: Partners in Power*. New York: HarperCollins, 2007.

Ehrlichman, John. *Witness to Power: The Nixon Years*. New York: Simon and Schuster, 1982.

Fulsom, Don. *Nixon's Darkest Secrets: The Inside Story of America's Most Troubled President*. New York: Thomas Dunne Books, 2012.

Higgins, George V. *The Friends of Richard Nixon*. Boston: Little, Brown, 1975.

Kissinger, Henry, and Clare Boothe Luce. *White House Years*. Boston: Little, Brown, 1979.

Nixon, Richard M. *RN: The Memoirs of Richard Nixon*. New York: Grosset & Dunlap, 1978.

Woodward, Bob, and Carl Bernstein. *The Final Days*. New York: Simon and Schuster, 1976.

CHAPTER 37: GERALD FORD

DeFrank, Thomas M., and Gerald R. Ford. *Write It When I'm Gone: Remarkable Off-the-Record Conversations with Gerald R. Ford*. New York: G.P. Putnam's Sons, 2007.

Nessen, Ron. *Making the News, Taking the News: From NBC to the Ford White House*. Middletown, CT: Wesleyan University Press, 2011.

Walsh, Kenneth T. *Air Force One: A History of the Presidents and Their Planes*. New York: Hyperion, 2003.

Woodward, Bob. *Shadow: Five Presidents and the Legacy of Watergate*. New York: Simon & Schuster, 1999.

CHAPTER 38: JAMES EARL "JIMMY" CARTER

Carter, Jimmy. *Keeping Faith: Memoirs of a President*. Toronto: Bantam Books, 1982.

Carter, William. *Billy Carter: A Journey through the Shadows*. Atlanta: Longstreet, 1999.

Kessler, Ronald. *In the President's Secret Service: Behind the Scenes with Agents in the Line of Fire and the Presidents They Protect*. New York: Crown Publishers, 2009.

Scheer, Robert, and Gore Vidal. *Playing President: My Close Encounters with Nixon, Carter, Bush I, Reagan, and Clinton—and How They Did Not Prepare Me for George W. Bush*. Los Angeles: Truthdig, 2006.

CHAPTER 39: RONALD REAGAN

Matthews, Christopher. *Tip and the Gipper: When Politics Worked*. New York: Simon & Schuster, 2014.

Reagan, Ronald, and Douglas Brinkley. *The Reagan Diaries*. New York: HarperCollins, 2007.

Reagan, Ronald, and Kiron K. Skinner. *Reagan: A Life in Letters*. New York: Free Press, 2003.

Shultz, George Pratt. *Turmoil and Triumph: My Years as Secretary of State*. New York: Scribner's, 1993.

Woodward, Bob. *Shadow: Five Presidents and the Legacy of Watergate*. New York: Simon & Schuster, 1999.

CHAPTER 40: GEORGE H. W. BUSH

Bush, Barbara. *Barbara Bush: Reflections*. Maine: Thorndike Press, 2003.

Bush, George. *All the Best, George Bush: My Life in Letters and Other Writings*. New York: Scribner, 1999.

Bush, George, and Jeffrey A. Engel. *The China Diary of George H. W. Bush: The Making of a Global President*. Princeton: Princeton UP, 2008.

CHAPTER 41: WILLIAM JEFFERSON "BILL" CLINTON

Branch, Taylor. *The Clinton Tapes: Wrestling History with the President*. New York: Simon & Schuster, 2009.

Clinton, Bill. *My Life*. New York: Alfred A. Knopf, 2004.

Matalin, Mary, and James Carville. *All's Fair: Love, War, and Running for President*. New York: Random House, 1994.

CHAPTER 42: GEORGE W. BUSH

Baker, Peter. *Days of Fire: Bush and Cheney in the White House*, New York: Anchor, 2013.

Bush, Barbara. *Barbara Bush: Reflections*. Maine: Thorndike Press, 2003.

Bush, George W. *Decision Points*. New York: Crown Publishers, 2010.

Bush, Laura Welch. *Spoken from the Heart*. New York: Scribner, 2010.

Minutaglio, Bill. *First Son: George W. Bush and the Bush Family Dynasty*. New York: Times Books, 1999.

CHAPTER 43: BARACK OBAMA

Obama, Barack. *Dreams from My Father: A Story of Race and Inheritance*. New York: Three Rivers Press, 2004.

Remnick, David. *The Bridge: The Life and Rise of Barack Obama*. New York: Alfred A. Knopf, 2010.

Index

387

W

Wade, Benjamin, 108
Waldorf-Astoria Hotel, 221, 276, 302
Wallace, Benjamin, 27
Wallace, George, 306
Wallace, Henry, 263
Wall Street, 4, 200–1, 236, 245, 250, 283
Wall Street Journal, 4
"Wall Street Wally," 250
Walsh, Kenneth T., 286, 313
War of 1812, the, 29, 38, 52, 77, 98, 101
Ward, Sam, 170–71
Ward's Tavern, 112
Washington Evening Star, 202
Washington, George, 1–11, 13, 18, 30, 37, 43, 56, 80, 87, 90, 271, 283, 294
Washington Post, 229, 233, 277, 285, 287
Washington's Crossing, 6
Washington, William A., 3
Watergate scandal, 299–300, 302–3, 305–6, 309–10
Watson, David, 22
Wayne, Mad Anthony, 75
Webster-Ashburton Treaty, 86
Webster, Daniel, 73, 84, 90, 95, 106, 108, 113
Weiner, Hermann J., 368
Welles, Gideon, 136, 139, 148, 182, 369
West Point, 257, 272–73
Whigs, Whig Party, 66, 71, 74, 78–81, 84, 87, 89, 97, 102, 106, 112–12, 115
whiskey, 1–4, 7, 14, 22, 29–31, 35, 43, 51, 56, 59, 61, 65, 68, 75–80, 83–84, 89–91, 93, 95, 97–99, 106–7, 113, 117, 119–21, 127–28, 130–32, 135–41, 143–44, 150, 153, 159–60, 162, 164–66, 176–77, 180–83, 185, 189, 191–92, 199–203, 211, 214–15, 219, 221–22, 227, 229, 232, 234, 238–39, 245, 250, 260, 265, 268, 262, 277, 289, 291, 293, 295, 298, 306, 319, 331, 334, 350, 360
Whiskey Rebellion, the, 1–2
Whiskey Ring, the, 153
whisky, 30, 59, 85, 106, 145, 183–84, 189, 198–99, 212, 214–15, 218–19, 224, 231–32, 253, 276, 284, 286
White House, 20, 32, 73, 77, 85, 128, 139, 150, 157–60, 163, 165, 173, 193, 199–201, 207–8, 213, 217–19, 221, 224, 228–33, 235, 237–38, 243, 250, 252–57, 263, 266, 276–77, 281, 284–86, 288, 291, 293–95, 300–4, 309, 311–13, 315, 318–20, 323, 331–34, 340–41, 348, 350, 360, 362–67. *See also* Executive Mansion
"White House Honey Ale," 362, 364–65
"White House Honey Blonde," 362
"White House Honey Porter," 362, 365–66

"Whitewater" scandal, 341
White, William Allen, 236
Willard Hotel, 113, 228
William Henry Harrison: His Life and Times, 78
Wilson, Edith, 218
Wilson, Woodrow, 187, 197, 204, 217–25, 228, 261, 350
wine, 1–2, 5, 7–8, 11, 14, 16–17, 19–34, 37–44, 48, 53–57, 59–63, 66–68, 70–71, 73, 76, 78–79, 81–82, 85–87, 93, 100, 102, 106–9, 112, 117–20, 122–23, 129–30, 140, 145, 147, 149, 151–52, 156, 159–60, 163–66, 169, 171, 177, 183, 185, 189, 192, 199, 202, 209–10, 220–21, 223–24, 234, 238–39, 242, 260–61, 274, 276, 283–86, 300, 305–6, 312, 319, 322, 326–27, 332–34, 337, 340, 348, 356, 358–59, 367–68
Winston, Robert W., 140
Wischnia, Bob "Wish," 356
Wisconsin, 98–99, 266, 363–64
Wise, Henry A., 114
Wise, John Sergeant, 85, 141, 156, 167–68, 183, 185
Women's Christian Temperance Union (WCTU), 158, 212–13, 284
"Wonder Boy, The" (nickname for Herbert Hoover), 236, 240, 242, 246
Wood, Leonard, 197
Woods, Randall, 294
Woodward, Bob, 310–11
World War I (WWI), 217, 250, 252, 273
World War II (WWII), 249, 272–73, 300, 335
Write It When I'm Gone, 312

X

Xiaoping, Deng, 302
XYZ Affair, the, 13

Y

Yale University, 118, 210–11, 335, 341, 350–52, 357
Yards Brewery, 11, 28
Yeltsin, Boris, 157, 347–48
Yuengling, 253, 363

Z

Zhukov, Georgy, 279